Better, Deeper, and More Enduring Brief Therapy

The Rational Emotive Behavior Therapy Approach

Better, Deeper, and More Enduring Brief Therapy

The Rational Emotive Behavior Therapy Approach

Albert Ellis, Ph.D.

BRUNNER/MAZEL, *Publishers* • New York

Library of Congress Cataloging-in-Publication Data

Ellis, Albert.
  Better, deeper, and more enduring brief therapy: the rational
emotive behavior therapy approach / Albert Ellis.
     p.   cm.
  Includes bibliographical references and index.
  ISBN 0-87630-792-6 (hc)
  1. Rational-emotive psychotherapy.   2. Brief psychotherapy.
I. Title.
RC489.R3E427   1995
616.89'14—dc20   95-44400
                                                                      CIP

Published by
BRUNNER/MAZEL, INC.
19 Union Square West
New York, New York 10003

Manufactured in the United States of America

10   9   8   7   6   5   4   3   2   1

For Janet Wolfe

Who has enormously supported me for the past thirty years and has greatly helped me to develop some of the best aspects of Rational Emotive Behavior Therapy. She has also been my living mate, adding considerable love and laughter to my life while maintaining a full and accomplished life of her own.

Contents

Acknowledgments

Several of my friends and colleagues have read the manuscript of this book, have made valuable comments on it, and have contributed greatly to its improvement. Some of them have spent considerable amounts of time perusing my first draft and have suggested editorial, stylistic, and content changes that have been most helpful. None of them, of course, are responsible for the content or style of this final version.

My reviewers, to whom I am most grateful, include Shawn Blau, Ted Crawford, Dominic DiMattia, Ray DiGiuseppe, Michael Edelstein, Kevin E. Fitzmaurice, Barry Morris, Stevan Nielsen, Phillip Tate, Emmett Velten, and Paul Woods. A varied and valuable set of helpers!

The whole staff at the Institute for Rational-Emotive Therapy in New York greatly contributed to get this book ready for the presses—especially Dominic DiMattia, Janet Wolfe, Christopher Ludgate, Jeffrey McHugh, and, above all, Ginamarie Zampano. At Brunner/Mazel, Natalie Gilman suggested that I do this book and gave me some excellent suggestions on it.

Most of all I want to thank the scores of writers and clinicians I have learned from over the years and without whose help I am sure I would have never developed Rational Emotive Behavior Therapy (REBT). Some of their names appear throughout the book and in the extensive bibliography at its end. There are others I have neglected to name but whose influence has been most rewarding and useful.

Let me repeat what I said in the Acknowledgments to *Reason and Emotion in Psychotherapy, Revised and Updated:* This book is hardly an individual project; it is also very much a social creation. As it should be!

About the Author

Albert Ellis, born in Pittsburgh and raised in New York City, holds a bachelor's degree from the City College of New York and M.A. and Ph.D. degrees in clinical psychology from Columbia University. He has been adjunct professor of psychology at Rutgers University, at United States International University, and at Pittsburg State University of Kansas. He served as chief psychologist of the New Jersey Diagnostic Center, chief psychologist of the New Jersey Department of Institutions and Agencies, and as a consultant in clinical psychology to the New York City Board of Education and to the Veterans Administration. Dr. Ellis currently holds the position of president of the Institute for Rational-Emotive Therapy. He has practiced psychotherapy, group therapy, marriage and family counseling, and sex therapy for over fifty years and continues this practice at the Psychological Clinic of the Institute in New York City.

A fellow of the American Psychological Association, Dr. Ellis has served as president of its Division of Consulting Psychology and as a member of its Council of Representatives. He is a Fellow (and past president) of the Society for the Scientific Study of Sex, as well as a Fellow of the American Association of Marriage and Family Therapists, the American Orthopsychiatric Association, and the American Sociological Association. The American Association of Sex Educators, Counselors, and Therapists has qualified him as a Certified Sex Educator and a Certified Sex Therapist. He is a Diplomate in Clinical Psychology of the American Board of Professional Psychology, in Clinical Hypnosis of the American Board of Psychological Hypnosis, and of the American Board of Medical Psychotherapists.

Several professional societies have honored Dr. Ellis: He holds the Humanist of the Year Award of the American Humanist Association, the

Distinguished Psychologist Award of the Academy of Psychologists in Marital and Family Therapy, and the Distinguished Practitioner Award of the American Association of Sex Educators, Counselors and Therapists, as well as the Award for Lifetime Achievement of the American Academy of Clinical Sexologists. The American Psychological Association has given him its major award for Distinguished Professional Contributions to Knowledge, and the American Counseling Association has given him its major Professional Development Award. He is a member of the National Academy of Practice in Psychology. In 1991, he was ranked "Most Influential Psychotherapist" in a survey of Canadian Clinical Psychologists, while American Clinical Psychologists and Counselors ranked him the second "Most Influential Psychotherapist," with Carl Rogers first and Sigmund Freud third.

Dr. Ellis has served as Consulting or Associate Editor of many professional journals, including the *Journal of Marital and Family Therapy*, the *Journal of Individual Psychology*, the *Journal of Contemporary Psychotherapy*, *Cognitive Therapy and Research*, the *Journal of Cognitive Therapy*, and *Psychological Reports*. He has published over 700 papers in psychological, psychiatric, and sociological journals and anthologies. He has written or edited over fifty-five books and monographs, including, *Reason and Emotion in Psychotherapy, Humanistic Psychotherapy: The Rational-Emotive Approach, A New Guide to Rational Living, The Practice of Rational Emotive Behavior Therapy*, and *How to Stubbornly Refuse to Make Yourself Miserable About Anything—Yes, Anything!*

Better, Deeper, and More Enduring Brief Therapy

The Rational Emotive Behavior Therapy Approach

1

Introduction

Let me attempt the impossible: to describe a method of psychotherapy—Rational Emotive Behavior Therapy (REBT)—that is intrinsically brief and that also aims to help people achieve an intensive, profoundly philosophical and emotional change. Ridiculous? Well, nearly. But not quite. REBT, along with its sisters, cousins, and aunts—usually called Cognitive Therapy (CT) or Cognitive Behavior Therapy (CBT)—has already experimentally shown that many clients can often (not always!) significantly improve in a short period of time (10 to 20 sessions) and that they can do so in individual and group therapy.[1]

Pretty nifty? Yes, but—as I shall show later—various other kinds of psychotherapy (some of them damned "nonrational"!) can also be brief and effective. Few experimental studies, but many case histories and observations, have attested to this.

The question is: Are REBT (and CBT) *more* likely to help people bring about *deeper* and *more lasting* emotional and behavioral change than other popular methods of therapy? I shall prejudicedly say, "Yes, they are." But with the caveat: Only a few studies have indicated this, and none with wild strength and enthusiasm. Future research will tell more accurately if my hypothesis holds water or is leaky.

1

Meanwhile, largely on the basis of my 52 years of experience with several kinds of therapy—especially with eclectic, psychoanalytic, and Rational Emotive Behavior therapy—I daringly present and defend this hypothesis. Specifically: When REBT is actively and strongly used along the lines I shall detail in this book, it can significantly help clients to reduce their neurotic problems in relatively few sessions (from one to 20); and in more instances than can be achieved with other popular forms of therapy (particularly with psychodynamic or with person-centered therapy), it can help clients effect a profound philosophical-emotional-behavioral change and thereby make themselves less disturbed and less disturb*able*.[2]

Quite a claim! No? Yes, but wait till some of my "data" are in. I shall present theories, practices, live sessions, and other materials to partially substantiate my (grandiose?) assumptions. Consider them. Think about them. Try some of them with your own clients. Make your own conclusions. Don't just take *my* word for it. Being something of a postmodernist (and relativist), I "know" that I can't absolutely "prove" anything. I can only try to convince you—and to reaffirm my *own* prejudiced conviction. So hear me out. And reach—as you will, anyway!—your own verdict.

Psychotherapy, especially when it is psychoanalytic, ostensibly takes many sessions, as thousands of case histories have shown. Perversely or not, the great majority of clients stay for only a few—from five to 10. And they often even improve significantly in this "short" length of time.[3] For this and several other fairly obvious reasons, therapists from Mesmer, Charcot, Freud, and Janet to the present day have often tried to use briefer methods of therapy, and have published scores of reports of "successful" cases of doing so.[4] Fortunately—or, as you may see it, unfortunately—their methods of brief therapy greatly differ.

A number of practitioners, for example, have advocated using a highly "positive" relationship or positive "transference" with clients[5] and a number of other practitioners have urged much more direct confrontation, the use of environmental pressures, and quick focusing on preconscious or unconscious issues.[6] Few therapists exclusively use only one or another of these methods and most emphasize *selective* employment of various methods. Fine!

Much or most of the time, however, advocates of brief therapy stress specific "helpful" methods, and so shall I. Finding which techniques work best for which clients under which circumstances is at the heart of "effective" practice.[7] But let us face it: Most of us—including myself—strongly *believe* it a "fact" that methods A, B, and C usually work better with most clients most of the time and therefore we often use these first. These are likely our favorite techniques, with which we are most comfortable and skilled. When we meet with different or difficult clients (DC's) with whom A, B, and C do *not* work too well, we *then* try methods D, E, F (or X, Y, Z), and soon.

So do I. With "average" or "regular" clients, I usually (not always) try my main tested and "proven" REBT methods—tentatively and experimentally. If they work—as they often do—I continue with them; later, I include several other methods. I go along with Aubrey Yates in this regard and consider each session an *experiment*.[8] On the basis of a few such experiments, I then may downplay my favorite A, B, C methods and add to them or replace them with other "better" ones.

That is how I shall proceed in this book. I shall first describe the "best" REBT methods for helping people reduce their neurotic symptoms and achieve more fulfilling individual and social lives. I shall especially describe which methods often help people make themselves "elegantly" effective, including less disturb*able*.[9] Assuming, however, that my (and your) best laid plans will often go awry, I shall then outline some alternative approaches that may better hit the mark. Hopefully! I shall also include reasons why both my "best" and my less (or less often) workable suggestions may be disadvantageous or harmful. I shall try, you see, to cover all the bases!

What about brief therapy applications to group, marital and family, sex, and other special modes of therapy? These shall be included in many of the examples I give, because REBT has been shown to be quite effective in practically all such problem-filled areas.[10] For clarity's sake, however, I shall largely outline effective methods of better and more intensive brief *individual* therapy and not include special sections on other important counseling modes. Maybe in some later books!

Again, the techniques of better and more intensive brief therapy that I usually advocate are mainly for what I call "nice neurotics"—that is, the vast majority (perhaps all) of the five billion plus people in today's world. Yes, I shall contend that, with few exceptions, they all often needlessly defeat themselves (and their relatives, friends, and associates) by making themselves severely cognitively, emotionally, and behaviorally "disturbed" or "dysfunctional." Fairly often? Yes, but obviously not all the time!

These individuals with neurotic thoughts, feelings, and behaviors, I hypothesize, are both born and reared to act the way they do—*but* they are less innately and biologically disturbable than other seriously upsettable people whom we often describe as having "personality disorders" or "psychoses." Such people with *greater* malfunctioning can be significantly helped by REBT and CBT. But *brief* therapy helps them *less* often and less "elegantly" than it helps the "nice neurotics."[11]

This is sad. Also too bad. But still "true"! As scores of articles and books—including my own—have shown, people with personality and psychotic disorders can definitely be helped, and often considerably. With good methods and enough time, some of them can improve so much that they may be for the most part functioning "neurotically." This is especially true if they receive "good" therapy plus proper medication. So let's not sell them short![12]

Because, probably, of their own biological *and* environmental limitations, they usually require longer periods of psychotherapy than people with neurosis, and they do not become as *thoroughly* symptom-free. They more often fall back to dysfunctional thoughts, feelings, and actions.

Fortunately, however, the REBT and CBT methods described in this book *can* be successfully employed with difficult clients, including those we see as afflicted with personality disorders, psychotic states, organicity, and mental deficiency. Can be and often have been—as many studies have shown.[13] So consider these methods carefully and use them experimentally. But be skeptical about quick results!

Is REBT, in its own right, intrinsically brief? Yes, with "regular," "normal," or "average" neurotic clients. Why so? Because I originally designed it so in 1953, after I had almost entirely abandoned psychoanalysis.[14]

As I have often humorously said at my talks and workshops, but with more than a grain of serious "truth," poor Sigmund Freud was born and reared with a propensity for *in*efficiency, while I seem to have been born and reared with a gene for efficiency.[15] Problem solving—quick problem solving—is definitely my thing. So when I first started doing psychotherapy, including sex and relationship therapy, in 1943, I got straight to my clients' problems and helped most of them in a few sessions (rarely more than 15) of eclectic therapy. I saw that active-directive counseling worked, so I specialized in it.

A little later, alas, I wrongly assumed that liberal psychoanalysis—à la Horney, Fromm, and Sullivan—was "deeper" and "more intensive" than short-term therapy. So, in 1947, I began to be trained in psychoanalysis (by Charles Hulbeck, a training analyst of Karen Horney's American Institute for Psychoanalysis) and for the next six years practiced classical analysis and psychoanalytically oriented psychotherapy.

Well, neither of these two analytic methods worked—though to my surprise the second one, which was briefer and less passive, worked better than classical analysis.[16] So I intensively studied hundreds of other methods between 1953 and 1955, and came up with Rational Therapy (RT) in January 1955, which I changed to Rational Emotive Therapy (RET) in 1961, and to Rational Emotive Behavior Therapy (REBT) in 1993.[17]

Analytic, Gestalt, Adlerian, Rogerian, and other therapists have often tried to modify their long-term procedures and slice them down to sensible proportions.[18] Not so me and REBT. From the start, I designed it to be a brief *and* an intensive school of therapy. Brief, because I knew from my eclectic preanalytic work, as well as from some of my experiences with psychoanalytically oriented psychotherapy, that effective therapy could often take only a few weeks or months. Intensive, because I realized that psychoanalysis intensively deals with all kinds of *irrelevancies* of clients' lives while almost always missing their important *philosophical relevancies.*

From the age of 16 onward, my main interest was philosophy, not psychology. Because I was anxious myself—especially about public speaking and encountering suitable female partners—I read voraciously all kinds of philosophy, especially material on the philosophy of human happiness. You name it: Confucius, Lao-Tsu, Buddha, Epictetus, Cicero, Seneca, Marcus Aurelius, Immanuel Kant, Arthur Schopenhauer, Ralph Waldo Emerson, John Dewey, George Santayana, Bertrand Russell—I read and studied them all. For the most part, they had one central theme: You largely *create* your needless misery by irrational or dysfunctional *thinking.* Therefore, you can change this thinking and re-create emotional and behavioral fulfillment.

I found that few psychoanalysts stressed this *attitudinal* approach to alleviating disturbance and fulfilling yourself. Alfred Adler did in his Individual Psychology, but in America, in the 1940's, he was amazingly unpopular (although some of the "neo-Freudians" stole from him without giving much credit).

So psychoanalysis, I decided in 1953, was supremely unphilosophical— and therefore inefficient. It also almost completely neglected behavior therapy, which, as emulated by John B. Watson's experiments with children's phobias, I had used to rid myself of my public speaking and social anxiety when I was only 19 (see note 14). So, between 1953 and 1955, I started to load my therapeutic ammunition with lots of philosophy and in vivo desensitization, and became a full-blown Rational Emotive Behavior Therapist in 1955. On to intrinsically brief *and* intensive therapy I plowed!

In what ways is REBT intrinsically brief? In many ways, which I will describe in detail later, so I will barely mention them now:

1. It assumes that a good percentage of clients can quickly learn the REBT theory of human disturbance, acknowledge that they largely upset themselves (not just *get* upset) when they act neurotically, and quickly start to experiment with *un*upsetting themselves. It therefore has brevity as one of its chief goals.

2. Its main concepts—the ABC's of human neurosis—can be clearly and simply shown, easily grasped, and quickly put to therapeutic use.

3. It is active-directive. The therapist actively keeps trying to help her or his clients and aims to teach them how to alleviate their disturbances and to encourage them to fulfill themselves in the shortest feasible time.

4. When clients have practical problems—such as, how to get a good job, or addictive problems such as how to stop drinking—REBT quickly zeroes in on helping them with these practical issues, as well as with their longer-range and often underlying personality problems.

5. After clients actively and strongly use REBT cognitive, emotive, and behavioral methods for even a short while, they often clearly internalize healthy and undefeating philosophies and meanings and quickly react sensibly and fulfillingly to unfortunate life events. They quickly and semiautomatically can refrain from upsetting themselves about such events. They promptly are able to undisturb themselves again if they happen to fall back to self-defeating thoughts, feelings, and actions. They can rapidly learn the main REBT theories, can sometimes immediately begin to apply them, and after a matter of weeks or months can automatically use them to enhance their lives.

6. Emotional-behavioral problems have complex "causes" or "sources" that include psychological, sociological, ideological, and biological aspects. Many of these—especially the socio-

logical aspects–are, at the time you see your clients, unchangeable. Other aspects, such as dysfunctional beliefs, are
quite important and more changeable. Psychoanalysis and
some other therapies spend much time focusing on complex,
usually impossible to prove or disprove "causes" of disturbance. These may be interesting to know but (even when
"true") are not very helpful for personality change. Many
other therapies equate "deep" with endlessly digging up the
past. Instead, REBT focuses concertedly on dysfunctional
philosophies that not only more directly lead to serious
emotional problems but also can be directly challenged and
changed. In REBT, "deep" means that a fundamental belief
system or philosophy is involved. It is therefore briefer–and
usually more *efficiently* "intensive"–than many other therapies. As Steve de Shazer indicates, "simple" solutions to
therapeutic problems are often more realistic and effective
than some of the "deeper" solutions.[19]

In what ways is REBT intrinsically "deep" and "intensive"?

1. Its theory states that if people want to feel better, get better,
and stay better, they had best make a profound philosophical
change (particularly giving up their grandiose, rigid *shoulds*
and *musts*); that is a far better way for them to go than merely
to *feel* better.[20]

2. Like the other cognitive behavior therapies, it helps people
see and uproot their self-defeating beliefs–that is, their
personalizing, self-deprecation, catastrophizing, and
overgeneralizing. But it uniquely shows them that behind
these dysfunctional antiempirical and illogical beliefs are
specific absolutistic *musts* that they can find and change, or
else they will keep thinking irrationally. Thus, behind their
belief, "Because I have failed at this important performance
several times, I am *no good,* I will *always* fail and *never* have
any happiness," is the underlying philosophy, "I *must* under
no conditions ever fail at important performances–*or else* I am
no good, will *always fail,* and *never have* any happiness."[21]

3. REBT helps people work for the goal of letting go of their
present disturbances and then acquiring such an effective anti-
musturbatory and anti-awfulizing attitude that they make

themselves significantly less disturb*able*, now and in the future.[22]

4. It shows clients how to use a large number of cognitive, emotive, and behavioral methods, and how to use them *strongly* and *persistently* until they *automatically* tend to refuse to keep disturbing themselves.[23]

5. It teaches clients that even after they make themselves less upset and less upsettable they will sometimes fall back again—for that is their human nature—and gives them methods of promptly undisturbing themselves again.[24]

6. In REBT, "deep" results are not confused with digging in the past. It often (not always) discourages clients' longwinded recounting of their history, their complaints, their chitchat with their friends and associates, their philosophizing about general world conditions, their obsessions with therapy and their therapists, and other interesting material that sidetracks them from facing and dealing with their basic emotional-behavioral problems, while often helping to exacerbate them.[25]

REBT—and to a lesser extent similar CBT practices—are, of course, not the only therapies that are intrinsically brief and intensive. Religious conversion, for example, can be achieved quickly and can lead to some profound ("good" and "bad"!) personality changes. The problem is to devise a psychological treatment that includes both brevity and intensiveness, without commonly leading to less fortunate results as well!

A final introductory word. This book is largely about therapy theories and practices. As such, it could be endless. In 1955, when I published a monograph, *New Approaches to Psychotherapy Techniques*, I listed hundreds of methods. Raymond Corsini noted that there are now some 350 major "schools" of therapy.[26] Accordingly, this relatively short book, although I shall mention scores of methods, will be no encyclopedia.

Instead, I shall do my best to emphasize those psychotherapy procedures, REBT and others, that seem to be particularly useful for *brief* therapy. Many of them—such as active-directive techniques—can also, of course, be used in long-term treatment. If you so choose! But I shall emphasize their short-term advantages and disadvantages. Enough is enough in one medium-size book!

NOTES TO CHAPTER 1

1. Beck, 1991; DiGiuseppe, Miller, & Trexler, 1979; Dobson, 1989; Elkin, Shea, et al., 1989; Ellis, 1957b, 1979c; Engels, Garnefski, & Diekstra, 1993; Haaga & Davison, 1989; Hajzler & Bernard, 1991; Hollon & Beck, 1994; Lipsey & Wilson, 1993; Lyons & Woods, 1991; McGovern & Silverman, 1984; Silverman, McCarthy, & McGovern, 1992; M. L. Smith & Glass, 1977; M. L. Smith, Glass, & Miller, 1980; Steenberger, 1994.

2. Bernard & Wolfe, 1993; Dryden, 1994a, 1994b; Dryden & DiGiuseppe, 1990; Dryden & Hill, 1993; Dryden & Neenan, 1995; Dryden & Yankura, 1992; Ellis, 1962, 1972b, 1972c, 1973b, 1979d, 1980d, 1983c, 1991b, 1994c, 1995a; Ellis & Abrams, 1994; Ellis & Becker, 1982; Ellis & Bernard, 1985; Ellis and Velten, 1992; Walen, DiGiuseppe, & Dryden, 1992.

3. Bellak & Small, 1977; Bloom, 1991; Budman, Hoyt, & Friedman, 1992, Cade & O'Hanlon, 1993; de Shazer, 1985; Ellis, 1992a; Goulding, 1992; Janis, 1983; Kleinke, 1993; Koss & Shiang, 1994; O'Hanlon & Beadle, 1994; O'Hanlon & Wilk, 1987; Phillips & Wiener, 1966; Rosenbaum, 1994; Small, 1979; Wolberg, 1965; Zeig & Gilligan, 1990.

4. Bellak & Small, 1977; Ellenberger, 1970; Janis & Mann, 1977; Kardiner, 1941; Koss & Shiang, 1994; Small, 1979; Wolberg, 1965; Zeig & Gilligan, 1990.

5. Bellak & Small, 1977; Fenichel, 1954; Sifneos, 1972; Slater, 1964; Small, 1979; Wolberg, 1965.

6. de Shazer, 1985; Erickson, 1980; Erickson & Rossi, 1979; Goulding, 1992; Haley, 1963, 1973, 1990; Watzlawick, 1978.

7. Blatt & Felsen, 1993; Corsini, 1989; Ellis, 1984a, 1989b, 1994e; Young, 1984; Zilbergeld, 1983.

8. Yates, 1970.

9. See Note 2.

10. Broder, 1994; Crawford, 1988; Ellis, 1986c, 1988a, 1988b, 1991e, 1991f, 1991i, 1993i; Ellis & Harper, 1961; Ellis, Sichel, et al., 1989; Grieger, 1988; Hauck, 1974, 1977; Huber & Baruth, 1989.

11. Beck, Freeman, & Associates, 1990; Benjamin, 1993; Cloninger, Svrakic, & Przybek, 1993; Ellis, 1965a, 1965b, 1989e, 1994b, 1994d, 1994g; Kramer, 1993; Linehan, 1993; Robin & DiGiuseppe, 1993; Steketee, 1993; Winston, Laikin, et al., 1994.

12. Beck, Freeman, & Associates, 1990; Carey & DiLalla, 1994; Cuon, 1994; Ellis, 1994d, 1994g; Freeman, 1994; Greist, 1993; Langley, 1994; Laydon & Newman, 1993; Silver & Rosenbluth, 1992; Sookman, Pinard, & Beauchemin, 1994; Steketee, 1993; Winston, Laikin, et al., 1994.

13. Beck, Freeman, et al., 1990; Greist, 1993; Laydon & Newman, 1993; Linehan, 1993; Robin & DiGiuseppe, 1993; Steketee, 1993.
14. DiMattia & Lega, 1990; Dryden & Ellis, 1989; Dryden & Neenan, 1995; Ellis, 1962, 1965b, 1990d, 1990f, 1991d, 1992a; Ellis & Dryden, 1993; Palmer, Dryden, et al., 1995; Warga, 1988; Weinrach, 1980; Wiener, 1988; Yankura & Dryden, 1990, 1994.
15. Ellis, 1965b, 1990a, 1993b.
16. Ellis, 1957b, 1962.
17. Ellis, 1962, 1993b.
18. Bellak & Small, 1977; Koss & Shiang, 1994; O'Hanlon & Beadle, 1994; Wolberg, 1965; Zeig & Gilligan, 1990.
19. de Shazer, 1985.
20. Bernard, 1991, 1993; Ellis, 1972b, 1973b, 1975a, 1979c, 1993k, 1994e, 1995a; Ellis & Abrams, 1994; Ellis & Becker, 1982; Ellis & Harper, 1975; Ellis & Velten, 1992.
21. Bricault, 1992; Dryden, 1994a, 1994b; Ellis, 1987d, 1988a; Ellis, Young, & Lockwood, 1987; Young, 1974.
22. Ellis, 1973b, 1974b, 1975a, 1979d.
23. Bernard & Wolfe, 1993; DiGiuseppe & Muran, 1993; Ellis, 1965b, 1969, 1973a, 1974a, 1977a, 1980c, 1981, 1985b; Ellis & Abrahms, 1978; Ellis & Abrams, 1994; Ellis, Abrams, & Dengelegi, 1992; Ellis & Velten, 1992; Ellis & Whiteley, 1979; Walen, DiGiuseppe, & Dryden, 1992.
24. Dryden & Neenan, 1995; Ellis, 1972b, 1994e; Ellis & Dryden, 1987, 1990, 1991.
25. Ellis, 1975a; Ellis & Abrahms, 1978; Ellis & Dryden, 1991; Walen, DiGiuseppe, & Dryden, 1992.
26. Corsini, 1989.

2

Just What *Is* Rational Emotive Behavior Therapy?

When I created Rational Emotive Behavior Therapy (REBT) in 1955, I knew exactly what it was—and wasn't. Now, I am not so sure!

At first, REBT, compared to most other therapies, was amazingly simple. That is probably why it has become so popular. Therapists, their clients, and the reading and listening public really liked the ABC's of neurosis that I presented—and they usually still do. For these ABC's— which I honestly "stole" from ancient and modern philosophers—are beautiful and profound. They get at one of the main cores of human disturbance. They beautifully describe important aspects of social "reality." If you—and your clients—use them, they work. Not perfectly. But remarkably well.[1]

Unfortunately, the ABC's of REBT—and of countless other forms of psychotherapy—can be seen out of context, taken too literally, and over-simplified. Fortunately, I keep revising and amplifying them. But in their original, simple form they have a kind of life of their own. Therapists and their clients sometimes rigidly stick with them, perpetuate them. As I, at times, have wrongly done myself. So that my tail has sometimes wagged my dog!

11

Perversely, even in their original state, my ABC's of REBT have done immense good–especially in the field of better and more intensive brief therapy. Why? Because, probably, they are lucid, understandable–and partly "true." By "true," again, I mean that they work.

Let me state the ABC's of REBT in their original, clear-cut form. People, of course, live in an environment, physical and social. They usually have several main Goals (G) or purposes: (1) to remain alive, kicking, and enjoying; (2) to enjoy life by themselves and socially; (3) to have intimate relations with a few others; (4) to find meaning in life through education and experience; (5) to devise and carry through vocational goals; (6) to enjoy recreation and play. When they pursue these Goals, they frequently encounter an Activating Event or Activating Experience, or Adversity (A) that blocks them and helps them fail, be rejected, or experience discomfort.

When this unfortunate Activating Event (A) occurs, people–whether they realize it or not–have a *choice* of feeling a healthy or useful Consequence (C), such as feeling sorry, disappointed, or frustrated. Or they can *choose* to feel unhealthy or destructive Consequences (C), such as severe anxiety, depression, rage, or self-pity. They also, when experiencing A, usually have the choice of acting in a self-helping manner either to improve it or (when they can't change it) accept it (C). Or they can choose to act self-destructively by doing nothing about it, or by making it worse (C). They can act unhealthily and self-defeatingly (C), for example, by whining, procrastinating, drinking excessively, or avoiding coping with A.

If your clients (and you) choose to create a useful or beneficial Consequence (C) when they experience an unpleasant Activating Event (A), they largely do so by their Beliefs (B) *about* A. They can usually choose to have rational Beliefs (rB's) that encourage them to have healthy, functional feelings and behaviors at C; or they can choose to have irrational Beliefs (iB's) that encourage them to have dysfunctional, destructive feelings and behaviors at C.

Your clients' rB's that help them cope with unpleasant A's almost always consist of *preferences, hopes,* and *wishes,* and include *and/also* and *yes/but* meanings about the unfortunate A's they experience. For example, "I *wish* this unpleasantness (A) doesn't occur; *but* if it does, I can cope with it and still have some happiness in my life." Again: "I really *prefer* John to like me; *but* if he doesn't, too bad. I can still lead a good life."

People's irrational Beliefs (iB's) that help them create disturbed feelings and actions that sabotage their coping with unpleasant A's almost always consist of (conscious or unconscious) absolutistic *shoulds, oughts,* and *musts,* plus the "logical" but destructive awfulizing and people-denigrating derivative irrationalities that generally accompany these *musts.* Their three basic neurosis-inciting musts (which have almost innumerable unhealthy subheadings) are:

1. "I (ego) *absolutely must,* at practically all times, be successful at important performances and relationships—or else I, as a person, am inadequate and worthless!" Result: Feelings of severe anxiety, depression, despair, worthlessness. Actions of withdrawal, avoidance, addiction.

2. "Other people *absolutely must* practically always treat me considerately, kindly, fairly, or lovingly—or else they are no damned good and deserve no joy in their existence!" Result: Feelings of real anger, rage, fury, resentment. Actions of fighting, feuds, violence, wars, genocide.

3. "Conditions under which I live *absolutely must* be comfortable, pleasurable, and rewarding—or else it's *awful,* I *can't stand* it, and the goddamned world is no good!" Result: Feelings of self-pity, rage, and low frustration tolerance. Actions of withdrawal, procrastination, addiction.[2]

These ABC's of REBT, once again, are simple. But not exactly elegant. To make them "truer" and conform more to social "reality," I have revised—and complicated!—them in recent years, as I will show later in this book. In particular, I have shown how the A's (Activating Events), B's (Beliefs), and C's (Consequences) all importantly interact with and influence each other.[3] I have also shown how people's Beliefs (B's), which I originally saw mainly as self-statements or sentences that we tell ourselves, often actually are that—but they also are more subtle conscious and unconscious ideas, meanings, images, attitudes, symbols, and other kinds of cognitions.[4]

I have also added D (Disputing) and E (Effective New Philosophy, Emotion, and Behavior), which I originally formulated as the "answers" to clients' discovering their dysfunctional Beliefs, challenging and acting against them, and coming up with a new set of healthy philosophies and actions. Originally, I saw Disputing (D) mainly as cognitive. Thus, your clients may irrationally Believe (B), "I *absolutely must* win John's (or Joan's) approval and if I don't win it that proves that I'm an *inadequate person who will never achieve a good relationship!*" and may therefore feel severely depressed when John (or Joan) rejects them. If so, they can strongly Dispute (D) their irrational Beliefs (iB's) by asking: "Why *must* I win this approval? Does it follow that failing at this one endeavor makes me a totally *inadequate person*? Where is the evidence that if I fail to win John's (or Joan's) approval I'll *never* have a good relationship? If I keep strongly convincing myself of these absolutistic Beliefs, what results will my Beliefs most probably bring?"

Your clients' answers (at E, Effective New Philosophy) to this kind of logical, empirical, and utilitarian Disputing (D) will likely be: (1) "There is no reason why I *absolutely have to* win John's (or Joan's) approval, though that would be *highly preferable*—so I'll do my best to win it." (2) "Failing to win his (or her) approval makes me *a person who failed this time* but hardly a *totally inadequate* person." (3) "There is no evidence that, if I get his (or her) lack of approval, I'll *never* have a good relationship. Most likely, if I keep trying for one, I will succeed!" (4) "My Beliefs about my *absolutely needing* John's (or Joan's) approval will most probably keep me depressed, malfunctioning, and much less likely to win *almost anyone's* love and approval!"

If your clients (and you) use REBT Disputing in this fashion they will tend to significantly change their dysfunctional Consequences and make themselves less neurotic and happier. Hundreds of REBT and CBT experiments attest to this probability.[5] Try it and see!

Let's slow down, however. My early formulations of D (Disputing) and E (Effective New Philosophies, Emotions, and Behaviors) indeed showed people with neurotic (and personality disordered) dysfunctions how to change their grandiose *musts* to sensible *preferences* and how to thereby reduce their disturbances. Great! But, again, not quite elegant.

My later clinical work and research (and that of hundreds of other therapists using REBT and CBT) led me to see D (Disputing) more clearly. As I originally noted, in my first paper on REBT at the Annual Convention of the American Psychological Association in Chicago in 1956, what we call thinking, feeling, and behaving are *not* (practically ever) separate, but are integrated, conjoined, and holistic. When you *think* negatively ("I'm an inadequate person when I fail to win John's [or Joan's] approval!"), you tend to *feel* badly (e.g., anxious) and *act* dysfunctionally (e.g., beg for approval or avoid John [or Joan]). When you *feel* anxious, you tend to *think* negative thoughts and to *act* compulsively or avoidantly. When you *act* compulsively, you tend to *think* and *feel* negatively. Don't you?[6]

If so, D (Disputing your clients' dysfunctional Beliefs) can be *largely* cognitive (as shown above). That will often work. But for better results, they had also better include in D a good measure of emotive Disputing. Thus, they can—as I show in detail later—*forcefully* question and challenge their irrational Beliefs (iB's). They can use *strong* coping statements with which to *replace* them. They can use rational emotive imagery, shame attacking exercises, role playing, rational humorous songs, reverse role playing, and a number of other REBT *emotive* methods that I (and other CBT practitioners) describe later in this book.[7]

D (Disputing) can also—and often had better be—behavioral. Thus, your clients can *act* against their irrational Belief (iB), "I *absolutely must* win John's (or Joan's) approval and I'm an *inadequate person* when I don't!" They can use several REBT (and CBT) counteractions, such as: (1) Don't cop out: Keep *un*desperately trying to win John's (or Joan's) approval; (2) Try to win the approval of other people whose rejection would be troubling to them; (3) Try to remain in contact with John (or Joan) even when he (or she) isn't giving them the approval they desire; (4) Get some skill training in trying to win people's approval; (5) Reinforce themselves with something pleasant when they Dispute their dire need for approval and when they risk seeking acceptance that they probably won't get.

REBT, as you can see, now stresses a number of emotive and behavioral methods (as well as additional cognitive methods) that I didn't clearly or forcefully include in its early versions. Like CBT, it keeps growing and developing in these respects and has become—along with the therapy of Arnold Lazarus—more multimodal than it was in the 1950's. It still holds to its original ABC's of neurosis, though more complexly. But it has particularly expanded D (Disputing). It hypothesizes that people largely (not completely) make themselves neurotic with conscious and unconscious absolutistic *shoulds, oughts,* and *musts.* Therefore, if they persistently and vigorously change these to clear-cut—and often strong—*preferences*, they will make themselves less disturbed. How? By specifically Disputing their self- and social-defeating Beliefs—and doing so in several cognitive, emotive, and behavioral ways. With patience and fortitude—and with vigor![8]

This brings us to the three main, but not only, insights that have been stressed in REBT since the early 1960's.

Insight Number 1: Activating Events (A's) that are seen as Adverse or unfortunate (against your and your clients' Goals and Desires) contribute importantly to neurotic Consequences (C's), but do not exclusively "cause" them. Probably the most important "cause" for therapists (and clients) to look for is B, people's absolutistic and musturbatory Beliefs about A. B importantly interacts with A to bring about C. Because B is usually more changeable than A, it is especially to be looked for and Disputed (D) until the individual who is neurotic constructs E, Effective New Philosophies, Emotions, and Behaviors.

Insight Number 2: When your clients (or you) think, feel, and act neurotically (self- and social-defeatingly), they often first construct their irrational Beliefs (iB's) about unfortunate Activating Events (A's) during their early childhood. But they may not do so until later. When they presently create neurotic symptoms, they perpetuate their early dysfunctional Beliefs and/or construct new ones. They usually continually recreate and reestablish and reindoctrinate themselves with their iB's and thereby maintain or exacerbate their disturbances. Their past thoughts, feelings, and behaviors do not merely *stay* alive today. They also actively *modify* and *reconstruct* them. As Stevan Nielsen, when he read the manuscript of this book, noted:

> In REBT we don't travel to the past for a "deep" understanding of a client's problems or to effect a "deep" change. The past is memory recalled (reconstructed) and explored by therapist and client, not a place to which therapist and client time-travel! Many clients do, indeed, feel upset about the past. However, the past does not explain their disturbance. The past will be "deeply" disturbing if clients have profoundly upsetting beliefs about their memories of the past. In REBT, "profound" and "pervasive" are better synonyms for "deep" than are "past" and "historical."
>
> Clients get deeply disturbed primarily because they presently, pervasively, convincingly—that is, "deeply"—are constructing or reconstructing upsetting thoughts and strengthening "deep" beliefs about something. This is usually something they presently think about something they remember about the past, or it is something they presently think about the present, or it is something they presently imagine about the future. These somethings *may never have happened* or *may never happen* or perhaps *never could happen* at all!

Insight Number 3: It is usually "simple" and "easy" for you and your clients to discover the specific irrational Beliefs (iB's) that accompany neurotic behavior, and you can almost always Dispute and change them for functional preferential Beliefs. But to do so usually requires a good deal of persistent—and forceful—work and practice. Yes, no magic. Mainly, *work and practice!*[9]

These three major insights are usually required for effective REBT therapy—especially for better and more intensive brief therapy. Other REBT insights will be presented later, but here is another important one right now.

I particularly found, as I used REBT with my early clients, that often—in fact, very often—they upset themselves *about* their serious upsetness. This is expectable according to REBT theory, which says that neurotic clients (yours as well as mine) tend to hate and to *horrify themselves about* both their failures *and* about their disturbed feelings about these failures. Foolishly, to be sure; but "naturally" and "humanly." In fact, they may have biological tendencies that encourage them to make a "magical"—or shall I say "demoniacal"—jump from "I badly failed" to "I am a *failure*–a bad person!" Silly, of course—at least, from a sensible Martian standpoint. And needlessly self-sabotaging—at least, from a sensible human outlook. For they then tend to feel panicked, depressed, self-hating, and hopeless.

When they think this way, your clients first *see* and *feel* their neurotic symptoms and, as you would guess, they go beyond just disliking their symptoms and conclude that their severe anxiety is a dismal *failure* and that their depression encourages further rejection. They view their *symptoms* as decidedly "bad" or "uncomfortable," experience "symptom stress," and often upset themselves about their upsetness. To wit: "I'm *no good* for being so anxious!" "It's *awful* being depressed, and I *can't* stand it!" "I'm so enraged that no one will *ever* love me!"

A pickle about a pickle—which most "neurotics" much of the time create for themselves. Knowing that your clients will frequently *doubly* bind themselves in this self-manufactured kind of mess, you can use REBT to guess that they will do so, to look for their secondary disturbances about their primary disturbances, to find and show them their irrational Beliefs on both levels, and to help them—often quickly and intensively—improve. Again: more on this later.

Well, enough of these preliminary, general outlines of REBT theory. Let me now be more specific and describe some of the main cognitive, emotive, and behavioral methods of Rational Emotive Behavior Therapy and apply them not only to regular individual therapy but especially to how you, as a therapist or counselor, can use them to help your clients benefit from better and more intensive brief therapy.

NOTES TO CHAPTER 2

1. See Note 1 to Chapter 1. Also: Baisden, 1980; Dubois, 1907; Ellis, 1979c, 1987a, 1987d, 1989c, 1990e, 1991b; Ellis & Grieger, 1977, 1986; Epictetus, 1890; Kant, 1929; Lazarus, Lazarus, & Fay, 1993; Marcus Aurelius, 1890; Walen, DiGiuseppe, & Dryden, 1992; Walter, 1994; Warren & Zgourides, 1991; Wessler & Wessler, 1980; Wolfe & Brand, 1977; Wolfe & Naimark, 1991.
2. Bricault, 1992; Dryden, 1994a, 1994b; Elliott, 1993; Ellis, 1962, 1985b, 1987a, 1991h, 1991j, 1991l, 1991m, 1993d, 1994e, 1995a; Ellis & Dryden, 1987, 1990, 1991; Ellis, Krasner, & Wilson, 1960; Horney, 1950; Palmer, Dryden, et al., 1995.
3. Dryden, 1994a, 1994b; Ellis, 1991j, 1991m, 1992f, 1993d, 1993i, 1994e, 1995a; Walen, DiGiuseppe, & Dryden, 1992.
4. Barlow, 1989; Beck, 1976, 1991; Beck & Emery, 1985; Breuer & Freud, 1965; Ellis, 1994e, Ellis & Dryden, 1991; Freeman & Dattilo, 1992; Glasser, 1992a; Gutsch & Ritenoor, 1983; Hauck, 1973, 1974; R. Lazarus, 1966, 1994; McMullin, 1986; Raimy, 1975; Rorer, 1989; Rotter, 1954.
5. See Note 1 to Chapter 1.
6. Bernard, 1991, 1993; Ellis, 1962, 1994e; Ellis & Dryden, 1987; Schwartz, 1993; Walen, DiGiuseppe, & Dryden, 1992.
7. Bernard & Wolfe, 1993; Blakeslee, 1994; DiGiuseppe & Muran, 1993; Dryden, 1994a, 1994b; Ellis, 1969, 1973a, 1974a, 1980b, 1980c, 1990b, 1991b, 1991e, 1991f, 1991i, 1991k, 1992c, 1992d, 1992f, 1993d, 1993f, 1993g, 1993j, 1993m, 1995a; Ellis & Abrahms, 1978; Ellis & Abrams, 1994; Ellis, Sichel, et al., 1989; Ellis & Velten, 1992; Kayser & Himle, 1994; Lazarus, 1989, 1992; Maultsby, 1971a, 1984; Walen, DiGiuseppe, & Dryden, 1992; Yankura & Dryden, 1990, 1994.
8. See Note 7.
9. Bard, 1980; Bernard, 1991, 1993; Dryden, 1994a, 1994b; Dryden & Neenan, 1995; Ellis, 1962, 1965b, 1974c, 1991b, 1993d, 1993f, 1993g, 1993, 1994e, 1995a, 1995b; Ellis & Abrahms, 1978; Ellis & Abrams, 1994; Ellis, Abrams, & Dengelegi, 1992; Ellis & Velten, 1992; Ellis & Whiteley, 1979; Grieger & Boyd, 1980; Sichel & Ellis, 1984; Phadke, 1982; Walen, DiGiuseppe, & Dryden, 1992; Wessler & Wessler, 1980; Wolfe, 1992; Wolfe & Brand, 1977; Yankura & Dryden, 1990, 1994.

3

Probing for "Deep" Emotional Problems

As promised in the preceding chapters, I shall now present a number of "cognitive" methods that you can use to help your clients (and your friends and relatives!) to achieve better and more intensive brief therapy. Why do I put "cognitive" in quotation marks? Because, as I noted before, it is rarely pure, standing entirely on its own feet. The human condition—our biology *and* social conditioning—makes us almost always think, feel, and behave interactionally, mergefully.

Thus, when I think (and perhaps say) "I like (or love) you very much," I *feel* kindly toward you and tend to *move* closely to you. Cognition, especially in regard to promoting and reducing "mental" disturbance, includes evaluating, appraising, and rating one's own and others' behavior (and personhood)—all of which are "emotional" reactions. "Feeling" or "desiring" includes perceiving, being aware and conscious, and taking an attitude toward people and things—all of which are "intellectual" reactions. "Responding" includes noticing, recognizing, expressing, and experiencing—which are also cognitive and/or emotional reactions. So I shall use the term "cognitive methods" to describe therapeutic techniques that seem to be largely intellectual, rational, and problem-solving procedures, but that *also* have emotional and action aspects. Postmodern critics of some of these methods, like Michael Mahoney and Vittorio Guidano, rightly show that "rational" techniques are not absolutely "true" or "effective," cannot be consistently defined, and overlap with "emotional" and "behavioral" techniques.[1] I agree. But what I call "cognitive" methods of therapy can be very useful, especially to help bring about better and more intensive brief therapy. Here are some of them that REBT often favors.

I almost always listen carefully to my clients' main presenting problems and put them first, in my own head, into REBT's ABC framework. I start with C, their emotional-behavioral consequences, and practically force them to quickly—usually within five minutes!—come up with (acknowledge) a clear-cut "real" emotional and/or behavioral problem.

I consider, first, their *healthy* or *self-helping* negative feelings—such as their feeling sorry, disappointed, frustrated, or annoyed about important Adversities (A's) that have been happening in their lives. Suppose a male client says (or writes in our four-page Biographical Information Form), "My partner is acting obnoxiously and I feel very frustrated and disappointed about this." I respond along these lines:

AE: Do you *only* feel *frustrated* and *disappointed*, which in REBT we consider *healthy* negative feelings, when something like this goes wrong in your life? For if it does go badly, you'd better not feel *happy* about it or even just *neutral.*

Client: No, I feel that "healthy" way, too. But I also often feel *angry* at my partner.

AE: Ah, let's explore your *anger*, which is a feeling that will really upset you and can easily wreck your relationship with your partner. When do you usually experience *that* feeling, real anger, at your partner?

Client: Oh, quite often. Especially when he contradicts me in front of others.

AE: You mean, in front of your other employees?

Client: Yes, and in front of potential customers. I really *hate* that!

AE: And do you feel angry at *him* for frustrating you like that?

Client: Yes, *very* angry at him for acting so badly and frustrating me so much.

Notice, in this case, I first look *at and then beyond* the client's "healthy" feeling of frustration and disappointment and quickly ferret out his feelings of "real anger," resentment, or low frustration tolerance (LFT). For his frustration is a problem, and if he *only* had that feeling I might possibly—and "superficially"—try to help him deal "better" with his partner and thereby induce this partner to act less frustratingly. But helping him in this way, in REBT, might lead to helpful and brief, but not *deep and intensive*, therapy. As we saw before, however, there was a more intensive, deeper emotion—anger!

So I go directly for my client's emotional jugular. I *assume* probabilistically that if he bothers to come to therapy about his feelings when his partner contradicts him (at point A), he is feeling *more* than healthy frustration and disappointment (at point C). So, if he does not spontaneously reveal more himself, I *actively ask him* about his other, more extreme, disturbed feelings (at point C), and quickly help him acknowledge his "real" anger (or, as we soon discover, rage).

Suppose this same client refuses to admit his anger at his partner and keeps insisting that he is *only* disappointed and frustrated at this person's negative behavior. I will then tend to show him that (1) he may well feel frustrated *and* angry, as most of us would feel; (2) his feeling of "mere frustration" is "normal" or "healthy" and hardly merits psychotherapy; (3) if he really does feel angry and refuses to acknowledge it, he is wrongly viewing anger as a heinous crime (instead of a dysfunctional behavior) and is *un*healthily feeling ashamed and putting himself down *as a person* for experiencing anger. This is the kind of stress symptom I described earlier; (4) he likely is *really* disturbed about something else, so let's look for his *neurotic* feelings, to see what they are and how they can be changed.

Usually, after five to 10 minutes of this kind of REBT-oriented discussion, this client will fully acknowledge his anger at his partner—or else we will start looking for one of his "real" emotional problems. I will still try to keep his therapy brief; and he will most likely work toward some kind of *intensive* and *enduring* personal change.

Right from the start, then, REBT assumes that clients have healthy *and* unhealthy reactions to unfortunate Activating Events (A's), tries to unearth the latter reactions and works to reduce them, and thus deliberately *aims for* a rather profound cognitive-emotive change. Similarly, if a client says that she is very annoyed at dances and socials because men are interested only in having sex and not in having caring relationships with her, I will probe for more disturbed feelings of anger at males and of her self-deprecation at not being "able enough" to get suitable men to care for her. I will also probe for her "hidden" behavioral reactions—such as refusing to go to social events, running home from them early, avoiding attractive men who she thinks might reject her, and remaining unassertive with men. I will quickly seek out these possible disturbances and not let her "get away with" concentrating on her healthy negative feelings.[2]

Does the REBT technique of quickly probing for "real" and "deep-seated" symptoms have any disadvantages? Of course it does. Among other things: (1) It may frighten away some skittish and defensive clients; (2) it may encourage some clients to *invent* or *exaggerate* "deep" problems; (3) it may raise serious issues—especially with severely disturbed clients—that cannot easily be dealt with and had better currently be left unsaid; (4) it may raise for review and treatment issues that the therapist rather than the client wants to alleviate.

All these—and other—questionable outcomes may occur. But I have personally—and, of course, prejudicially—found that *not* bringing them up usually leads to superficial or poor therapy and sometimes does more harm than good. So consider the cost *both* ways. Consider your particular client. And consider the short-term *and* the long-term advantages of actively looking for and working with your clients' deep, pervasive, and underlying cognitive-behavioral problems.

What about clients' practical problems—like their getting a better job, finding a suitable mate, or deciding which house to buy? Of course, REBT deals with them, too, especially when they are pressing and lead to exceptionally bad results. Like child abuse, for instance. Or spouse-beating. Or prolonged unemployment. REBT is very practical—and definitely zeroes in on these issues and tries to help people solve them.[3] More of this later.

Largely, however, REBT first focuses on clients' emotional problems *about* their practical problems. For if your clients, at point A, want to quickly stop their partners from abusing them or their children, or to focus on how to get a good job or relationship, their problem-solving ability will usually be impaired by their feeling extremely panicked, depressed, or enraged about these practical problems, and they will have difficulty listening to you—or themselves—about possible "good" solutions. So, except in real emergencies, the REBT choice is: First deal with their "emotional" disturbances and, while doing so, also work on their "practical" difficulties. Not necessarily always, but usually.

Besides, as I will keep reminding you, "emotional" problems are "deeper" than practical ones in that they often create the latter and impair the "best" solutions to them. And this is why, for better or worse,

REBT is mainly concerned with brief *intensive* and *more enduring* therapy.

Stevan Nielsen suggested that I restate some of the main material in this chapter in the ABC format of REBT. So here goes:

When your clients (or others) experience Activating Events, and especially Adversities (A's), they are likely to feel both a healthy and an unhealthy negative emotion as a Consequence (C). Both these negative feelings are largely created by their Beliefs (B) about what is occurring in their lives at point A.

Usually, their healthy, though still negative, responses to Adversity (A) will stem from rational Beliefs (rB's), while their unhealthy negative responses or dysfunctional emotions will stem from their irrational Beliefs (iB's). Usually, too, they have *both* rational and irrational beliefs about Adversities, and they therefore have *both* healthy and unhealthy negative feelings about the same Adversities.

In the case of the male client mentioned above who upset himself about problems with his business partner, he probably had both an rB and an iB about these Adversities. When his partner acted obnoxiously (A), he first told himself the rational Belief (rB), "I wish he wouldn't act that way, but it's only frustrating and not as bad as it possibly could be." He then felt the Consequence (C) of the healthy negative feeling of frustration and annoyance at his partner's obnoxious behavior. But also, along with his rB, he had the irrational Beliefs (iB's), "He absolutely *must not* act that way when clients are around! It's *awful* when he acts so badly, and I *can't stand* it!" These iB's led to his dysfunctional or unhealthy feeling of intense anger or rage (C).

In the case of the female client mentioned above who has problems at dances, she again probably has rational and irrational Beliefs that lead to healthy and unhealthy negative feelings. Following Adversity (A), a sexual come-on at a dance, her rational Belief probably is something like, "I strongly *prefer* to have men treat me nicely at dances, so that I can save having intimate relationships for those that I have known for some time. But if they quickly indicate that they want to go to bed with me immediately, without any intimacy taking place, that is annoying and undesirable, but I don't have to take them too seriously and upset myself about this." With this rB, she would feel the Consequence (C) of annoyance and regret, which are healthy negative feelings.

Following the same Adversity (A) at dances, however, this woman often tends to tell herself irrational Beliefs (iB's), such as, "These men who are quick on the trigger for sex absolutely *must not* act in that abominable way! I must be coming across as *a brainless, worthless* slut if so many men at dances want to have sex with me immediately!" Along with this set of irrational Beliefs (iB's), she has the emotional Consequence (C) of feelings of rage and self-deprecation.

This woman's deep upsetness (meaning *pervasive* upsetness) at point C, which includes her feeling depressed and her withdrawal from further socializing, is a combination of her healthy disappointment and her unhealthy rage and depression. It stems from both her rational *preference* that men appreciate her for her intellect, sense of humor, and other aspects of her character and her *absolutistic demand* that they not go after her merely for sexual reasons.

In both cases, then, as well as in most other instances, people make themselves, at point C, feel healthily sorry and frustrated when Adversities occur in their lives at point A. They largely do this by *wishing* and *preferring* that these Adversities not occur. But when, following the same Adversities, they make themselves unhealthily and self-defeatingly panicked, depressed, enraged, and self-hating, they largely do so by adding to their sensible, realistic preferences a set of *instant musts* and *demands*. Their feelings, when faced with Adversities, quickly tend to follow and to be largely negative. But helpful and unhelpful emotions they experience in dealing with these Adversities are tied to their *sensibly preferring* that the Adversities not occur and to their *foolishly commanding* that they absolutely must not exist. Actually, however, they rarely react in a rigid either/or manner, but almost always in an and/also way. They simultaneously have healthy *and* unhealthy reactions to obnoxious Activating Events, and they fairly obviously have the innate capacity to react both ways. REBT tries to show them their double-headed emotional and behavioral reactions and to intensively provide them with ways that will help them minimize their unhealthy and maximize their healthy negative feelings. Then, as I shall show later in this book, they can proceed to leading more enjoyable, more self-fulfilling, lives.

NOTES TO CHAPTER 3

1. Guidano, 1991; Mahoney, 1991.
2. Bernard & Wolfe, 1993; Crawford & Ellis, 1982; Cramer & Ellis, 1988; Dryden, 1994a, 1994b; Ellis, 1988a, 1990a, 1990f, 1991d, 1991e, 1991k,

1991m, 1992d, 1992f, 1993d, 1993g, 1993i, 1994e; Ellis & DiGiuseppe, 1994; Ellis & Dryden, 1987; Ellis & Grieger, 1977, 1986; Ellis & Hunter, 1991; Ellis & Knaus, 1977; Ellis & Lange, 1994; Ellis & Velten, 1992; Ellis, Wolfe, & Moseley, 1966; Grossack, 1976; Low, 1952; Shibles, 1974; Yankura & Dryden, 1990.
3. See Note 2.

4

Discovering Important Antecedents That Lead to Disturbances

As noted in the previous chapters, finding the ABC's of emotional-behavioral disturbances, and using them for better and more intensive brief therapy, usually starts with "deep" or "real" Consequences (C's). But you usually cannot understand and help minimize self-defeating C's without your finding some relevant and important Activating Events (A's) that precede or accompany them. If your clients do not spontaneously and quickly give you such A's—as they usually actually do—open your big mouth and ask for them. At least, if you do REBT.

Joann, a 36-year-old teacher, said during our first session that she had been severely depressed pretty much so "all my life about everything." "About nothing in particular?" I asked. "No, just about everything."

Joann's vagueness sabotaged my clearly understanding the ABC's of her depression because when I looked for her irrational Beliefs (iB's) and asked, "What do you usually think or tell yourself when you feel quite depressed, she answered, "All kinds of negative things." "Nothing special?" I asked. "No," she replied. "All kinds of negative things. Nothing special." Not very helpful!

I refused to give up, and I persisted:

AE: I doubt whether you're equally depressed about "all kinds of negative things." Almost everyone has *some* special things they often depress themselves about.

Joann: I'm sure they do. But not me. Nothing special that I can see.

AE: Well, let's explore a few possibilities. How about your profession, your teaching?

Joann: Not too good or too bad. Okay, I'd say.

AE: Your family? Father, mother, older sister?

Joann: All gone now. All dead. Used to bother me, but not any more. Sort of glad they're not around.

AE: How about your relationships with men?

Joann: Also haven't had any for several years. None to speak of.

AE: And how do you feel about *that*?

Joann: Oh.

AE: Oh!

Joann's eyes filled with tears. The lost kitten was out of the bag. She cried for almost five minutes as she told me about how miserable she was about having only one fairly long relationship in her whole life, having her lover end it five years ago, and not being able to replace it since that time. George, her lover, shied away from a lasting relationship, as did a few later men in her life.

I went on to ask the usual REBT questions: "What are you telling yourself when you think about your past relationship and its loss? How do you feel about yourself as a loner? What comes to mind in regard to your having a lasting relationship in the future?"

Somewhat to my surprise, Joann's answers indicated that it wasn't a partner's companionship, love, or sexuality that Joann missed. No, she got along pretty well without all that. But she *had to* be a mother, and she *had to* have a kind, doting father for her child. At 36, and with irregular periods, she might *never* fulfill that lifelong dream. And that would be *perfectly awful*.

Well, I had smoked Joann out. She easily gave me her C, severe depression. I got her reluctantly to acknowledge A, lack of any permanent relationship. Then her B's spilled out all over the place, and by the end of the first session we were already going on to D, Disputing her B's about the *absolute necessity* of her having a fine child and a wonderful father for it.

Within 12 sessions of REBT exploring and of my teaching Joann how to actively and forcefully Dispute her dysfunctional Beliefs and change them to preferences instead of arrogant demands, she came up with several important Effective New Philosophies, Emotions, and Behaviors (E's):

1. "I don't *need* my strong desires for a child and a husband to be fulfilled. I never *need* what I greatly *want*. No matter *how* strongly I want it!"

2. "George was *not* a louse for leaving me five years ago, though I think he acted badly and led me on for some time. He probably would have made a fine father, and it's very sad that he had such a fear of marriage and fatherhood. But he has a right to his fears—just as I have a right to mine. It's very bad, but not *horrible* that I lost him."

3. "I'm going to have a hell of a time, at my age, finding a suitable husband, becoming pregnant while I am still fertile, and raising a healthy, happy child. But it's not impossible, just difficult, to do so. And depressing myself about this difficulty will hardly help me find a mate!"

4. "I most probably will get pregnant—even if I have to be a single mother to do so. George or some other suitable man will most likely help me out, especially if I assume full economic and other responsibilities for the child. Raising a kid alone will be tough—but, if necessary, I can do it!"

5. "If the worst comes to the worst and I *never* have a child, that will be most unfortunate. It's unlikely, but it *could* happen. What a loss! The worst I will ever suffer, no doubt. But I could still bear it—and make my life *reasonably* happy. I could switch to teaching young children. Or run a nursery school. Or steadily volunteer at a home for orphans. No matter what, *I could* still make myself into a happy human being. With much determination and work!"

By achieving, and really believing in, these and several other antidepressive philosophies, Joann made herself undepressed for the first time in 16 years and began to look upon her quest for a suitable husband as a fascinating challenge instead of a dismal hardship. Oddly enough, she still at times depressed herself about the state of the school system in which she worked and about worldwide poverty. But not often and not for long, as she kept using REBT's misery-attacking methods with regard to these unfortunate problems too.

Back to finding the A's (Antecedents or Adversities) in your clients' lives. Usually, they give them readily—often all too readily. They may describe a long series of "unfortunate" Activating Events—may see little frustrations as "huge" and big ones as "horrible." Because they are clients and not "normal" happy humans—if such people really exist!—they usually have more, bigger, and longer-lasting misfortunes and losses. Or *see* them that way. Or *make* them that way. Being neurotic—which usually means whining, howling, and panicked—they are often unusually talented at *creating* and *exacerbating* problems and difficulties.

Joann, for example, communicated her terror of being childless, bearing a deformed child, and having an unkind father for her child to George (and other lovers), thereby considerably helping these men to terrify themselves about marrying her, and to break off their relationship. Other panicked, semisuicidal, and enraged neurotics also ineptly bring about job losses, car accidents, or physical disabilities. So, with or without their own "help," their "awful" Activating Events may indeed be hazardous. Sometimes deadly!

Suppose your clients easily relate their "gruesome" A's or you somehow, in the first few sessions, lead them to do so. How do you first deal with them in your own mind in order to help these clients view them less neurotically? Ask yourself several important questions, especially:

Are your client's A's probably accurate ("factual" to their "social reality") or inaccurate (invented or grossly exaggerated)? If you view them as "false" to their "social reality" or exaggeratedly negative, you may decide to show your paranoid or exaggerating clients that their A's actually did not occur or were not as "bad" as they seemed. But watch it! If your clients are really paranoid, you may waste valuable time trying to talk them out of their "false" descriptions. Brief therapy doesn't always allow you so much luxury! You can try to *quickly* intersperse some doubts about their "false" or "exaggerated" A's and help them agree that they are really "not that bad." If so, they may—or may not—stop horrorizing about them.

Or you may use a more elegant approach: Agree with the client that her A's "really are" as "bad" as she makes them out to be, but show her that they are not *awful,* that she *can* stand them, that she can actually *enjoy* the challenge of coping with them, that she is quite *capable* of improving them or of nicely dealing with them in their present state, and that she can *accept* without *liking* them.

These kinds of philosophical solutions to coping with A's that are not "really" as grim as your client*s* *see* them are usually preferable to the empirical or "realistic" solutions of showing them that their A's are not "stupendous." One of the basic aims of "elegant" or "deeper" therapy—and particularly of "better" REBT—is to teach clients, as the title of my popular book says, *How to Stubbornly Refuse to Make Yourself Miserable About Anything—Yes, Anything!* Not all—or even most—clients are likely to construct a no-holds-barred, no-matter-what-happens-I-shall-show-my-self-how-to-ward-off-deep-misery. No, not all! But to the degree that they do achieve this desirable goal, they will tend to minimally awfulize about present *and future* unfortunate A's and will thereby make themselves less disturb*able*. Or so I hypothesize![1]

Let me give an illustrative case. Jonathan, a 50-year-old ex-banker, had enough real problems to encourage most people to depress themselves. He had emphysema, was still smoking, lived on meager disability payments, and was practically deserted by most of his old friends because they blamed him for creating his own problems and rarely wanted to be with anyone who still foolishly smoked. I accepted, of course, that his Activating Events were quite dismal and gave him some reason for strong feelings of sorrow and frustration. But (as usual), I was prepared to push him to give up his feelings of rage, depression, and worthlessness.

First, however, I was dubious about some of his Activating Events. For instance, he claimed that many of his old friends were deliberately enticing him to keep smoking, because they were angry about his encouraging them to smoke in the past and because, even after they had stopped smoking, he purposely invited them to his small apartment and practically blew cigar smoke in their eyes. They kept plotting with each other, he insisted, to tempt him to keep smoking, and even sent him anonymous gifts of fine, aromatic cigars—especially after he had told everyone he was about to quit.

To make matters much worse, said Jonathan, most of the people in his apartment house, even those he had no personal contact with, viewed his smoking as a severe fire hazard, and kept plotting and scheming to have him willingly leave or unwillingly be thrown out of his apartment. They fiendishly made loud musical and unmusical noises on all sides of his apartment. They rudely bumped into him in the hallway and elevator. They had their children jeer him and play pranks on him. They—well, you name it and they certainly did it. Viciously. With undoubtable intention.

Though I didn't see Jonathan as completely paranoid, as he convincingly showed that some of his old friends really *were* angry at him—because, partly, of his anger at them—and that they possibly were, at times, moderately vindictive, I thought that he went too far in implicating most of his neighbors, their children, his landlord, and even some strangers who noticed him smoking cigars in the street or in Central Park.

I got nowhere in trying to show Jonathan how much he was exaggerating—not to mention sometimes fabricating—innumerable people's hostile and combative actions. Being bright, he often beat me at my skeptical game by saying, "Yes, I agree with you that I *sometimes* exaggerate and see hostility where there is little or none. But the rotten things I keep telling you about happen *so* often—sometimes 20 times a day—that they can't *all* be a product of my imagination."

No dice. My attempts to help Jonathan accept social "reality" got me—and him—nowhere. So I tried two different therapeutic tracks. First, I acknowledged that most of his nasty A's were probably happening—but that he, by his own hostility, was helping to make them happen more often and more viciously than if he were less—and especially less noticeably—angry at his persecutors. He partly acknowledged this, so I first collaborated with him on a palliative plan of changing his "vicious" A's—other peoples "attacks"—in several ways: (1) He forced himself to tame his expressions of anger and to show much more "acceptance" and "approval" for people's "obnoxious" behavior than he really felt; (2) I taught him the "fogging" method of *seeming* to agree with others' views even when *inwardly* he disagreed; (3) I showed him how to be much more assertive rather than hostile—and to quickly ask people for what he wanted and politely refuse to do what he didn't want to do—instead of *un*assertively biding his time and building up so much frustration and anger that he finally reacted furiously.

These social-skills training methods worked so well that within a few weeks Jonathan appreciably changed some of his A's. His "old friends" became less critical, more caring, and were sometimes doing nice things for him instead of nasty things against him. He got such good benefits, in fact, that he saw that his own newfound niceness was quite reinforcing. It got great results and encouraged him to repeat his efforts to be agreeable and pleasant rather than disagreeable and sour to his "old friends." To his surprise, he found that he *liked* being friendly and warm much more than he previously *liked* being oversuspicious and unfriendly.

All to the good. Jonathan, within a few weeks, was happy with his therapy. So was I—though not *too* happy. I liked Jonathan's skill-training progress and liked the fact that it reduced his paranoid thinking. Now that he treated others well and they often returned this treatment in kind, voilà! he had few "horrors" of which to accuse them. My palliative methods had helped change his grim social "reality." He still, of course, had his emphysema and meager disability income. But many of his other annoying A's almost disappeared. And, along with them, his exaggerated and paranoid complaints. In only a few weeks' time, his therapy had really worked. Great.

Yes, Jonathan's brief therapy was great–but not "deep" or "elegant." Not enough for me. For Jonathan felt much better mainly because, by his own efforts to be sure, his nasty A's had changed. Was he yet able to live reasonably happily with *rotten* A's? No. Was he ready to face new troubles–such as lung cancer–that could happen to arise? No. Was he changed *philosophically?* Not very much. Jonathan was less disturbed– but not really less disturb*able*.

Noting this–because I *look* keenly for signs of less disturbability in virtually *all* my clients–I proceeded to implement Plan Two, which I had thought about during Jonathan's first session and had begun to partially employ as I was also working on Plan One. No, let me correct that. Plan One was to help Jonathan get more in touch with social "reality" and to acknowledge how paranoid he was. That didn't work–for even when he became less oversuspicious he did so not because he saw that he was exaggerating other people's "heinous crimes," but because they were treating him better. Had his skill training not worked and had others kept (in his eyes) treating him harshly, he still would have jumped to some paranoid thinking about *how* badly they were treating him. In fact, after his first therapeutic successes, he still blew people's criticisms out of proportion and often accused them of imaginary skullduggery.

Anyway, my Plan One failed. Plan Two–my cleverly "agreeing" with Jonathan and showing him how to skillfully induce people to be less hostile than they presumably were–worked very successfully and increased his faith in my willingness to help him and my adeptness at doing so. Fine. Now on to Plan Three. Plans One and Two were designed to help Jonathan deal with his Activating Events (A's). Plan Three went on to his dealing with his Beliefs (B's)

Plan Three–yes, "deeper" and "elegant" Plan Three–was designed to tackle Jonathan's basic emotional vulnerability, to help him be significantly less vulnerable to almost *any* appalling set of A's. To implement it, I first went out of my way to agree with Jonathan that he *was* being sorely and "nastily" put down by his "old friends," his neighbors, strangers in the street, and "you know who." Naturally, he ate up this agreement—which two other "stupid" and "rotten" therapists before me had refused to give him.

Just because his victimizers were "truly" oppressing him, and *wanted* him to feel very upset about this, I tried to convince Jonathan that he owed it to himself *not* to feel angry and depressed. If he managed to feel healthily *sorry* and *disappointed* about their persecutions, instead of unhealthily *horrified* and *frantic*, he would accomplish two important things: First, he would save himself a great deal of endless anguish; second, he would stop his persecutors from gloating over his upsetness. Ironically, Jonathan was more enthusiastic about this second possibility than about the first. Because he hated his victimizers so heartily, he wanted to deprive them of the satisfaction of gloating over his pain. So taking away their pleasure by *refusing* to upset himself about their cruel machinations appealed to him greatly. He decided to work with me on achieving *only* the healthy negative feelings of sorrow and disappointment.

Terrific! Jonathan and I enthusiastically collaborated on his acquiring several anti-awfulizing philosophies, which he steadily pursued and largely acknowledged in the course of the next two and a half months. And they were? These:

1. "I *can* dehorrify myself about my old friends' and other people's withdrawing from and persecuting me and I *can* take the steam out of their pleasure in bothering me and making me upset. Ironically, instead of their bothering me, I shall be bothering them. That will be marvelous!"
2. "Even if I don't bother my persecutors by making myself less disturbed about their rotten deeds, it will be wonderful if I stop plaguing myself about them. Dr. Ellis is really right: This is an even more important goal—to first think of *me* and *my* upsetness and reduce that for *my* sake. Damn it, I will really work on that!"
3. "It is certainly *bad* what my old friends and others are doing to me and they are very *wrong* for doing it. But, as REBT keeps saying, humans have the right to be wrong. They are—like all humans—very fallible. So they will *often* act badly. But their putrid *acts* never make them *rotten people*."
4. "It's really deplorable the way many people are persecuting

me. But it's not *horrible* or *awful.* It could be *worse* than it is. More of them could be violating me, and could do it more often. So it's not *totally* bad. And, although it's unfair, it *should* be unfair–because it *is.* So my insisting that it *must* not be as unfair as it indubitably *is* unfair is silly. It still *is*–and therefore *has to* be. Unfairness is practically the human condition. Even for me!"

As Jonathan continued to work on these philosophies, he made himself less and less angry and depressed. He still was far from happy when he remembered what his friends and others had done to him in the past–but he was also delighted that he had cleverly stopped most of them from currently continuing to persecute him. He never completely forgave what they *did,* but he forgave *them* for doing it.

I, too, was fairly happy. For rather than stopping after I helped Jonathan to change moderately, to stop his "persecutors" in their tracks, and thereby to achieve better relationships with them, I went for a much more "elegant" solution: to show him how to make himself less disturbed *and* less disturb*able.* That is my usual goal for my clients and though they by no means always achieve it, I feel damned good–and my clients feel delighted–when they do.

So short-term therapy *can* be intense and profound. Sometimes!

Can your accepting your clients' "horrible" Activating Events as "factual" when they may be paranoid or exaggerated have real disadvantages? Indeed, it can. It may encourage them to become more paranoid. It may lead, as it first did in Jonathan's case, to superficial philosophical changes. It may encourage your fictionalizing clients to make themselves angrier, and possibly violent.

So be careful. Don't use this method indiscriminately. Even when it works, try to help your clients make profound philosophical changes. Help them, for example, accept the "sinners" who are "persecuting" them– though not necessarily their "sins." Help them see the "naturalness" of others' "persecutory" behaviors. Help them see that they themselves are sometimes mean and vindictive–and can be forgiven for their own "sins."

Philosophical changes, such as these, is what REBT usually strives for. And often can, in brief time, help to effect.

NOTES TO CHAPTER 4

1. Bard, 1980; Bernard, 1991, 1993; Bernard & Wolfe, 1993; Dryden, 1994a, 1994b; Dryden & Neenan, 1995; Ellis, 1962, 1965b, 1972a, 1979e, 1980c, 1991b, 1994e; Ellis, Young, & Lockwood, 1987; Shedler, Mayman, & Manis, 1993; Walen, DiGiuseppe, & Dryden, 1992; Wessler & Wessler, 1980; Wolfe, 1993.

5

How to Deal with Real Traumas in Your Clients' Lives

Most of your clients—and perhaps those you can especially help in brief therapy—keep whining and screaming about relatively minor unfortunate Activating Experiences (A's). A boss, for example, criticizes them harshly when their work is "mediocre," but never threatens to fire them. A daughter insists on dating the "wrong" guy. A friend keeps forgetting to pay back fifty dollars he owes them. A mate has sex only once a week when they want it twice. Horrors! The end of the world ensues.

But not always! Some clients experience *real* traumas at point A. *Serious* accidents, incest, rape, loss of the best job they ever had, or poverty. Or *continual* setbacks: a series of colds and sore throats, being steadily dunned by creditors, betrayal by several close friends, three bad marriages in a row. You name it and some of your clients—indeed, quite a few—suffer from harsh Adversities. Only then do they carp, complain, and castigate life.[1]

What to do, then, when you *agree* that your clients' A's are indeed deplorable, uncalled for, and downright cruel? Well, naturally, you quickly try to help them improve these dismal A's. If you can!

36

But suppose you can't help? You can't show them how to reduce their woes. You can't, and they can't even stop their woes from continuing. What then?

Well, you can try to use, and to help your clients achieve, various REBT palliative and elegant outlooks. Such as those I tried with Jill.

Jill, a 20-year-old college student, had several bad A's. She was crippled in an auto accident when she was 16 and could walk and exercise only with real pain. Her parents were divorced, and she and her younger brother lived with their mother, who worked as a secretary and had little money for herself and her children. Her father was remarried and, although he lived close by, visited Jill and her brother infrequently and refused to contribute to their support because he was angry at their mother for divorcing him. Jill was dyslexic and, though she wanted very much to be a teacher and tried hard at college, she had great difficulty in keeping up with her schoolwork. Finally, the males she was really attracted to were friendly but did not date her because of her physical problems and their belief that they could not have good sex with her.

Well, quite a kettle of handicaps! No wonder Jill felt depressed, kept almost entirely to herself, ground away desperately at her schoolwork, and often thought about suicide. Oh, yes, before her car accident Jill had been very beautiful, was fondled on several occasions by her father (whose wife divorced him when she discovered it), and now felt herself to be a cripple who was quite unattractive.

I naturally agreed with Jill that she had much more than her fair share of woeful A's. I even wondered to myself, once in a while, whether her thoughts about killing herself were somewhat rational, because though she could still have some degree of enjoyment, her two great interests—getting excellent grades at school and dating attractive men—were sabotaged by her disabilities and, at best, she might well end up with a pain-ridden, quite deprived life. Seeing this, she could "rationally" ask herself, "Is it really worth it? Shall I bother to go painfully on?"

Because Jill was desperate, and because she might possibly kill herself before she managed to see some daylight, I particularly aimed to help her as rapidly as possible. So I agreed that her plight was indeed sorry, but insisted that she still *could* make a happy existence for herself and she *could*, though with difficulty, get her main goals fulfilled.

"Nonsense!" she exclaimed. "Let's not be pollyannaish about this. Be realistic!"

I'm a tough cookie myself, so I persisted:

AE: I *am* being realistic. One of your main goals is to be a teacher. Right?

Jill: Yes, very right.

AE: And you're having trouble, especially with your dyslexia, getting the good marks you want to get. Right?

Jill: Bully for you! Right again!

AE: Fine, but you don't need very good marks to pass your courses and get your B.S. in education.

Jill: I don't?

AE: Of course you don't. You just have to *pass*, not get all A's.

Jill: True, but I even have trouble passing some of my courses. What about *that*?

AE: How many of them have you actually failed in your three years of college?

Jill: Well—well, none.

AE: Oh! So, for all your trouble passing, and all your lack of A's, you still pass, pass, pass. No?

Jill: (*very softly and reluctantly*) Yes.

AE: So what about *your* nonsense? It looks like, with continued hard work, you have at least 9 out of 10 chances—maybe 99 out of 100—of getting through.

Jill: You really think so? That good a chance?

AE: Definitely. Wanna bet. (Jill was silent for a while. Then she began again.)

Jill: Okay. Let's suppose you're right. I may well get through school.

AE: And be a teacher.

Jill: Okay. Let's suppose that. But what about my dating and winning a guy I really want? Not the basket cases who now occasionally want me. But a real good guy?

AE: Well, you most likely can—if you'll stop being a hermit and go to a little trouble to get what you want.

Jill: A *little* trouble?

AE: Yes, more than you—like most women—are willing to do.

Jill: And that is—?

AE: Be assertive. Don't be passive. Forthrightly go after a few men whom you really want. Let yourself be rejected and rejected—as happens to all of us in this dating game—and wind up with one or two you really want who also, for one reason or another, want you.

Jill: You really mean that–get myself rejected and rejected? How horrible!

AE: That's just the point. It's *not* horrible–only a pain in the ass! Most women, even when not at all handicapped, won't do this, and many wind up settling for someone they don't really want but who assertively wants *them*. The few who do what I'm trying to get you to do–as I originally advocated in 1963 in the first edition of *The Intelligent Woman's Guide to Dating and Mating*–get plenty of rejections, *don't* put themselves down for getting them, and finally usually do get what they want.[2]

Jill: They do?

AE: Yes, with much effort. And, usually, after many rejections. But these kinds of rejections are always good and beneficial.

Jill: Like hell they are!

AE: No, they *are*. Because you then get rid of the men who *don't* want you *fast*. See?

Jill: Oh.

AE: Oh!

Jill: But you forget one important thing that I told you before. One of my male friends frankly told me that two other men he knew thought I was very attractive but thought that because I am so restricted in movement and in so much pain that they couldn't ever have good sex with me.

AE: No, I remember that very well. But you have a very good answer to that handicap, too–if you use it.

Jill: And that is.

AE: Simply let all the males you're interested in know that having good *sex* doesn't mean having *intercourse*. Does it?

Jill: Well–uh, no.

AE: See what I mean?

Jill: You mean that I can let them know that I can do what me and my boyfriends did before my accident, when I was 15? Pet to orgasm.

AE: Right! Use your hands–or even your mouth–to give them some of the greatest orgasms they've ever had!

Jill: Yes, I could do that. But suppose that some of them mainly or only want intercourse. What then?

AE: Then they are not for you. Too bad–but you can't win them all! Don't forget that if you only liked intercourse, some men would reject you for not loving oral sex.

Jill: I see. I guess I can't win them all.

AE: But you *can* win a hell of a lot of them if you show how hot you are for oral, manual, and other kinds of sex.

Jill: I never thought of that!

AE: Well give it some real thought!

Jill did give it some real–and rational–thought. Without any further urging, she started to approach a number of men whom she thought attractive–and let some of them know very quickly that she loved oral sex, loved giving and receiving it, and got some of her greatest orgasms going down on a suitable man. Within a few weeks she had more dates than she could handle–and was almost neglecting her schoolwork.

My plan was quite successful in showing Jill that her real handicaps were hardly fatal and could be overcome–so that she could most probably finish school, become a teacher, and get into a sex and love relationship with a "good" man. She quickly became–or made herself–undepressed and was even a little guilty about previously looking at her life so dismally and thinking about suicide. She now had a forward-looking attitude and often felt disappointed when life was hard and things didn't come her way. But she was basically content, in spite of her remaining handicaps.

Fine and dandy. I was pleased with Jill's and my efforts, happy that she was no longer in the throes of her worst symptom–depression. But I was still aware that she could have theoretically made a much deeper and more elegant solution to her emotional problems. Thus, she could have been able to still be reasonably happy *without* graduating from college, *without* being a teacher, and *without* a good relationship. Even under such *rotten* conditions, she could make herself feel sad and frustrated, but not depressed. For depression, according to REBT theory, usually stems from the rational Belief (rB), "I really don't like what's happening to me!" *plus* the irrational Belief (iB), "Therefore, it *must* not be happening! It's *awful* that it is occurring. I can't bear it."[3]

Theoretically, and more elegantly, Jill could make herself only healthily *sad* and not unhealthily *depressed* about the highly deprived state she at first was in and thought that she had to continue. Should I bother, since she was doing so well, to try to help her to achieve this elegant solution?

I decided not to try too hard. Because if I stressed that even under the worst conditions she need not depress herself, she might focus too much on how bad some of her remaining restrictions really *were* and might make herself depressed again.

I did, however, keep mentioning to her, from time to time, that other handicapped people–like Christy Brown of the *My Left Foot* documentary fame–had even worse handicaps than she had, and that they managed to fare quite well. She read several articles and books about such people, and she voluntarily read my book *How to Cope with a Fatal Disease.*[4]

She then brought up the subject of making an elegant philosophical change herself. "I'm doing very well," she said after three months of therapy. "I even have a steady boyfriend who I really like. And we're having great sex together. He tells me that he's never had it so good! But suppose, because of my physical handicaps, he doesn't want to marry me. Suppose other good males feel the same way–as most of them may. What can I do then to refuse to depress myself?"

"Then," I answered, "you use what we call the *elegant* REBT solution."

"You mean focus on other enjoyable things in my life and not on that dismal one."

"Right. And try to get and retain a vital absorbing interest that will keep you creatively busy for many years to come."

"Oh, I've already thought of one and I'm sure I'll love it."

"And that is?"

"Teaching handicapped children. After I finish college, I'll go for a Master's degree in that area. And I would greatly enjoy teaching all kinds of handicapped children–mentally, emotionally, and physically handicapped–how to lead a happy life in spite of their disabilities. Including teaching them REBT."

"That would be fine!" I said. "But suppose these kids keep telling you, 'I see that I can do several things that I enjoy. But what am I going to do about the important things that I can't enjoy because of my handicaps? How am I going to stop depressing myself about that?' What will you answer them?"

"Well," said Jill, "I guess I'll tell them, 'It's really *rough*. You *do* have unusual limitations. But you can't have everything. Now why not *accept* the disadvantages you don't *like*? See that they're bad but not *awful*–or *more* than bad. And take the *challenge* of getting what you *can* out of your life while *realizing* but also *accepting* what you *cannot* get. Now begin to focus on your available enjoyments!'"

"That's excellent!" I said to Jill. "You'll really help many of those children if you talk to them like that. But see that, if you keep talking to *yourself* along similar lines, you've basically found a solution to your *own* problem."

"Yes," said Jill. "I guess I can see that."

She kept working on this kind of REBT outlook and, two boyfriends later, she found one who wanted to live with her. Mainly, he said, because of her rational philosophy and her low degree of upsetability.

So once again, in this case, Jill and I achieved a fairly elegant solution to her emotional problems–after her original depression had been nicely dissipated by her training herself to work on some important practical considerations while she stopped complaining that answers to them could not be found. Jill could have stopped her therapy only a few weeks after starting it. But she determinedly stayed for four months longer until she felt that she was then, even if very bad events should keep recurring, much less depressible.

How about the dangers and disadvantages in treating clients in the way I treated Jill? Indeed, there are dangers. If you press your traumatized and handicapped clients to make an "elegant" philosophical change, and to undisturbedly accept the *worst* possibilities that may occur, some of them will obsess about these "horrors" and upset themselves more.[5] Some of them may accept only an unrealistic or pollyannaish "solution" and soothe themselves by insisting that things will certainly improve.[6] Other will "see" things as less "bad" than they really are. Still others will *too* readily accept their handicaps and, therefore, give up trying to ameliorate them. Others will fully accept the *facts* of their disabilities but refuse to accept the *nonhorror* of these facts and may resort to abysmal self-pity.

Your trying to help your client achieve "elegant" REBT solutions to their emotional problems is fine–for some of them, some of the time. Others won't work at achieving this "elegance," will disturb themselves more by facing "awful" handicaps, or will take so long to "really" accept grim reality that brief therapy is precluded.

In the case of Sidney, who had an avoidant personality disorder, I believed that he was capable of "elegantly" accepting his life in spite of his becoming totally blind at the age of 27, but I realized that he would do so only after prolonged therapy, which was too expensive for him and was impractical for him to arrange. So I focused mainly on his improving the quality of his life by composing songs and making friends through computer network correspondence, both of which he found very enjoyable. I also directed him to REBT reading and cassette listening and had occasional phone sessions with him. After two and a half years of this kind of intermittent REBT activity, Sidney got closer to the "elegant" solution of unconditional acceptance of himself and his severe handicaps, but never "made it" as fully as he might have done with more intensive and prolonged therapy.

NOTES TO CHAPTER 5

1. Ellis, 1994b, 1994e; Goleman, 1993; Lazarus & Folkman, 1984; Moore, 1993; Resick & Schicke, 1993; Warren & Zgourides, 1991.
2. Ellis, 1979b.
3. Ellis, 1962, 1987a, 1994e; Hauck, 1973; Simon, 1993; Walen, DiGiuseppe, & Dryden, 1992; Walen & Rader, 1991.
4. Brown, 1985; Ellis & Abrams, 1994.
5. Ellis, 1994b.
6. Taylor, 1990.

6

Exploring Clients' Belief Systems:
Ego-Driven Musts

According to REBT theory, people rarely, if ever, have "emotional" and "behavioral" problems without contributory Belief systems—B, in the ABC's of Rational Emotive Behavior Therapy. For even when they have a "chemical imbalance" and, let us say, "just" get depressed, they are probably *made* to see and judge things worse because their neurotransmitters and other physiological factors are "off key." And when "biochemical" states of depression occur, people often cognitively observe and judge their "feelings"—and thus often create *other* disturbed feelings about their depression.

REBT fully acknowledges the importance of the A's as well as the B's in the ABC's of "emotional" disturbance—and of the C's as well. For, as just noted, when your clients experience disturbed Consequences *for any reason*, they usually react badly to them and thereby create additional disturbance about their disturbances—C's about C's.[1]

We could easily argue about the *prime* importance of our Beliefs in the ABC's of upsetness. Environmentalists and radical behaviorists argue for the priority of Activating Events (A's); cognitivists for the B's; and experientialists for the C's. All are at least partly right, and who is righter depends to some extent on how you define each one of these entities.

In REBT, and especially in brief and intensive REBT, we usually stress the B's. For REBT theory says that people, when they are disturbed, can often *quickly* find their dysfunctional or irrational Beliefs (iB's) and can sometimes *profoundly* change them in short order. This theory is backed by literally hundreds of REBT and CBT studies that show significant changes in individuals in individual and/or group therapy in from 10 to 20 sessions. Few of these studies, however, assessed *intensive and long-lasting* change.[2]

More to the point is the vast literature that shows that almost innumerable individuals, over the centuries, have listened to a sermon, read a book, spoken to a friend, or otherwise imbibed a new idea, attitude, or philosophy and have, as a result of thinking about and acting on this idea, radically changed their lives. Some, moreover, have done so quickly, within a few days or weeks of acquiring a new outlook. They have literally been converted—or converted themselves—to communism or capitalism, Christianity or Moslemism, Shamanism or skepticism. You name it and they have done it. Radically, permanently, often rabidly. Sometimes from one extreme (e.g., devout Catholicism) to another extreme (devout Atheism).[3]

Didn't these people who made revolutionary changes have predispositions and prior experiences that fomented or aided their changes? Indeed, many of them did. But didn't their new cognitions often spark their changes and lead to their new actions and experiences? Indeed they did.

What about new experiences themselves instigating radical "personality" and philosophical changes? Well, they certainly often do! Near death experiences. Failing in a career. Falling in love. Succeeding in a sport one previously "couldn't do." Being raped or tortured. Witnessing a murder. Again, all kinds of dramatic—but also "ordinary"—experiences.

With such "crucial" experiences, however, go thoughts. You think about these experiences—and often *make* them "vital." You think about what they "mean," how you can use them as "signs" or "guides," what you can "learn" by them. So, as REBT hypothesizes, your thoughts flow from, add to, accompany, affect, and change your feelings, actions, and "experiences." That is why therapeutic "experiences"—especially relationships with a therapist—may (or may not) significantly help you and your clients to change, as I shall specifically show later, and as many studies have already indicated.[4]

In this and several other chapters, we shall optimistically consider Beliefs. Some theorists—including radically different ones like George Kelly, Fritz Perls, and Wilhelm Reich—think that trying directly to change people's Beliefs about themselves and the world is futile and that only helping them to modify their feelings, experiences, bodies, and actions will work.[5] This may partly be "true"—but, obviously, most of these therapists used talk, persuasion, and teaching to induce their clients to "experientially" change. *Didn't* they?

REBT says that *one* way, and probably the *main* way, to help clients reduce their "emotional" disturbances and make themselves less disturb*able* is for them to make a strong and consistent change in some of their important irrational Beliefs (iB's). They usually hold several basic iB's, and the Devil knows how many derivatives. Primarily, as noted in Chapters One and Two, they tend to accept and construct the three main Jehovan commands: (1) "*I* must perform well!" (2) "*You* must treat me nicely!" and (3) "*Conditions* must be favorable!"

REBT hypothesizes that if your clients change any or all these *must*urbatory ideas to mere, though still strong, preferences—yes, really and truly *prefer* rather than *demanding*—they can remarkably and "deeply" change themselves in a few weeks or months. *If!*

Let us consider, in this chapter, the most common—and most deadly—dysfunctional Belief that your clients frequently (consciously and unconsciously) hold: "*I* (ego) *absolutely must* do well at important endeavors and be approved by significant others for doing so, and if I fail in these important ways, I am an inadequate, insignificant person!" What percentage of the five billion people in the world fairly often believe this notion and thereby sabotage themselves? Approximately 100%.

Take, for example, Trudi. Thirty-one years of age, a manager of a large office, attractive, mother of a "darling" seven-year-old daughter, living with a loving second husband, she had "nothing to complain about." But she had been "terribly anxious" all her life, she frantically rushed around all day, night, and weekends to "keep things under perfect control," and she constantly worried about her job, her daughter, her husband's love, and other "crucially important" things. Whatever she did was "not good enough" and she incessantly predicted, though never achieved, "dismal and total failure." Trudi strongly believed Irrational Belief Number One of REBT, acknowledged that she did so after reading my book, *A New Guide to Rational Living*, and wrote under "presenting problem" on the Institute's intake biographical form, "Perfectionism. Must do well all of the time."[6]

Well, that was fast! Bolstered in advance by some REBT reading, Trudi told me about her main iB's during our first session, acknowledged that her big problems were "perfectionism and performance anxiety," and said that she had come to therapy "to work on that." Good!

But not so fast! Trudi was bright and hardworking. She had cognitive therapy for a year before she came to see me, had read *A New Guide* at the suggestion of her therapist, and had worked to give up her perfectionism. To little avail. What was wrong? What could she do? How could she *really* change?

Using REBT theory, I took a chance, assumed that Trudi had a problem *about* her problem, and asked a few questions to test my hypothesis.

I was right. She had a *big* problem about having and giving up her perfectionism. Her self-defeating Beliefs that created this second problem—her symptom about her symptoms—included:

1. "I *must* not be as anxious as I am!"
2. "Because I am more anxious than I *should* be, I am an *anxious person*, an *inadequate individual.*"
3. "Being anxious is very uncomfortable and *awful.* I can't bear it!"
4. "If other people see how anxious I am they will despise me and often boycott me. And they are right!"
5. "My anxiety is disabling and will make me perform badly and be seen as an incompetent individual. That makes me even more worthless!"

After I questioned Trudi about her feelings and her ideas *about* her anxiety, she soon realized that this secondary problem was even worse than her primary one (acting imperfectly) and that she was usually so upset on this second level that it interfered with her working against her first-level anxiety. As she put it during our third session:

"I now see that every time I ask myself, 'What's so awful about performing imperfectly,' I answer, after reading *A New Guide*, 'It's really not awful—only damned inconvenient. So I'm still fallible!' I feel good for a minute or two. But then I think, 'But is my Disputing *really* working? Suppose it isn't. Suppose I'm still anxious. Let's see if I still am. Oh, my God! I think I still am! Hell, this Disputing isn't working! I'm still anxious! And everyone will see that I am! That's *really* terrible. I'll *never* get rid of this anxiety! How horrible!'

"I then focus so much on *my still* feeling anxious, and *how* awful that is, that I distract myself from my original perfectionism and *its* horrors. I'm so anxious about my anxiety that I can't think of anything else."

"Right," I said. "But not *can't.* You *don't* think of anything else. And you really don't have to. Focus, if you will, on the secondary anxiety—on your anxiety about your anxiety. And Dispute the horror of *that.*"

"Forget about my original perfectionism?"

"Yes, temporarily. Go to your *present* perfectionism. It's the same thing—but this time about your being perfectly unanxious."

"So I'm telling myself, 'I must be perfectly unanxious! I must be perfectly undisturbed.'"

"Aren't you?"

"Well—yes, I guess I am!"

"And you can Dispute that nutty idea by doing what?"

"Why *must* I be perfectly unanxious? Where is *that* written?"

"Exactly. Keep Disputing along those lines."

That was quite a breakthrough for Trudi. She temporarily forgot about her perfectionism about her original performances, and strongly focused on her perfectionistic demand that she absolutely *must not,* under *any* conditions, be anxious. When, on this second level, she fully gave herself permission to be anxious, stressed out, and panicked *about* her anxiety, she enormously relaxed. Much of her primary anxiety vanished, too, and she was then able to successfully Dispute it when it returned.

Trudi's case shows the multilevel aspect that Irrational Belief Number One often, probably usually, takes. Once your clients devoutly believe, "I *absolutely must* do well at important tasks!" and once they bring on poor performances (e.g., anxiety and inhibition) *by* this Belief, they will "logically" see their disturbed feelings as "rotten" performances, and bring on emotional-behavioral problems about them. The emotionally blind creating more blindness!

In these cases, one of the quickest and best methods, again, is to assume that secondary disturbances exist, check them out, and tackle them first if they actually do exist. Not necessarily, of course. If Trudi's primary anxiety was that she absolutely had to be a perfect mother, and if she made herself so panicked about this that she couldn't take care of her daughter at all and her husband was therefore about to divorce her, I might quickly and intensively push her to Dispute her child-rearing perfectionism, to modify it considerably, and *then* proceed to tackle her perfectionism *about* her motherhood perfectionism ("I must not be anxious about motherhood!"). Perhaps. But even then, if her anxiety about her anxiety were really high, she might be practically unable to get to and to Dispute her anxiety about being an imperfect mother.

So the REBT rule is: You often work with the secondary disturbance first, but sometimes you reverse this order. How do you determine *which* order? Use your clinical judgment.

Back to primary ego-driven *musts*. These are often endless. The two basic ones tend to be: "I *must* perform well!" and "I *must* be approved by significant others!" With hundreds of variations. And many common results: anxiety, depression, self-loathing, inhibitions, phobias, shyness, unassertiveness, withdrawal, etc. Practically all these neurotic symptoms involve strong "I musts" and "I must nots," which you can easily and quickly figure out by using REBT ABC theory.

Figure out? Yes, deduce, guess, infer, hypothesize. Given a negative Activating Event or Adversity (A) by your clients, and given a neurotic feeling or (in)action (C)—such as those C's listed in the previous paragraph—you can almost always make a good guess about your client's B's. For example:

> A–Failure at school, sports, or work.
> C–Depression.
> B–?

Fairly obviously: "I *should* have succeeded! There's no excuse for my failing! I'm no damned good for letting myself fail! I'll never succeed at this important endeavor!"

> A–Rejection by a lover, mate, family member, friend, or
>   boss.
> C–Withdrawal from getting involved in or looking for a good
>   job.
> B–?

Fairly obviously: "I must not get rejected! How awful! I'm a real loser! I'll never get accepted the way I have to be!"

Easy? Can you always find B's when you discover a client's unfortunate A's and self-deprecating C's? Yes, practically always if you ask yourself these simple questions:

- What are his absolutistic shoulds, oughts, musts, supposed to's, got to's?
- What are her awfulizings, terribilizings, horribilizings?
- What are his can't-stand-it's and can't-bear-it's?
- What are his self-downings, ideas of inadequacy, worthlessness, slobhood?
- What are her overgeneralizations, allnesses, and nevernesses?

Is that it? Yes, that's pretty much it for quickly figuring out your clients' dysfunctional ego-oriented Beliefs. Further details may—or may not—be important. But fill in, in your own head, this outline. Pronto. Fast. Almost immediately.

Don't get sidetracked. Don't fool around. Answer the above questions. To your own tentative satisfaction. Now! Usually, in a session or two.

To be more precise and to give you detailed instructions about finding your clients' Beliefs (B's), and especially their neurosis-inciting irrational Beliefs (iB's), let me present some excerpts from the article by Ted Crawford and myself, "A Dictionary of Rational-Emotive Feelings and Behaviors," which appeared in 1989 in the *Journal of Rational-Emotive and Cognitive-Behavior Therapy*. In this article, we point out that when your clients have disturbed, destructive emotions—such as severe anxiety, anger, depression, self-hatred, and self-pity—they almost always have *both* a set of rational Beliefs (rB's) *and* a set of irrational Beliefs (iB's) that accompany these dysfunctional feelings. Their rB's usually lead to healthy, self-helping feelings—such as sorrow, regret, frustration, and annoyance—and their iB's, as noted in the previous sentence, usually lead to disturbed feelings.[7]

For example, when your clients have feelings of inadequacy, self-hatred, ego-deflation, unworthiness, Ted Crawford and I say that they tend to have these main rB's and iB's:

1. (rB) I want you to approve or like me.
   (iB) You *must* approve of me because if you don't I cannot accept myself.
2. (rB) I want you to approve or like me.
   (iB) (a) I *need* your approval but because I perform so badly you *must* not, cannot, or *should not* approve of me.

(b) Because my bad performing, which I *must* not do, shows I am a rotten person.

3. (rB) I want success.
  (iB) (a) I *must* succeed but because I don't have the ability always to do so I *can't stand* my inadequacies and hate myself for being deficient.
  (b) Therefore, I am a rotten person!

4. (rB) I like doing well and I dislike failing or acting immorally.
  (iB) When I fail at important things or act immorally, as I *must not*, I am an undeserving, rotten person.

When your clients feel severe anger, rage, or fury, they tend to have these main rational Beliefs (rB's) and irrational Beliefs (iB's):

1. (rB) I want what I want you to do and I feel frustrated when you don't do it.
  (iB) Therefore,
    (a) You absolutely *should* not frustrate me.
    (b) You are a *rotten person* for frustrating me.

2. (rB) I want what I want and I don't want to go without it.
  (iB) Therefore, things *should* go my way and give me exactly what I want and definitely *need.*

3. (rB) I want you to give me exactly what I want.
  (iB) Consequently,
    (a) Life is *awful* if you don't exactly give it to me.
    (b) You are *no good* for not exactly giving it to me.

4. (rB) Life should preferably bring me joy.
  (iB) Therefore,
    (a) If things aren't the way they *should* be, it's *awful!*
    (b) Life is hell when it doesn't give me what I want and what it *should* give me!

5. (rB) I don't like not getting what I want.
  (iB) Therefore,
    (a) I *must* get what I want for me to be okay.
    (b) If I don't get what I want, I am *worthless.*
    (c) Rather than my seeing myself as worthless, *you're* worthless if you do not give me what I need to make me worthwhile!

6. (rB) If I don't get what I want, I may suffer a serious loss.
   (iB) (a) I *can't stand* this loss that I *must* not suffer.
       (b) How horrible for you or the world to deprive me and make me suffer!

7. (rB) I may feel badly if I don't get what I want.
   (iB) That will mean that
       (a) I have little ability to get what I want.
       (b) I have little worth as a person.
       (c) Rather than feel I have little ability and am worthless for suffering a serious loss, I feel better thinking that you, who frustrate me, are worthless.

8. (rB) I want you to treat me fairly and properly, and I won't like it if you don't.
   (iB) Therefore,
       (a) You *should* treat me fairly and properly.
       (b) If you don't, I *can't stand* it!
       (c) You are no damned good for making me feel horrible!

9. (rB) You behave unfairly and I don't like it and feel annoyed.
   (iB) Therefore, I *must* feel angry at you and *must* let you clearly know how angry I feel.

10. (rB) I dislike not getting what I want and therefore feel frustrated.
    (iB) Consequently, I *must* feel angry or else I am a weakling.

11. (rB) You keep acting wrongly and I don't like your behavior.
    (iB) Therefore, you *mustn't* do that wrong thing and *must* not bother me!

12. (rB) I dislike it when you *should* me.
    (iB) You *must* not lay your should on me and are no good if you do what you *must* not.

13. (rB) I dislike it when you *should* me.
    (iB) (a) Underneath, I agree with you and I *shouldn't* act badly. Therefore, I feel guilty, and I think I *should be* condemned.
        (b) Therefore, you *must not* make me feel bad (by

reminding me of how worthless I am) and, you're a *rotten person* when you remind me of my guilt!

14. (rB) I dislike it when you *should* or *must* me.
    (iB) (a) I don't agree with your *must* because musts deprive me of freedom.
    (b) I *can't stand* musts that deprive me of freedom.
    (c) So, I'll eliminate your musts on me by thinking you have no right to hold them and thereby making myself angry at you.

When your clients have low frustration tolerance or what I have also called discomfort anxiety, they tend to have these rational Beliefs (rB's) and irrational Beliefs (iB's):

1. (rB) I don't like existing conditions.
   (iB) (a) Therefore, they *should* or *must* change to give me what I like.
   (b) Otherwise I *can't stand* it and I can't be happy at all!
2. (rB) I would like immediate gratification.
   (iB) (a) Therefore, I *must have* immediate gratification and *have to* get it.
   (b) Or else I *can't stand* it and my life is *awful!*
3. (rB) I find hassles and frustrations inconvenient.
   (iB) (a) They *must* not exist!
   (b) They are awful when they do exist!
   (c) I can't stand them!

Let's suppose that you do quickly find your client's absolutistic musts and some of their main derivatives—his awfulizing, can't-stand-it-itis, self-damnation, and overgeneralizing. Do you immediately show them to him, with no nonsense about it?

Usually, yes. Why not? What have you got to lose? What does he have to gain if you do show him his irrational Beliefs?

Answer to this last question: Quite a lot.

If you are right about your client's main iB's, if you present them to her, and even if she only lightly agrees that she holds them, you have probably helped her:

1. To see some of the main reasons for (that is contributions to or "causes" of) her disturbances (C's).
2. To see that, at least in part, she *owns* her iB's and *chooses* to believe them. Her choice may be automatic or "unconscious" but she still largely *selects* it.
3. To see that she can therefore *disown* her iB's and change them to rational or self-helping *preferences*.
4. To see that she can *feel against* and *act against* her iB's, and change them emotionally and behaviorally, as well as cognitively.

If you are wrong about your client having certain iB's that you think she has, she can still benefit by:

1. Testing your hypotheses, to see how wrong they are.
2. Coming up with other, different reasons for her disturbances.
3. Showing you what your errors are, and inducing you to change your hypotheses about her iB's.
4. Collaborating with you to explore her disturbances further and encouraging both of you to come up with other iB's or other explanations for her disturbances.
5. Seeing that you, her therapist, are willing to shift your therapeutic gears and to serve as a flexible model of scientific thinking.

According to REBT, then, you will probably quickly and helpfully guess at and arrive at "good" iB's for you and your client to work on and to change. But as long as you *quickly* do so, your mistakes in this regard will still most likely help you and your client to find other and "better" reasons and explanations for her disturbances (C's) and to still quickly work to help her change. So, again, what have you—and she—got to lose by your quickly figuring out and tentatively showing her her "important" iB's? Very little.

However, if you bungle this job and lead your client up the garden path, you may help bring about these dangers:

1. Delay. Your "brief" therapy may be prolonged.
2. Standoff. Even if you are "correct" about your client's iB's, he may not buy your views, may fight against them, may agree

with them *lightly* but not really work to Dispute and change them.

3. Harm. You may convince your client of the wrong iB's—convince him, for example, that he hates himself for failing when he really finds failing *awful* or *more than* bad. His giving up his "self-hatred" may, therefore, do no good and, by distracting him from reducing his low frustration tolerance, may possibly harm him. Again, if his feelings of depression (C) are not really created by his self-hatred but by a chemical imbalance influenced by his biochemical deficiency, you had better reveal to him his self-downing, but also encourage him to get proper antidepressant medication.

So, whether you are right or wrong about your client's dysfunctional Beliefs, pointing them out and encouraging her to change them may not be helpful. So what? I still say: Take a chance. Look for her iB's, presumably find them, and then *un*dogmatically show her that they *probably* exist, that they *probably* help create her ego-downing, and that she *probably* can reduce her anxiety, depression, phobias, and withdrawal by actively and forcefully Disputing and acting against her iB's. This indeed may not work. But if your client desires *quick* and *intensive* results, try it and see. Briefly and experimentally. If this isn't effective, you can always go on, a little later, to some of the other methods that I shall soon describe.

Again: Find your client's main iB's that accompany his self-deprecation and, usually, quickly show him what they probably are. Then teach him REBT Disputing. In particular, empirical, logical, and pragmatic or practical Disputing. Like this:

EMPIRICAL DISPUTING

Your client's ego-oriented iB's are almost always "false" or "unrealistic," because they do not conform to her "reality." Actually, "objective reality" may not "truly" exist or at least be "provable" because it is always perceived, as Kant showed, by fallible, limited humans.[8] It may possibly exist "in itself" and be equally "knowable" to humans, other animals, and Martians. But that seems "objectively" unprovable.

What does exist, largely by human consensus, are various kinds of *social* "reality." Thus, humans are "alive" or "dead" because much of the time we agree on our definitions of these terms and few of us, therefore, would allow a "dead" person to vote, make out a will, or share our meals. "Aliveness" and "deadness" may indeed be "intrinsically" different. But they also have a *social* meaning and significance. We *humans* partly create this meaning, and we can always change it—as when we decide to ignore or to worship our ancestors.

Anyway, *social* "reality" seems to exist, although it is not invariant or immutable, and largely exists by consensus. To a large extent, then, our "rational" (self-helping) and "irrational" (self-defeating) Beliefs can be empirically tested in terms of this "reality." For example:

Your client Believes, "I *absolutely must*, under all conditions, perform well at important tasks, be especially competent at my job, and consistently please my boss." So you actively Dispute his Belief and show him how to keep disputing it.

"Where is the evidence that you always have to be competent at your job and consistently please your boss?"

You and he quickly check with his social reality and he comes up with this answer: "Doing well on my job is 'factually' important (because I *choose* this goal). It is, therefore, 'good' (beneficial) if I perform to my boss's satisfaction, don't get fired, and get salary raises. Considering the 'reality' of my preferences, of my job, and of my boss, these things are 'true.' *But* I clearly don't *have to* always do well and please my boss. I *can* do poorly, can *often* perform badly, won't die if I do, and may even possibly keep my job and get raises if I sometimes screw up."

Your client's *social reality*, therefore, usually (not always) "proves" that there is no reason why he *absolutely must* always do well on his job (or anything else), no matter how *preferable* his succeeding would be.

Similarly, your client's derivative iB's, which accompany his absolutistically demanding that he *must* succeed, can fairly easily be revealed and *empirically* Disputed by you and by him. Thus:

Awfulizing: "Because I am doing poorly on my job and displeasing my boss as I *must not* do, it's *awful and horrible.*"

Disputing: "It's 'bad' for me to do my job poorly and displease my boss, but where is the evidence that it's *awful and horrible*?"

Answer: "There is no such evidence. If it were *awful*, it would be 100% bad, as *bad as it can be*. But just about nothing is *that* bad. It would also be *more than bad*, 101% bad—which, of course, it cannot be. It would be badder than it *must* be. But it clearly *has to be* just as bad as it actually now *is*.

I-can't-stand-it-itis: "Because I am doing poorly on my job and displeasing my boss, as I *must not* do, I *can't stand it!* I *can't bear* his disapproval. I *can't tolerate* losing my job."

Disputing: "Prove that I *can't stand* doing poorly, displeasing my boss, and losing my job. Is my finding it *unbearable* true to my social reality?"

Answer: "Of course not. If I couldn't *stand* failing, displeasing my boss, and getting fired, I would die. If I survived, I wouldn't be happy *at all.* But I won't die (unless I foolishly kill myself); and I *can* work to find some happiness even under such unfortunate circumstances."

Self-damnation: "Because I am doing poorly on my job and displeasing my boss, as I *must not do,* I *am* a complete failure, a totally inadequate person. I don't *deserve* any good things in life. Everyone will thoroughly despise and boycott me."

Disputing: "Am I really a *complete failure* who is incapable of *ever* succeeding? Is my *total person* worthless because my job *behavior* is poor? Will the universe call me *undeserving* and make me eternally suffer? Will *everyone* thoroughly despise and boycott me?"

Answer: "Hell, no! All these views of my *self,* my *personhood,* are unrealistic, no matter how much I *see* them as 'true.' In spite of my failing and being rejected by my boss, I *deserve* to live and enjoy myself, just because I *think* I do and because I *can* work to do so."

Overgeneralizing: "If I fail at my job, gain my boss's disapproval, and get fired, I'll *always* fail and *never* succeed at important projects. I can't succeed again."

Disputing: "Where is the evidence that I'll *always* fail, never succeed, and *can't* succeed again?"

Answer: "Only in my nutty head! Almost always, if I give up this crazy Belief, I can often succeed in the future."

LOGICAL DISPUTING

In addition to being contradicted by your clients' social reality, their self-sabotaging, irrational Beliefs (iB's) are usually illogical non sequiturs. They don't follow from the premises and assumptions on which they are based. Thus, if your clients assume that "All trees are healthy" and "This is a tree" it "follows" that this tree is "healthy." But only if their *assumption* is correct! If it isn't, their "logical" conclusion, "This tree is healthy," doesn't necessarily follow and may well be unfactual or false. So you and they would check their assumption or premise, "All trees are healthy"—which is false, because all trees are not healthy—and show that their observation "This is a tree" doesn't *prove*, by its social reality, that it *has to be* healthy. Similarly, you and your clients can logically rip up most of their self-defeating irrational Beliefs (iB's). For example:

Illogical Belief: "Because I *very much want* to do well at my job and please my boss, I *always absolutely have to* do so."

Disputing: "Granted that I *very much want* to do well at my job and please my boss, does it really follow that I *always absolutely have to* do so?"

Answer: "Of course it doesn't! There is no law of the universe that declares that my wants always *must* be fulfilled. Often, they aren't. No matter how strong my desire is, the assumption that the universe *has to* fulfill it doesn't follow. My *assumption* that my life at all times *must be* the way I *strongly want* it to be is *only* an assumption, not a fact."

Illogical Belief: "I am a *deserving person* who merits happiness only when I do well on my job and please my boss. I am now doing poorly and displeasing my boss. Therefore, I am an *undeserving person* who can achieve *no* personal worth or happiness."

Disputing: "Prove that I am a *deserving person* who merits happiness only when I do well on my job and please my boss."

Answer: "I can *believe* this but cannot *prove* it. This is my unprovable and unfalsifiable *assumption. If* I assume it, I will *make myself* feel *undeserving* and *worthless* when I do poorly on my job and displease my boss. But it is my unprovable *premise*, and not my failing at my job, that will *make* me "undeserving" and "worthless.""

PRAGMATIC AND PRACTICAL DISPUTING

In REBT, "irrational" basically means "unworkable," "inefficient," and "impractical." So you check to see whether your clients' Beliefs are likely to lead to "good" or "pragmatic" results. For example:

Impractical Belief: "*I absolutely must not* do poorly on my job and displease my boss or else I am worthless. I'll always fail, and will get nowhere at work and in life!"

Disputing: "Where will this Belief get me? Will it help me at work? Will it improve my life? Will it make me a happier person?"

Answer: "It will most probably get me nowhere. It will help make me anxious and depressed, and thereby hinder me at work. It will tend to sabotage my life. It will make me miserable and unhappy, even if it sometimes helps me to succeed on my job. If I keep this Belief as a *preference* but not as a *necessity*, I then may find it helpful at my work and in my life."

Using REBT, therefore, you can quickly zero in on your clients' irrational Beliefs (iB's), and show them how to Dispute them empirically, logically, *and* pragmatically. REBT definitely uses realism and logic in these respects. But it does so *in the service* of helping clients lead more useful, happier lives. It does not deify empiricism or logic, as Michael Mahoney, Vittorio Guidano, and other social constructivists have claimed at times. Instead, it uses several kinds of Disputing–including, as I shall show later, emotive and behavioral Disputing of iB's.[9]

Following the lines of REBT's empirical, logical, and pragmatic (or functional) Disputing, Ann Marie Kopec, Don Beal, and Raymond DiGiuseppe have included the following table (Table 1) in their article,

TABLE 1
Disputing Strategy

RHETORICAL STYLE	Logical	Empirical	Practical or Functional	Rational Alternative
Didactic	Just because you weren't perfect, it doesn't follow logically that your father wouldn't have molested you.	You're telling me that if you were perfect, your father wouldn't have molested you. But we don't have any evidence that this is true. Indeed all of the evidence suggests just the opposite.	It appears that you are experiencing several negative emotions (guilt, shame, and depression) by holding the belief that if you were perfect, your father wouldn't have molested you.	Perhaps you can think I was a normal, fallible child who made mistakes like all five and six year old's but those mistakes do not devalue me as a person.
Socratic	Does it follow logically that your father wouldn't have molested you, even if you were perfect?	Where's the evidence that if you were perfect, your father wouldn't have molested you?	What does this belief (If I were perfect, my father wouldn't have molested me) get you?	What might be a more realistic belief that you might construct about that situation, specifically concerning your fallibility and your father's disturbed behavior.

Reprinted with permission from Kopec, A. M., Beal, D., & DiGiuseppe, R. (1994). Training in RET: Disputational Strategies. *Journal of Rational-Emotive and Cognitive-Behavior Therapy, 12,* 47–60.

"Training in RET: Disputational Strategies," in a recent issue of the *Journal of Rational-Emotive and Cognitive-Behavior Therapy*.[10]

Because REBT is not merely a cognitive method of therapy, but just about always includes several emotive and behavioral techniques as well, it particularly emphasizes your working out homework assignments with your clients—especially if you want to help them become *self*-changers and to get into the habit of *continuing* to modify their thoughts, feelings, and actions for the rest of their lives. Therefore, you show your clients the ABC's of their disturbances, and how—as this chapter shows—to Dispute their irrational Beliefs. But you also agree with them to *keep* actively looking for these iB's when they behave dysfunctionally and to *keep* challenging and questioning them.[10]

To help them do this kind of homework, REBT has always encouraged clients to monitor their disturbed thoughts, preferably to clarify them by writing them down, and also to record the Effective New Philosophies (E's) that they thereby construct. Since 1968, REBT has devised and used several Self-Help Report forms for client use. The one most commonly used was created by Joyce Sichel and myself in 1984 and has been shown to work with many clients. It is reproduced here as Figure 1.[11]

When your clients use this Report, you often can go over some of the filled-out forms with them, to see if they are doing them adequately. Consider trying this Report as homework for some of your clients, to see how useful it is.

Even the best kinds of Disputing of your clients' ego-oriented problems may reach them *briefly* but not *intensively*. So let me show you in the next chapter how you can focus on teaching them "deep" and "elegant" Disputation and still achieve this kind of change in a relatively short period of time.

FIGURE 1
REBT SELF-HELP FORM

(A) ACTIVATING EVENTS, thoughts, or feelings that happened just before I felt emotionally disturbed or acted self-defeatingly: _____

(C) CONSEQUENCE OR CONDITION—disturbed feeling or self-defeating behavior—that I produced and would like to change: _____

(B) BELIEFS—Irratio-nal BELIEFS (iBs) leading to my CONSE-QUENCE (emotional disturbance or self-defeating behavior). Circle all that apply to these ACTIVATING EVENTS (A).	**(D) DISPUTES** for each circled Irrational BELIEF (iB). Examples: "*Why* MUST I do very well?" "*Where is it written* that I am a BAD PERSON?" "*Where is the evidence* that I MUST be approved or accepted?"	**(E) EFFECTIVE RATIONAL BELIEFS (RBs)** to replace my Irrational BELIEFS (iBs). Examples: "I'd PREFER to do very well *but I don't* HAVE TO." "I am a PERSON WHO acted badly, *not* a BAD PER-SON." "*There is no evidence* that I HAVE TO be approved, though I would LIKE to be."
1. I MUST do well or very well!	....	....
2. I am a BAD OR WORTHLESS PERSON when I act weakly or stupidly.	....	....
3. I MUST be approved or accepted by people I find important!	....	....
4. I NEED to be loved by someone who matters to me a lot!	....	....
5. I am a BAD, UNLOV-ABLE PERSON if I get rejected.	....	....
6. People MUST treat me fairly and give me what I NEED!	....	....

7. People MUST live up
to my expectations or
it is TERRIBLE!

....
....
....
....

8. People who act
immorally are
undeserving,
ROTTEN PEOPLE!

....
....
....
....

9. I CAN'T STAND
really bad things or
very difficult people!

....
....
....
....

10. My life MUST have
few major hassles or
troubles.

....
....
....

11. It's AWFUL or
HORRIBLE when
major things don't go
my way!

....
....
....
....

12. I CAN'T STAND IT
when life is really
unfair!

....
....
....

13. I NEED a good deal
of immediate
gratification and
HAVE to feel
miserable when I
don't get it!

....
....
....
....
....

**Additional Irrational
Beliefs:**

....
....
....

(F) FEELINGS and BEHAVIORS I experience after arriving at my EFFECTIVE
RATIONAL BELIEFS: _____

_____

**I WILL WORK HARD TO REPEAT MY EFFECTIVE RATIONAL BELIEFS
FORCEFULLY TO MYSELF ON MANY OCCASIONS SO THAT I CAN
MAKE MYSELF LESS DISTURBED NOW AND ACT LESS SELF-
DEFEATINGLY IN THE FUTURE.**

NOTES TO CHAPTER 6

1. Barlow, 1989; Barlow & Craske, 1989; Beck & Emery, 1985; Walen, DiGiuseppe, & Dryden, 1992; Ellis, 1962, 1979c, 1986a; Ellis & Abrams, 1994; Ellis & Velten, 1992; Wachtel, 1994.
2. Ellis, 1991b.
3. Ellis, 1983a.
4. Dryden, 1994a, 1994b; Horvath & Luborsky, 1993; Reandreau & Wampold, 1991.
5. Kelly, 1955; Perls, 1969; Reich, 1960.
6. Beck, 1976; Burns, 1980; Ellis & Harper, 1975; Hendlin, 1992; Walen, DiGiuseppe, & Dryden, 1992.
7. Crawford & Ellis, 1989.
8. Kant, 1929.
9. Ellis, 1990b; Guidano, 1991; Mahoney, 1991; Piaget, 1954.
10. Cohen, 1992; DiGiuseppe, 1991a; Kopec, Beal, & DiGiuseppe, 1994.
11. Sichel & Ellis, 1984.

7

Treating Clients with Ego and Self-Rating Problems "Deeply" and "Intensively"

Mark, a 33-year-old attorney who had serious ego problems, was schizoid and withdrew from competing for female partners, for intelligent friends, and for clients. An expert in tax law, he made a good deal of money for his firm, but never became a partner because of his shyness with clients and in his social life. He took to the ABC's of REBT and to the Disputing of his irrational Beliefs very well, because he enjoyed logical questioning of these Beliefs and almost always came up with the correct answers to the REBT self-help form. Unfortunately, he never quite believed these answers. He *saw* that he was not a worm for copping out on dates and having sex only in massage parlors, but he still *felt* worthless and "dirty." No matter how many times he told himself, and wrote on the REBT self-help form, that nothing terrible would happen if he got rejected by women and by clients, he made no effort to approach them. Then, as you might expect, he also mercilessly beat himself for his "stupid" avoidance.

So regular REBT Disputing helped Mark a little. But not much. He forced himself to have a few dates, then quit and went back to the massage parlors and to watching good movies on his VCR. Little else but this and his work.

Theoretically or "intellectually"—or what I call, lightly—Mark used REBT Disputing to conclude:

1. "I don't *have to* win attractive females or good clients, though I damned well would like to!"
2. "My shyness and anxiety about rejection are very inconvenient—but not *awful!*"
3. "I can view myself as a *good person* no matter what my serious deficiencies."
4. "I'll often fail, if I try to get contacts I really want, but not always."

However, Mark believed these sensible philosophies only somewhat—and *not* when he had a chance to approach a woman he found attractive. Then he had almost opposite Beliefs! So he copped out. After a few sessions of REBT, in spite of his "intellectual" insight and Disputing, we were stumped.

So I encouraged him to use several *forceful* Disputing methods:

Forceful Taped Disputing. He recorded some of his main irrational Beliefs—especially, "It's *too* hard to approach a woman when I'm very anxious. I *can't* make myself *more* uncomfortable when I already *feel* horribly discombobulated. I *must not* feel so nervous, so I *have to* run away!"

At first, Mark Disputed these ideas namby-pambily, as he acknowledged when he listened to his five-minute recording of them and his Disputations. Then, with my coaching, he much more vehemently put on tape, "I don't give a damn *how* anxious and uncomfortable I am when I think of approaching a woman. I *can*, yes, I definitely *can* talk to her! No matter *how* terrible I feel! No matter *how* anxious I am! I *never* have to run away. Never, never, never!"

Mark not only did this forceful Disputing and answering of his iB's at home, in the safety of his apartment, but was surprised to see that he could do it at singles bars and at a dance. The more he did it, the more he believed his answers—and the more overtures to women he began to make.

Forceful Coping Statements. From both his regular and his forceful

Disputing, Mark came up with some brief but vigorous coping state-ments—Effective New Philosophies—which he vigorously repeated to him-self many times. Such as, "It's *only* hard and *never* too hard for me to approach!" "To hell with my discomfort! It only lasts a *short* time if I bear it, and lasts *forever* if I escape from it!" "So I'm anxious. Tough shit! Let me plunge in *with* my anxiety!"

Again, Mark vigorously repeated these rational coping statements until he really felt them and acted on them.

Reverse Role Playing. Whenever Mark tended to relapse to his irratio-nal Beliefs or his lightly held rational ones, I took over his role, power-fully declaimed and rigidly held on to his iB's and gave him practice at talking me out of them. Thus, I would say, "Let's face it. I can't ap-proach attractive women. I'm *too* anxious and tongue-tied. I can't even open my mouth. Even with it closed, she sees how terrified and what a jerk I am. She wouldn't give me her number if I were the last man on earth. And she's right about that. What a complete fizzle I am! How hopeless!" Mark would then have to try to vigorously talk me out of this outlook.

Challenging Rational Beliefs. When Mark came up with rational an-swers to his Disputations, I would push him to stop parroting these Be-liefs, to think about *why* they were sensible or "true," and to keep chal-lenging them and "proving" their usefulness. Thus, he came up with, "It's not *awful*, only a pain in the neck, to get rejected by a very desirable woman!" "Fine!" I would say, "But *why* isn't such a pain in the neck *awful?*"

> Mark would then proceed to dialogue with himself, "Well, it's only *bad*, hardly awful."
> "But it's *so* bad, considering how great she is, it really seems to be *awful!*"
> "You mean as bad as it can possibly be?"
> "Well, no. But still *awful.*"
> "Awful? *More* than bad?"
> "No—but...still horribly bad."
> "Very bad, yes. But is that what you mean by 'horribly bad'?"
> "Well, yes. Very bad."
> "*Only* very bad. Not really awful?"
> Yes, I guess so. *Only* very bad."

By challenging and questioning his *good* answers to his Disputing, Mark was often able to make them stick. Yes, really stick.

Acting on Rational Beliefs. We arranged for Mark to write down some rational Beliefs—such as, "I *can* force myself to socialize better with some of my clients," to go over them a number of times, and to keep talking to "fearsome" people while strongly repeating them to himself. Sometimes, he would deliberately make himself, no matter how uncomfortable he felt, arrange a lunch or dinner date with a client so that he could socialize for an hour or two at a time.

After using these forceful methods of Disputing for two months and employing other REBT emotive and behavioral methods (which I shall describe later), Mark loosened up by tightening up his "intellectual" Beliefs. He not only approached a number of women and clients whom he previously "couldn't" approach, but did so with less and less anxiety and discomfort. It was this lesser feeling of harrowingness, more than the approaches themselves, that convinced him that he *really* was believing his thought-out healthy ideas.

Does "deep," "intensive," and vigorous Disputing of irrational Beliefs always work? Of course not. Some clients, no matter what you and they do, improve only slightly or moderately—as Mark at first did. Some never improve. Some get worse! My own experience in using REBT with literally thousands of clients shows that the kind of Disputing described in this chapter often works, and often with difficult customers (DC's). Sometimes, only after many months, even years. But sometimes after a few weeks or months.

Does forceful and vigorous Disputing of clients' iB's have disadvantages? To be sure, it does. People may come up with the "wrong" or inelegant answers—and vigorously believe them. Janice, for example, hated herself for almost everything she did and finally came up with the powerful idea, "I do many *good* things, not all *bad* ones. Therefore, I'm a darned good person." Good—but inelegant. She achieved only *conditional* self-acceptance and was in danger, in case she fell back to doing *more* "bad" things, of renewed self-downing.

John did even worse. From believing he was a thoroughly *bad person*, he strongly came to believe that most other people were really bad and that therefore he was okay. Not so great a solution—though his anger at *them* was in some ways "better" than his self-rage.

So, strong Disputing has its disadvantages and limitations. Recommend and teach it cautiously and selectively. Check–and have your clients check–its results.

Let me say at this point that a number of REBT therapists–including some I have trained myself–seem allergic to its hard-headed, forceful methods, and almost always practice it less vigorously. Still, they often help their clients to get good results. My hypothesis says that highly active-directive and vigorous REBT, by both therapists and clients, usually gets quicker and more intensive results. But just because it seems to do so with me and my clients doesn't prove that it mostly or always does. Again, experiment and see.

8

Disputing Angry and Hostile Musts Directed at Others

Irrational Belief Number Two that practically all people—and quite a few of your clients—hold much of the time is their rage-creating *must*: "Because I treat other people fairly and kindly, they *absolutely must* treat me nicely and justly, and it is *terrible* when they don't! I *can't stand* it! Their unfairness, particularly when it is frequent, makes them rotten, undeserving, damnable people! Even when I don't treat others too well, they *must* act kindly and fairly to me—or else they're no damned good!"

This *demand* that other people, including your intimates, do your bidding and treat you properly often makes you—and your clients—angry, resentful, enraged, furious, argumentative, violent, vindictive, and warring. It does immense harm to human relationships, leads to enormous inefficiency, and helps bring on a host of physical ills that are figuratively, and even literally, deadly.[1]

Anger and rage are not always foolish. Particularly when people and institutions *do* treat you abominably, your revving up your fury may motivate, push, energize, and almost compel you to deal with stupidity and injustice. Tyrants, of course, are usually angry, but so are those who work to overthrow them. So let us not say that rage is invariably inept and wrong. Not always! Strong displeasure against tyranny, rather than total damnation of tyrants, might lead to "rational" and more humane revolutions.

Don't forget, however, that when someone treats you "unfairly," you can bring on highly useful, healthy, and appropriate feelings—including strong feelings—of displeasure, frustration, and even "anger" at their *behavior* without damning *them* for this behavior. Speaking in REBT terms, what we call anger—and especially rage—normally condemns the *sinner*, the *person*, not just his or her *sins*. Quite different! And, usually, quite pernicious.

Tom was typical in this respect. An EAP (Employment Assistance Program) counselor, he dealt with angry members of his company very often—and usually very well. He used REBT and cognitive behavior therapy (CBT) methods to show them how harmful their rage was, how they largely created it in response to "unfair" happenings, and what they could do to tone it down and change it to irritation and annoyance at others' "bad" acts. He even used his counseling methods on himself and rarely enraged himself at his superiors and co-workers when they treated him and other company members "unjustly." Which they often (in his eyes) did.

At home, Tom was quite different. Being a "good" son, husband, and father, in his own and other family members' view, and often making real sacrifices for his original and current family, he *couldn't stand* their "unappreciativeness" and "selfishness" and lashed out at them for "indulging" in it. When one of them acted "unfairly," he frequently screamed, vituperated, punished, and even assaulted. Later, he was contrite and apologetic. But not during!

John came to see me because he knew that he was "too" angry too often and that he was ruining some of his intimate relationships and harming himself physically. He used REBT with his EAP clients—"but rarely on myself at home."

Actually, that was an overstatement. He often used REBT antiagression methods at home. But often not. Sometimes, with his "difficult" family members, he disputed his irrational Belief (iB) that they *shouldn't* be the way that they indubitably were. But not frequently enough.

I asked John, during our first session, what he usually told himself to enrage himself at home and he gave expectable answers: "Whenever my wife or son acts unfairly to me, I immediately recall how *many* times I've gone out of my way, often at great sacrifice, to be kind and fair to them. Then I immediately think, 'How *could* they be that way? After all I've done, and am still doing, for *them.* How incredible! How unfair!'"

"Yes," I said, "but you may be right about that. Compared to you, they may be very unfair."

"They are!"

"Let's suppose they really are. But that's just a description, albeit perhaps accurate, of their behavior. What *else* are you saying *about* this behavior that makes you really enraged?"

"Oh, yes, REBT, of course, is right about this. 'They *absolutely should not be* that unfair!' Then I get enraged."

"Right. And when you Dispute this godlike demand, as you tell me you sometimes do, you come up with—what?"

"Oh. *When* I Dispute it, I come up with practically all the right answers: 'They *should* be unfair—because that's the way they now are. They have a right to be wrong—that's their human fallible nature. They *have* to do me in—when they're actually doing so.' All the right REBT answers."

"And how do they work?"

"Fine—when I actually get to them and use them. I quickly calm down and feel what you call *healthily* sorry and disappointed with their behavior."

"But not incensed at them?"

"No, that goes right away. But not for long! The very next time they act unfairly, I go right back to my fuming and seething. Before I have a chance to think. Immediately!"

"So you *automatically* go back to your demandingness?"

"Yes. Without thinking."

"Well, not quite," I said.

"You mean?"

"I'd guess that you *temporarily* give up your basic, underlying philosophy—'My wife and son *shouldn't* act that unjustly!'—but you never quite erase it. It's still there, ready to pounce on you—and on your wife and son!—again."

"So I only *temporarily* banish it?"

"Yes, temporarily—and often *lightly.* But because you naturally, like most humans, think that commanding way, and because you've *practiced* doing so thousands of times, you *easily* sink back to it once again. Not always, of course."

"No, I sometimes pass over their unfairness and don't erupt about it."

"But often not!"

"Yes. Back to my, uh, as you call it, demandingness I go."

This is typical of anger-creating *musts*. Probably because they are partly protective and built, through centuries of evolution, in the human race. Because whatever rules of behavior society, the family, and other institutions agree upon and define as "fair" and "just," members of these groups supposedly *should* follow them. And our angry feelings, when they don't do what they *should*, help us check and try to correct them.

Morality's *shoulds*, however, are *preferable*, not absolute. If John truly treats his wife and son kindly and fairly, they *preferably* should act similarly to him. Good. But they obviously don't *have* to, and his rage says that they *do* have to do what they're indubitably (in his eyes) not doing. Very crazy, this rage, because it stems from his *demand*, not from the *preference* that precedes it and sparks it. John—and the rest of us humans—had better retain that preference. But give up his accompanying demands.[2]

Because John already knew and sometimes used the anti-anger Disputing of REBT, I at first had him review it. One of the first homework assignments that he agreed to do was to make a list of reasons why his wife and son (and other intimates) often *should* and *would* act unfairly to him. His initial list went like this:

1. They often don't see their acts as unfair, but think they are "all right" and "fair."
2. They sometimes see that they are wrong, but still insist on unfairly getting their way. They *have to* get it.
3. They think that I am unfairly treating them and that they have to stop me.
4. They are angry at other people and take it out on me.
5. They are anxious or depressed and can't think straight. They screw up.
6. They easily forget the things I have done for them.
7. They have low frustration tolerance when deprived of what they want from me. They think that, no matter what, they *need* what they want.
8. They're fallible humans!
9. They are not thinking straight because they are tired, moody, or ill.
10. They often will put themselves first and naturally do what *they* want, not what *I* want.
11. They may feel so guilty and self-damning about their previous unfairness that they punish themselves by acting badly again and bringing on my wrath.

As soon as he made this list and went over it several times, John's angry outbursts at his family members decreased. But not to zero! A week after he brought in the list, his son, Don, and some of his friends left the family's house in a mess when John and his wife went away for the weekend and warned Don to invite practically no one in and to take good care of the house. John berated Don for 20 minutes, and came within a hair of beating him. "How *could* he have been so careless! And after all those warnings! And his 'sincere' promises!"

John's falling back to extreme rage, however, was therapeutically "good"—because it showed him what we had previously discussed: his underlying, often unconscious, basic demandingness.

So he went back to the REBT Disputing and filled out several self-help forms on his occasional outbursts and on his honestly acknowledged feelings of rage, even when he forbore from expressing these feelings. This again helped cut down—but not cut out—his outbursts.

John and I agreed that, like Mark whose case I presented in the previous chapter, he *lightly* held a number of rational Beliefs (rB's) about his family's injustices to him but that he *strongly* still held a few irrational Beliefs (iB's) about them. Especially: "After *all* I do for my wife and son, how could they treat me *so* unfairly? My God—such incredible unfairness!"

This is what I call a *subtle* iB that *seems*, on the face of it, to be sound but really isn't. Thus, if John believes, "No matter how I treat Don, I am his father and therefore he *absolutely must* treat me well," he (and everyone else) may easily see how unreasonable—and unfair—this Belief is and John may give it up. But suppose he believes, "I treat Don *so* well *so much* of the time that the least he can do is to treat me well in return. Therefore, he *must!*" This *subtle* must *seems* correct but is still a non sequitur. It is a demand and just *doesn't* follow from the facts that because John actually treats Don *so* well *so much* of the time that *therefore* Don *absolutely must not* be unfair.[3]

I explained the notion of *subtle* irrationalities to John and we agreed that he often had several of them. For example: "Because I *really* care for my wife, Martha, and show her that I do in *so* many ways, she *absolutely should* care very much for me and always show me that she does!" When John found these *subtle* irrationalities and figured out why they were still senseless, he made more inroads against his rage. He was able to laugh at these subtle but powerful musts, change them, and make himself less underlyingly horrified at the "unfair" behavior of Don and Martha.

In fact, he realized, for the first time, that his *demanding* that they *always and only* be "fair" actually *made them*, in his eyes, "terribly unfair," when they were often being normally self-interested and not *really* as "unfair" as he saw them to be. By decreasing, in his head, the extent of their "unfairness," he made himself much less prone to rage at them when they were normally inconsiderate. In the process, he gave up the subtle demand, "Because I am *so unusually* considerate of them, they *should be* very considerate of me; and because they are not, they are *really* unfair—as they *must not* be!"

When John saw his subtle, but still strong, irrationalities and agreed that he'd better do some *vigorous* Disputing, we used some of the emotive-evocative Disputations that I had shown Mark how to use, as noted in the previous chapter of this book. Thus:

Forceful Taped Disputing. John recorded his strong demands that Don treat him considerately and fairly, vigorously Disputed them on tape, and came up with these powerful Effective New Philosophies: "No matter *how* kind, loving, fair, and sacrificing I am for Don, he *never has* to treat me in kind! He is his own person and easily *can*—and often will—act 'worse' than I do. Too damned bad. But I can live with it!"

Forceful Coping Statements. From his taped and written Disputing, John came up with a number of other coping statements, which he strongly repeated to himself until he truly felt them. One of the most effective forceful coping statements was: "I *can* bite my tongue and shut my big mouth when I foolishly incense myself at Martha and Don. Later, I'll work at surrendering my rage. But even while I feel it, I *can* shut up and do something else. Shit, I can't! I *can, can, can!*"

Reverse Role Playing. At times I role-played as if I were John, acted as if I were enraged, and dogmatically held on to his irrational Beliefs that his wife and son *absolutely owed* him considerateness and fairness and were *despicable people* when they failed to give it. He, playing me, had to talk me out of his own rigid views. Thus, in playing me, while I played his role, he very powerfully was able to say, "You can say anything you want, but your wife and son *should* be the rotten way they are. Or, rather, *aren't* that way—because they have other traits as well. But they *will* act badly—yes, often! No matter *how* well you treat them. They *should* see things *their* way, not yours! They *should* see you as wrong—even when you act rightly. They *should* be ungrateful! People often are! Ingratitude is one of the main human conditions. Including theirs!"

These forceful Disputing methods helped John give up his rage—and rarely go back to it. I used other, palliative REBT methods with him and they also worked—somewhat. I taught him some relaxation techniques, which he used whenever he felt a fit of fury coming on. I showed him that he could take 15-minute time-out breaks and read or take a walk whenever he began to feel enraged. At my suggestion, he got a punching bag to hit when he got close to hitting his son.

All these methods worked to distract John from his anger and to reduce it. But they only mildly interrupted his core philosophy—that when he (or anyone else) was unusually fair, others should reciprocate in kind. "That," he once exclaimed after he had slipped back to another fit of rage, "is a hard one to give up!"

"Yes," I agreed. "But it's a hard*er* line to keep!"

"Not for my head," he said smilingly. "But for my family relationships!"

We both agreed.

Does your clients' Disputing of their anger-creating Beliefs sometimes lead to questionable or poor results? Sure. They may convince themselves that there is no "right" and "wrong" and may fail to assert themselves when others act "wrongly." They may give up damning others, but still berate themselves for being too passive with offenders. They may put themselves down for not being "macho" enough and for *not* being vindictive against trespassers. They may go to extremes, cop out, and not fight against obnoxious political, economic, or ecological conditions.

In these and other respects, your clients, in working against their rage, may block their effective feelings of real displeasure at people's *doings* while minimizing their horror at the *doers*. They may then condone, or abet, immoral behaviors.

Some of your clients may even nicely manage to forgive "sinners" by ruthlessly, and "calmly," punishing their "sins." Rosalee, for example, never condemned her two teenage daughters for disobeying her "sensible" rules. But she unangrily gave them their "due" by grounding them for a week, depriving them completely of their allowances, and making them eat tasteless food when they flouted these rules in minor ways. She was quite surprised when both her daughters began to hate her and sometimes deliberately acted against her rules in order to try to upset her. Finally, I had to treat her for her severe depression.

Help your clients, then, forgive the sinners but still, often, hate their sins. Help them change their core rage-creating philosophies—while not passively tolerating depredation and aggression. This may take some length of time. But not always. With some hard work—yes, hard work—by you and them, they may fairly quickly achieve a profound philosophic-behavioral change.[4]

NOTES TO CHAPTER 8

1. Berkowitz, 1990; DiGiuseppe, 1990; DiGiuseppe, Tafrate, & Eckhardt, 1994; Dryden, 1990; Ellis, 1977a, 1988a, 1988c, 1991f; Nye, 1993; Tavris, 1983.
2. Ellis, 1987a, 1994e.
3. Ellis, 1987b, 1994e.
4. DiGiuseppe, 1990; Dryden, 1990; Ellis, 1977a; Nye, 1993.

9

Disputing Low Frustration Tolerance Musts

The third irrational idea that REBT looks for in virtually all clients, including those whom you want to help intensively improve in a brief period, is: "Conditions absolutely *must* be the way I prefer them to be, *must* never frustrate me considerably, and *must* arrange to give me exactly what I want when I want it." The main derivatives of this iB are: "It's *awful* if conditions are not exactly the way that I demand that they be! I can't stand it! The goddamned world is no good for being the rotten way that it is, and I can't be happy at all unless it changes!"[1]

Take Jane, for example. She wasn't too much of a self-downer and she usually didn't make herself too angry at other people (because she accepted the fact that they, like herself, were very fallible humans who would often do wrong and stupid things). But when traffic conditions were bad, or when the school in which she taught had screwed-up rules and procedures, or when she couldn't get to play tennis because there were too many other people waiting to play, she became very impatient, complained bitterly, and felt angry and depressed about the world being the way that it definitely *should not* be. She often realized that her complaining about unfortunate things did not change them and only upset her own gut, but she rarely stopped doing so; and because several areas of her life really were quite frustrating, she led a pretty miserable existence.

Jane at first thought that she was merely wishing and wanting conditions to be better than they were. But it didn't take me more than a few sessions to show her that her "wants" were really arrant and arrogant demands and that it was her demandingness, and not her wantingness, that was really doing her in. So we went through the usual Disputing of her irrational Beliefs and she felt somewhat better as her impatience and her depression decreased.

Jane's seeing that her absolutistic demandingness would rarely work to relieve her impatience and depression was fine. But seeing it–getting insight into it–didn't exactly change it. She still kept falling back to indulging in it. What finally did work was getting her to make a list of the real disadvantages of continuing her demanding rather than preferring. She agreed to make such a list and actually took two weeks to come up with a fairly complete one. It included these items:

1. I shall keep making myself impatient and depressed.
2. I will be preoccupied with how awful traffic and other conditions are instead of spending time and energy trying to do anything to change them.
3. Even if I feel motivated to try to change these bad conditions, I shall still feel very upset while I am doing so.
4. By continually bitching to other people about rotten conditions I shall keep boring them and turning them off.
5. The more bored and turned off they get, the less they will really help me to try to change the poor conditions.
6. Horrifying myself about these conditions will make me focus on them more than ever and will increase my frustrations about them. Low frustration tolerance, which is what I have, almost always significantly increases my frustrations and annoyances.
7. Stewing while I am caught in a traffic jam will not make the jam any better and will stop me from listening to my car radio, figuring out important plans, and doing anything else that I may possibly benefit from.

At first, Jane dealt effectively only with her minor frustrations, such as being stuck in a traffic jam for 10 or 15 minutes, and agreed with herself–

and the world—that traffic jams should exist, that they were not terrible, that she could stand them, and that her environment was not absolutely horrible even though she lived in New York and could not very well avoid quite a number of hassles. But when she was stuck, as she sometimes was, for a whole hour returning from her school in Brooklyn to her apartment in Manhattan, she went right back to her complaining and to her extreme impatience.

During our first few sessions, Jane kept arguing with me that mild frustrations certainly need not be seen as awful and horrible, but that when things were so stupidly arranged that gridlock kept occurring constantly, and when nothing was ever done about it although many things could be changed for the better, such needless great frustrations were *really* horrible, and she would be wrong not to upset herself about them. "Only when people like me get upset," she contended, "are rotten conditions like this actually ever changed. Isn't that so?"

I agreed that upsetness such as hers was often motivating and that it sometimes helped people harass traffic officials, so that something was finally done about bad situations. But I tried to show her that strong displeasure about such conditions would do just as much good, be just as motivating, as intense impatience and low frustration tolerance. She didn't agree.

Jane also insisted that saying that conditions *preferably* should be changed instead of *absolutely must* be changed was just a quibble. If they were really bad, as of course they often were, they *absolutely should* be changed, else chaos would keep ensuing. I tried to show her that she was substituting a conditional should for an absolutistic should; and that was okay as long as she agreed that it was conditional.

"What do you mean?" she asked.

"Well, you are really saying, 'If we want to get anything done about serious gridlocks and other rotten conditions, we then must and should do something about them—else they will never get changed.' True. But then, when you're very impatient and upset, you really change that conditional sentence into an absolutistic one."

"How come?"

"Well, when you're upset you really mean, 'Because it would be good if something were done, and because I strongly want it to be done, therefore it absolutely must be done!' But this, of course, doesn't follow. No matter how good it would be for situations to be changed, no matter how legitimate is your desire to have them changed, and no matter how many people agree with you about this, there still is no reason why they *have to be* changed. The world, and its poor situations, are just not subject to this absolute rule that you are setting up and that you imagine really exists. Do you see that?"

"No, not exactly."

"Well, let's put it this way. If I said to you, 'Unless you give up your absolutistic demands, you will almost certainly keep suffering from impatience and depression,' that is probably a conditional and a realistic statement. For if you don't give up your demands, and if things still don't change—as we can be pretty damned sure that they won't—you will definitely keep upsetting yourself. If X (your demandingness) persists, and if the changes you demand don't occur, then Y (your upsetness) results. Your demandingness and the stubbornness of the conditions in spite of this demandingness lead to (in all probability) your upsetness."

"Yes, I see that."

"Good. But if I say, 'Because I *want* you to see that your demandingness leads to your upsetness, and I *want* you to change it to preferringness, therefore you *have to* do so,' I then really say that my wish is your command—which, of course, it never has to be. So I am making my preferential rule into an absolutistic rule—which won't work."

"I'm now beginning to see what you mean. My demandingness frequently will bring about and be a condition for my upsetness. But your demanding that I have to change my demandingness, not merely to make myself unupset but to kowtow to your demandingness, is a different kind of absolutistic thinking, and that will rarely work."

"Right!"

When she kept reading over her list of the disadvantages of her demandingness and when she really saw how she was making her life worse rather than better, Jane was motivated to work harder at Disputing her irrational Beliefs that went with her upsetness. Doing so, she finally got very clear about the difference, which I mentioned above, between her conditional shoulds—"People should work hard to change traffic and other bad situations if they are really to effect any such changes"—and her absolutistic shoulds—"Because these traffic conditions are so abominable, they *absolutely should not* exist and *have to be* quickly changed!" Jane stuck to her conditional, energizing shoulds and gave up her unconditional absolutistic shoulds, and got absorbed in political activity that might spur the traffic bureau to do something about the "impossible" gridlock conditions.

Showing your clients, then, that they have irrational Beliefs that lead to their low frustration tolerance (LFT) and to their needlessly suffering from unfortunate situations will often quickly help them to change these iB's and to make them feel better. But not necessarily! Getting them to prove to themselves, in more ways than one, that their iB's are not only unrealistic and illogical but definitely self-defeating and impractical will often be a better route to take with them. When they are fully convinced of the ineffectuality of their Beliefs, they are more likely to work at changing them for more effective Beliefs.

Once again, does helping your clients to see how impractical their irrational Beliefs are have real disadvantages? Yes, it sometimes has. For example:

Some clients may acknowledge the great disadvantages of their holding their irrational Beliefs and then put themselves down for holding them. Their secondary symptom—self-immolation—then becomes so obsessive that they get hung up, dwell on it, and stop themselves from getting back to work on their primary iB's.

Sometimes clients have low frustration tolerance about their self-downing. "I *can't stand* my self-downing and the time and energy it takes me to give it up. I *shouldn't have* it, and find it *too hard* to change it. I'll live with it and won't bother to go to the trouble of working against it!" Their low frustration tolerance about their self-deprecation then stops them from working for self-acceptance.

Some clients think that no-goodniks like themselves don't deserve to change their irrational Beliefs that lead to their low frustration tolerance and that therefore they *have to* keep suffering from their LFT.

Other clients think that it's so foolish for them to keep holding on to their iB's that it really *is* impossible for them to change them. So what's the use of their even trying to do so?

For reasons such as these, you may show your clients what bad results they will get from holding on to their irrational Beliefs that go with their low frustration tolerance. Then, perversely enough, some of them may hold on to them even more and refuse to do the hard work of giving them up. In other words, their Catch-22 is that their abysmal low frustration tolerance blocks their working to give up their abysmal low frustration tolerance!

So, explaining to your clients that they have low frustration tolerance and that they will most probably defeat themselves by having it is sometimes not enough. You still have to persuade many of them to give up this LFT. And that itself may be quite a problem! Motivating them to become motivated is often not very easy! Not impossible, but damned difficult. It can sometimes be done in a short series of sessions. But don't count on it!

What can you do to hasten and deepen this process? Several things:

1. Don't only focus on your clients' ego or identity problems. Usually, these exist and are of prime importance. But not always. Some clients have conditional self-acceptance (CSA) and are in no trouble because they usually do well and therefore accept themselves for the "wrong" reasons. But you may decide to not fix it when it works. A few clients even have a decent degree of unconditional self-acceptance (USA) and really do respect themselves even when they screw up. Not many do. But some.

2. Both clients with CSA and USA generally have quite a bit of low frustration tolerance. Why? For one thing, they are human—and humans are talented avoiders, procrastinators, and short-range hedonists. Do you know any who never are?

3. For another thing, your clients are *clients*. They're in trouble, otherwise they wouldn't see you. When their trouble is not ego-oriented—which it usually *is*—you can bet on the next "best" thing: other-demandingness. Either they are insisting— yes, insisting—that other people act better than they often do act and/or that external conditions not be the way that they indubitably (and incredibly!) are. Why else would they get disturbed—or, rather, be self-disturbing? If they truly accepted themselves, *no matter what*, and they accepted (not liked!) unchangeable obnoxious people and execrable situations, *no matter what*, how would they unduly disturb themselves? Damned little!

    So assume that your clients, and particularly your difficult ones (DC's), have considerable low frustration tolerance—or what I often call discomfort disturbance—and collaborate with them on finding it and the irrational Beliefs (iB's) that accompany it.

4. Persistently—but unnaggingly—bring their low frustration tolerance to your clients' attention. Help them fully acknowledge it. No cop-outs! No denials! No excuses! Quickly track it down. Ferret out clear-cut examples of it. Many examples. Show them how ubiquitous it is. As I often say, the blasted human condition!

5. Show your clients that they *can* ease up on their low frustration tolerance (LFT). But not easily ease up! For their LFT

usually impedes their working consistently on their LFT. It's *too* hard! It's harder than it *should* be! Isn't it?

6. So they don't *have to* reduce it. But they'd better! Otherwise, it has great disadvantages and hazards like *increasing* their feelings of frustration. Like giving up and resting "in peace." Like pissing away much of their lives. Like not getting to enjoyment. Like alienating others. Like—well, encourage them to list their LFT's dangers.

7. Help your clients to Dispute the irrational Beliefs (iB's) they brilliantly invent to create and develop their LFT. "My family is jealous of me and will hate me if I push my ass better than they push theirs." "I'll lose my friends if I don't drink and dawdle with them." "Why should I have to *work* for real enjoyment?" "Life is too boring without food and television." "I'm going to die anyway, so I might as well smoke and avoid exercise."

8. Endorse your clients' hedonism, but mainly their long-range hedonism.

9. Show them how *strongly* they favor immediate gratification—and bring on ultimate pains. Teach them to *vigorously*, forcefully think, feel, and act against their LFT-bolstering Beliefs.

10. Watch your own LFT! You can *easily* avoid avoidant clients—or keep them forever while you lazily go along with their self-defeating rides. It won't cost you anything to let things slide. Or will it?

11. Accept the *challenge* of working with difficult customers and helping them reduce their LFT. Sell them, if you can, on the *challenge* of minimizing their discomfort disturbance.

12. Remind yourself and your clients that *enduringly* good and enjoyable outcomes—as particularly shown in academic activities and in sports—almost always include a considerable degree of tedious hard work. Why should therapeutic change, working for their goal of more happiness in life, require less persistent effort than the happiness that an academician or an athlete may have to work hard to gain?

13. Try to persuade some of your avoidants and procrastinators to acquire a vital absorbing interest—some long-range goal, cause, or interest. Like building a family or a business. Like working for a political or social cause.

Will all these plans work? Not with all of your customers all of the time. Some will work briefly—but not intensively and elegantly. Some will work deeply—but not briefly. Try for both. See for yourself!

NOTES TO CHAPTER 9

1. Ainslie, 1974; Danysh, 1974; Dryden & Gordon, 1993; Ellis, 1976b, 1978, 1979a, 1980a, 1982, 1983c, 1994a; Ellis & Abrams, 1994; Ellis & Knaus, 1977; Ellis & Velten, 1992; Hauck, 1974; Knaus, 1974; Pietsch, 1993; Prochaska, DiClemente, & Norcross, 1992; Trimpey, 1989, 1993; Trimpey & Trimpey, 1990; Wolfe, 1993, 1994; Woods, 1990a.

10

Using REBT Emotive Methods for Deep and Intensive Change

Rational Emotive Behavior Therapy (REBT) has always been unusually cognitive or philosophical. But, right from the start, as I particularly point out in the revised and updated edition of *Reason and Emotion in Psychotherapy*, it has also been highly emotive. For I discovered, early in the game, that most clients quite strongly and forcefully hold on to their irrational Beliefs and thereby cling to them in a highly provocative emotional manner. Especially provocative to you, their therapist!

We can easily predict this from the very nature of what we call "emotional disturbance." For in order for you (and your clients) to upset yourself about almost anything, you almost always first have to get blocked in one of your strong desires. If you mildly or moderately wish to succeed at anything—such as to mildly want to win someone's approval or to succeed at a game—you will rarely upset yourself when you lose. Too bad—but it's hardly the end of the world.

Ah, but suppose you definitely and strongly want to win So-and-So's approval and you get solidly rejected. Or suppose you really, really want to win a tennis game and you get beaten to a frazzle. Is it still only too bad? Or is it much closer to being the end of the world?

Guess!

Even to suffer a mild loss at a project leads to an "emotional" feeling—say, regret or disappointment. But to suffer a big loss frequently results in a disturbed feeling—such as anxiety, depression, or self-loathing. That is because you are quite likely to think, in this case, "I *absolutely must* win, and it is *awful,* and I am *no damned good* if I don't!" Thinking this, you make yourself feel, and really feel, disturbed.

Healthy negative feelings of regret and disappointment, moreover, are often short-lasting and easily forgotten. Not so with unhealthy feelings of panic, horror, and self-hatred. They are not easily or quickly put aside. And they are often obsessed about!

The absolutistic musts, shoulds, and oughts that accompany disturbed feelings are usually "hot" cognitions—strong self-statements or images. Disputing them logically, empirically, and pragmatically, as we are showing in this book, often works well—and sometimes quickly and dramatically. But sometimes it doesn't. Therefore, REBT uses quite a number of forceful cognitive methods, which might well be called cognitive-emotive methods, to tackle disruptive hot cognitions. Some of these I have already described and others I shall consider in this chapter.[1]

Take the case of Chana. A 19-year-old college student, she was so anxious every time she had to take a test that she avoided studying, then did poorly at remembering the material, then was overly anxious during the entire test, and then got barely passing marks even in the subjects she liked and knew a great deal about. She came to therapy anxious, depressed, and at times nearly suicidal.

The first few therapy sessions showed that Chana had a case of extreme performance anxiety. Partly as a result of her parental upbringing, but mainly stemming from her own perfectionistic tendencies, she believed that she *absolutely had* to do well in all her important subjects, thought that she was a total idiot when she did poorly, and almost always brought on severe test-taking anxiety. Her main musts were obvious:

1. "I *must* get good marks in all my important subjects!"
2. "I *must* show my parents how bright I am!"
3. "I *must* not be anxious, nor show others how anxious I am!"
4. "I *must* perform well in order to respect myself and be a worthwhile person!"
5. "I *must* not have such a hard time studying when other students find it relatively easy to do so."

With my help, Chana started to Dispute these musts and made some real progress in being less anxious within a few weeks. But neither studying nor giving up her anxiety came easily. So she put herself down for still having such difficulty and for not being completely cured in a short length of time. Her boyfriend, Sumi, was a particularly good, and thoroughly unanxious, scholar; whenever she saw how easily he took tests, enjoyed them, and did well on them, she immediately berated herself, concluded that she was hopeless, and thought about suicide.

Fortunately, Chana was a talented artist, did exceptionally well in her art classes, and won several prizes in school exhibitions. So it wasn't too hard to convince her that she was not a totally incompetent or stupid person, because her achievements were obvious and well recognized. Her original irrational Beliefs, "I'm a thoroughly inadequate person for being so anxious and inept in most of my subjects," could easily be Disputed. So she was helped to conclude, "I am inadequate in test-taking and in keeping myself unanxious, but I also have some unusual artistic talents and therefore am not really an incompetent or unworthy individual." This Effective New Philosophy made her feel much better than when she first came to therapy. But her test-taking anxiety and her depression after failing each new test decreased only moderately.

I used the forceful Disputing methods with Chana that I have described in Chapters 7, 8, and 9, but they worked only moderately well, largely because she was often so anxious when using them that she didn't think too straight or come to any vigorous rational conclusions. Her anxiety about her therapy also interfered with her reasoning consistently or well.

As I usually do with many of my clients and particularly with those who resist vigorous Disputing or seem prone to do it poorly, I used a number of REBT emotive-evocative techniques with Chana, especially the following ones.

RATIONAL EMOTIVE IMAGERY

Rational Emotive Imagery was created in 1971 by Dr. Maxie Maultsby, Jr., one of the first psychiatrists to regularly use REBT. His version is strong on imagination and on feeling, but it seems to me to be more close than I would like it to be to regular REBT Disputing. So I have devised the following special version of Rational Emotive Imagery (REI), which we train our supervisors to use at the Institute for Rational Emotive

Therapy in New York, and which often brings about quick and intensive results.[2]

To do REI, you have your clients imagine, vividly imagine, the occurrence of an Activating Event that is likely to encourage them to react with an intense disturbed feeling and/or behavior—especially, with severe anxiety, panic, depression, or self-loathing. You ask them what this emotion is, tell them to really get in touch with it and fully experience it, and then you instruct them to keep the same "gruesome" image but to change their feeling about it to a healthy negative emotion—such as feeling sorry, disappointed, regretful, or frustrated. For if something obnoxious really does happen, as they are now imagining that it happens, you would want them to feel not happy or indifferent, but rather "appropriately" or "healthily" negative.

In the REBT version of REI, you do not prescribe the disturbed feeling that your client is to achieve when he or she imagines some unfortunate event occurring; but you do prescribe the healthy negative feeling that they can substitute for their original disturbed one. When they report that they truly have changed their feeling to a negative but still self-helping one, you then ask them *how* they changed it—what they *did* to change it. But you do not ask them what they *told themselves* to change their feeling, because this makes it too easy for them and often leads to their saying that they told themselves something to change it when they really did nothing of the sort.

So you allow them to spontaneously and intuitively work on changing their feeling—which they almost all seem to be quite capable of doing—and you then ask them, "How did you change it?" You can almost always tell, by their answers, whether they really did change their unhealthy negative feeling to a healthy, appropriate one, because to do so they usually have to use some kind of sensible, rational coping self-statement. If they merely relax, meditate, or change the Activating Event that you gave them to work on, they can indeed give up their original dysfunctional feeling—mainly by distracting themselves from it. But they can't really change it to the new healthy negative feeling that you have prescribed for them unless they change their *evaluation* of A.

Thus, if I had stressed relaxation or meditation with Chana, doing this might have distracted her temporarily from her irrational Beliefs—until another A (such as another test) came along. Ignoring or being distracted from her stressful A's would make her feel comfortable and unanxious. But it would not create a "deep" change—which would occur when she firmly convinced herself, cognitively *and* emotionally, that her irrational

Beliefs were self-defeating and when she replaced them with rational Beliefs (rB's).

To help Chana make such a cognitive-emotive change, I used Rational Emotive Imagery with her in this manner:

"I am now going to show you how to use Rational Emotive Imagery, which is one of our most valuable REBT techniques. Once I show you how to do it, you can often use it on your own, and you will usually find that it works well and gives you good results. Okay, now: Close your eyes, close your eyes. Now think of one of the worst things that might happen to you. Imagine, for example, that you have an important test to take, and that as soon as you look at the test questions you see that they are much more difficult than you thought they would be. They really are quite hard! The other students in the room are taking the test well and promptly getting to work on it, but you see that right from the start you are having a great deal of trouble figuring out the correct answers.

"Vividly imagine that this is happening. Really see this very difficult test, see that you are having trouble with it, and see your fellow students taking it in stride. Can you vividly imagine that this is happening?"

"Yes, I can," Chana replied.

"Okay, fine. Keep imagining this. See yourself in great difficulty with the test. Vividly imagine this!"

"I'm seeing it clearly. I'm in great trouble."

"Good. Now how do you *feel* as you imagine your trouble with this test? What is your feeling? Get in touch, let yourself get really in touch, with your feeling. What are you feeling?" After a minute of obvious tension and grimacing, Chana replied, "Anxious. Panicked. Very anxious!"

"Good. Let yourself feel anxious: very anxious. Let yourself feel as anxious and panicked as you can feel. Really, really *feel* it. Make yourself as panicked as you can. Feel it, feel it, feel it!"

"I do!"

"Fine. Hold it a minute. Feel it, feel it. Now, keeping your image the same, don't change your image, let yourself feel, instead of anxious and panicked, only sorry and disappointed about how hard the test is. Only sorry and disappointed—not anxious or panicked. You can do it. You can change your feelings. You control your emotional destiny about what's happening to you. So make yourself, now, *only* feel sorry and disappointed about what you're imagining. Not anxious, not panicked. Just sorry and disappointed, just sorry and disappointed. And when you're really feeling this way, only feeling sorry and disappointed and not panicked, tell me that you have achieved this healthy negative state. Tell me when you've changed your anxiety to sorrow and disappointment."

Chana, after another minute: "All right. I changed it."

"And you're not feeling panicked any longer, but only sorry and disappointed about what's happening to you? Is that right?"

"Yes."

"Fine! *How* did you change your feeling? What did you *do* to change it?"

"I told myself, I said to myself, 'It really *is* sad and disappointing that the test is so hard and that I may not be able to do it well. But it's not the end of the world. Too bad. I'll do my best with it and see what happens.'"

"That was really fine!" I said. "You did that very well. That's one good way to change your feeling, and you managed to come up with it on your own. Great! Now what I want you to do is to take a minute or two every day—for you see it only takes you a minute or two—so take a minute or two every day for each of the next 30 days, to do exactly what you just now did. Close your eyes. Imagine one of the worst things that could happen to you, such as taking a very hard test. Let yourself feel whatever you naturally feel—such as anxiety, panic, depression, or whatever you feel. Let yourself be disturbed, if you are still disturbed, about what you are imagining. Then, just as you again did, change your feeling to one of sorriness and disappointment by using a coping statement like the one you just used. Or you can use several other similar coping statements that you can devise. There are 10 or 20 of them and you can use any of them that you want to use.

"Do this once a day, usually for a minute or two, and keep making yourself feel healthily sorry and regretful, instead of unhealthily panicked. If you do this rational emotive imagery exercise once a day, for only a few minutes a day, you will find that after awhile you automatically begin to feel sorry and disappointed, instead of anxious and panicked, when you do it.

"Now will you do this once a day, for 30 days, until you begin to feel automatically sorry and disappointed whenever you imagine the worst thing that could happen? You will also find, if you keep doing this, that if you actually take a difficult test, or some other negative event actually happens, you again will tend to feel automatically sorry and disappointed, instead of anxious and panicked. Will you try this, to see for yourself?"

"Yes, I will."

Chana did use Rational Emotive Imagery with a test-taking image, and after doing this for 15 days in a row she did begin to feel, automatically, naturally much less anxious and panicked, and usually only sorry and disappointed. She thus discovered on her own, how she could decrease her anxiety by changing her Belief to, "I may not be able to do it too well. But it's not the end of the world. Too bad," and thus make a philosophical shift. An emotional–philosophical shift of this sort seems to be crucial to bringing about *deep*, and often *lasting*, changes.

With many people, I increase the probability of their actually doing REI steadily by telling them to pick a reinforcer—something they consider pleasurable, such as reading, exercising, or listening to music—and allow themselves to experience it only contingently –*after* they have done their REI for that day. Also, if they still tend to avoid doing it, they can give themselves a punishment, such as cleaning the house or talking to an obnoxious person, or a penalty, such as burning a 20-dollar bill each day that they fail to do REI. Most people do not require these kinds of reinforcements, punishments, and/or penalties. But some do!

SHAME-ATTACKING EXERCISES

I realized, soon after I started doing REBT in 1955, that what we call "shame" is the essence of a great deal of our emotional disturbance. When we do something that we consider "shameful," we normally criticize our acts and tell ourselves, "That is bad. I'd better stop doing this and prevent myself from doing it again." We then feel sorry, regretful, or uncomfortable about doing this "shameful" thing, and we help ourselves refrain from repeating it. So defining one or more of our acts or behaviors as "shameful" is often useful; and our human tendency to experience this kind of act-directed shame has helped to socialize us, to prevent us from doing "wrong" or "antisocial" actions, and probably to help to preserve our communities and the human race. Unless we naturally and easily sometimes felt shame, embarrassment, humiliation, and similar emotions about some of our actions, we would not tend to follow many useful and self-preservative rules and would get into fairly steady trouble.

However, partly because of the human tendency to overgeneralize, just about all of us—including you and your clients—tend not only to rate our deeds, acts, and performances (*Good!*) but also to rate and measure our selves, our being, our personhood (*Incorrect and inefficient!*). That is what we do with shame: label our foolish and antisocial acts as "rotten" but also, when we feel really ashamed, measure our entire selves as "rotten" or "shameful." Seeing this, I created my widely used shame-attacking exercise in 1968. Perhaps millions of people, especially psychotherapy clients, have done this exercise and trained themselves to feel ashamed or sorry about what they *did* and about the public disapproval that often went with it, but *not* to put themselves down and not to feel humiliated about their personhood.[3]

I explained this shame-attacking exercise to Chana as follows:

"In REBT we try to help people to stop putting themselves, their whole person, down no matter how badly they behave and no matter how much other people look down on them for so behaving. In your case, one of the reasons for your panic about tests is that you know full well that other people—your parents, your teachers, your schoolmates—will discover how badly you do on such tests, and perhaps how panicked you are about taking them, and will view you as an incompetent or lesser person for your poor performances. So you are afraid or ashamed not only of *your* knowing about your test-taking problem but about *other people* knowing as well. And that is all right as long as you merely try to do well and win people's approval without convincing yourself that you absolutely, under all conditions, *have to* perform adequately and that if you don't, especially if other people see that you don't, your failure and their perceiving this failure make you an RP—a rotten person. Right?"

"Yes," Chana answered, "I just about always rate myself as well as my failings, and particularly feel ashamed—or, as you say, down myself—when others rate me badly, too."

"Right. Well, this shame-attacking exercise that I am going to encourage you to do will help you forego your *self*-rating and rate or measure only your *performance*. By regular social standards, the latter may indeed be 'poor' or 'inept.' But you are never a *poor or inept person*."

"Even if I do some very bad acts, such as cruelly kill some people?"

"No, *not* even then. Your acts, under those conditions, would be evil and shameful. But you would still be a *person who* behaved badly, and never, really, a bad person."

"But suppose that I usually or practically always do evil acts? Wouldn't I then be a pretty bad person?"

"Yes, you could define yourself as such and call yourself, your entire being, bad. But actually and technically, a "bad person" would *always* do bad acts, would be undeserving of any satisfaction in his or her life, and would be damnable to the universe. These, again, are either overgeneralizations or unprovable and unfalsifiable propositions. So we'd better not uphold them."

"But how do I stop viewing myself as a totally bad individual?"

"By using several REBT methods. But let's, right now, try a shame-attacking exercise."

"Okay."

"Think of something that you really consider shameful. Something that you normally wouldn't do in front of other people and that, if somehow you did do it, you would feel quite ashamed of doing. Now don't think of or imagine anything that would harm you, such as walking naked on the street and getting arrested. Or telling one of your professors that she is a real shit. And don't do anything that would harm someone else—such as slapping someone in the face or telling lies about them. Think of something 'shameful,' like telling someone that you just got out of the mental hospital. Or doing a jig on the sidewalk. Or trying to borrow a hundred dollars from a total stranger. Something that almost anyone, including you, would consider shameful but that would not get you or anyone else into any kind of trouble."

"You mean like the famous REBT shame-attacking exercise that I've heard about: yelling out the stops on the subway or on a bus and then staying on the train or bus."

"Yes, that's one of our mainstays, which many of my clients have tried and benefited by. Do you want to try that one?"

"No, I don't think so. But how about my asking a stranger for even a dollar bill. I would be quite ashamed to do that."

"Fine. Let's get you to try that one. Go out on the street, right in front of the Institute if you want, or any place else, and try to borrow a dollar from a stranger. But that's only the first part, the easy part."

"What's the second and harder part?"

"While asking a stranger for a dollar bill, work on yourself to *not* feel ashamed. Work on your possible feelings of embarrassment and humiliation—which you choose to feel but don't have to feel—and make yourself feel unashamed and unembarrassed."

"Is it all right for me to feel uncomfortable?"

"Yes, that will be fine. Feel uncomfortable, sorry, regretful, a bit foolish, or even ashamed of your intruding on the stranger. But not guilty, self-downing, or really ashamed of *yourself.*"

"Can I really do that?"

"Of course you can! Try it and see!"

Chana at first hesitated and only did this shame-attacking exercise a week later, just before she came to her therapy session. She kept telling herself that she would be too uncomfortable doing it, and she might never have done it at all had she not had a regularly scheduled therapy session when I would ask her about doing it. But she finally bucked up her courage and did it.

"How did you feel while doing the exercise?" I asked Chana.

"Oh, very uncomfortable at first. I could hardly get the words out of my mouth. I was practically tongue-tied. And the first time I did it, my mouth was so dry that the person I picked, a very respectably dressed man walking outside the Waldorf Astoria Hotel, couldn't hear what I had to say. So I very uncomfortably had to repeat it."

"And then?"

"Then I did what I thought I heard you telling me to do: I said to myself, 'He probably thinks I'm a perfect nut. Or maybe one of the dirty homeless people. But I'll never ever see him again, and I don't need his goddamned approval. Let him think what he thinks!' I then felt a lot better and by the third time I tried it I really began to feel shameless. By the fifth time, I saw the whole thing as sort of a joke, and I actually enjoyed it."

That's what frequently happens when people do REBT shame-attacking exercises. They soon feel much less uncomfortable—and sometimes downright enjoyment. In Chana's case, she soon saw that she could do shame-attacking exercises with people who knew her, as well as with those who didn't. She deliberately, at my suggestion, began telling her school friends how anxious she was about test-taking, how she kept procrastinating on her studies, how she refused to take some important subjects at school because she knew that taking then would entail taking several tests during the term. The more she confessed these weaknesses, the more she saw that most people fully accepted her with them; she then began to accept herself. She still very much disliked her panic and her avoidances, but she put *herself* down less and less for them. Her anxiety about her anxiety appreciably decreased, and so, too, did her primary horror of test-taking. The shame-attacking exercises particularly helped her to see that, on both her primary level of disturbance (panic about failing at tests) and her secondary level (horror of her original anxiety), shame was the essence of her upsetness. She saw that when she worked to reduce this shame, much of her disturbance disappeared. Her New Effective Philosophy, sparked by her shame-attacking exercise, was, "I don't need their goddamned approval. Let them think what they think!" This led her to make both a brief and *philosophically deep* change.

THE USE OF HUMOR

REBT assumes that people had better take things seriously, but not too seriously. It therefore encourages clients to lighten up and see that some of their main "problems" are gross exaggerations and really, in a sense, funny.[4] Thus, I frequently show my clients that it is very funny when they say things like, "I can't change my feelings. They get out of control and are too much for me." But, at the same time, these same clients are "sure" that they can change other people's thoughts, feelings, and actions—and that when these others do not let them do so, these others are stubborn, "impossible people."

Chana at first couldn't see anything funny about her test-taking panic and about her panic about her panic. Few panic-driven people can. They are so caught up in their "horrible" anxiety that they think, at the time they feel it, of nothing else, and they see no particular humor in it. In Chana's case, moreover, she kept contending that if she didn't do well at school she would not be able to go to graduate school and never become the art professor that she very much wanted to become. So that was very serious!

I acknowledged this but still insisted that when she panicked herself, as she often did over minor quizzes in subjects that she had no interest in and that didn't count for much in her general average, she was truly making a mountain out of a molehill. I quoted Montaigne's famous saying to her: "My life has been filled with terrible misfortunes—most of which never happened!" She laughed, but not very heartily.

I persisted: "You keep saying that you absolutely must get good marks or else you cannot be happy at all. But you also keep saying that if you cannot be a great professor of art, your life is hardly worth living, and once again you cannot be happy at all. Obviously, getting good marks will help make you happy—but there will still be many rotten things in your life. And, obviously, not being a great art professor will help make you sad, but it will not take away your talent, will not stop you from enjoying the art that you do, and will not in itself keep you from having any other pleasures in life. Your *demands*, and little else, are keeping you miserable—and, of course, are interfering with your getting good marks. The more demanding you are, the worse marks you will probably get and the fewer enjoyments you will allow yourself. So you are the master of your own misery; and you think that failing a test or being disap-

proved of *by others* truly creates your anxiety and depression. How funny!"
Again, she didn't quite get the joke.

I persisted, until one day Chana broke through on the humorous front.
"I see what you're trying to point out to me," she said. "I obsess myself
with good marks, with other people's approval, and even with the tests
that I hate. I occupy practically all my time with this kind of crap. This
leaves me, ironically enough, very little time for the one thing that I say
I enjoy and that I want to accomplish: producing a great deal of art,
finding out for myself what is great art and lousy art for me (and maybe
for the world as well), and enjoying the paintings that I do turn out. I
produce so many shitty thoughts and shitty feelings—and so little real art.
You know, that really is funny!"

Chana was also talented at music and poetry. She became interested
in my rational humorous songs, which combine music and lyrics in a
satirical manner. We give all our clients at the Psychological Clinic of
the Institute for Rational-Emotive Therapy in New York a sheet of these
songs to use when they feel quite upset, both to distract them from their
anxious and depressed feelings and to create "deeper" change by
laughing at their dismal philosophies and helping provide them with
more functional ones.[5] Chana took some of these songs and sang them
to herself hilariously when she found that she was overwhelmed with
anxiety.

One of the antianxiety rational humorous songs that Chana used to
good effect was this one:

I'M JUST WILD ABOUT WORRY
(*Tune*: "I'm Just Wild About Harry," by Eubie Blake)

Oh, I'm just wild about worry
And worry's wild about me!
We're quite a twosome to make life gruesome
And filled with anxiety!
Oh, worry's anguish I curry
And look for its guarantee!
Oh, I'm just wild about worry
And worry's wild about
Never wild about,
Most beguiled about me!

Another antianxiety and antiperfection song that Chana enjoyed singing to herself and that had good effects for her was PERFECT RATIONALITY, to the tune of Luigi Denza's "Finiculi Finicula":

> Some think the world must have a right direction
> And so do I! And so do I!
> Some think that, with the slightest imperfection,
> They can't get by—and so do I!
> For I, I have to prove I'm superhuman,
> And better far than people are!
> To show I have miraculous acumen—
> And always rate among the Great!
>
> Perfect, perfect rationality
> Is, of course, the only thing for me!
> How can I ever think of being
> If I must live fallibly?
> Rationality must be a perfect thing for me!

When Chana thought that she would literally go crazy with her incessant worrying and panicking, she found I WISH I WERE NOT CRAZY, sung to the tune of Dan Emmet's "Dixie," very useful:

> Oh, I wish I were really put together—
> Smooth and fine as patent leather!
> Oh, how great to be rated innately sedate!
> But I'm afraid that I was fated
> To be rather aberrated—
> Oh, how sad to be mad as my Mom and my Dad!
> Oh, I wish I were not crazy! Hooray, hooray!
> I wish my mind were less inclined
> To be the kind that's hazy!
> I could agree to really be less crazy.
> But I, alas, am just too goddamed lazy!

REBT rational humorous songs that are antidotes against depression were also at times very useful to Chana. Here are two that she particularly found would jog her from a depressed to an almost cheerful mood:

I'M DEPRESSED, DEPRESSED!
(*Tune*: "The Band Played On," by Charles B. Ward)

When anything slightly goes wrong with my life.
I'm depressed, depressed!
Whenever I'm stricken with chickenshit strife,
I feel most distressed!
When life isn't fated to be consecrated
I can't tolerate it at all!
When anything slightly goes wrong with my life,
I just bawl, bawl, bawl!

BEAUTIFUL HANGUP
(Tune: "Beautiful Dreamer," by Stephen Foster)

Beautiful hangup, why should we part
When we have shared our whole lives from the start?
We are so used to taking one course,
Oh, what a crime it would be to divorce!
Beautiful hangup, don't go away!
Who will befriend me if you do not stay?
Though you still make me look like a jerk,
Living without you would take so much work!–
Living without you would take too much work!

Lyrics by Albert Ellis. © 1977–1989 by The Institute for Rational-Emotive Therapy, New York City.

From time to time, I also employed other emotive-evocative methods with Chana, as I often do with many of my other clients, both in brief therapy and in longer-term therapy. I used strong language, fables, stories, and metaphors; a number of experiential exercises; and several of our cognitive-emotive workshops that we regularly give at The Institute for Rational-Emotive Therapy. Chana found that the most useful of these in her own case was my regular Friday Night Workshop, Problems of Everyday Living, where I interview volunteers from the audience in front of a hundred or more people, and then open the discussion to all the members of the audience, who are free to talk to me and to the volunteers. Chana, as a shame-attacking exercise, once came up to be a volunteer herself, and had an excellent session with me in public. The fact that she was able to confess her anxiety problems and talk about them in public in front of so many people, and to clearly see, right there and then, that she was not a *shameful person* while doing so made a great therapeutic impression on her.

More regularly, however, Chana came almost every week for several months to the Friday Night Workshop and participated from the audience by giving advice to almost all of the other volunteers that I talked with. She presented some very rational arguments to them, especially when they had problems involving anxiety and panic; by talking them out of some of their nonsense, she got good experiential practice in talking herself out of some of her own.[6]

TEACHING UNCONDITIONAL SELF-ACCEPTANCE (USA)

I used, with Chana, the main technique that practitioners of REBT use with virtually all their clients: unconditional acceptance, or what Carl Rogers called unconditional positive regard.[7] Chana, like most clients of her type, strongly hated herself for failing at tests, for being anxious, for supposedly being rejected by other people for her failures and for her anxiety, and for almost every other deficiency that she was sure she had. As her therapist, I of course did not deny nor try to cover up these deficiencies. In fact, I often brought them to her attention—as when I showed her that she had secondary as well as primary severe anxiety—anxiety about her anxiety.

I can afford to do this with most of my clients because I feel and display unconditional acceptance to them. That is to say, I often deplore what they do, but I fully accept *them* with their *doings*. No matter how bad their performances are, including their working poorly at therapy and not doing their agreed-upon homework in between sessions, I show them that they are never stupid, inept, worthless *individuals*. They can soon see, as Chana soon saw, by my manner and my tone, that I do not judge *them* as people and that I accept them as "sinners," in spite of their somewhat obvious "sins" against themselves and others.

Many therapists, following Rogers, do this same kind of thing but they—including the Rogerians—get few good results because their clients, alas, take their acceptance as conditional rather than as unconditional. Thus, when a person-centered follower of Rogers shows clients that he or she accepts them with their failings, these clients very often wrongly conclude, "Because my therapist fully accepts me, that proves that I can accept myself and that I am an okay person." But this, of course, is *conditional* acceptance—because it depends on the therapist accepting the clients and not on their unconditionally accepting *themselves*, whether or not the therapist, or anyone else in the world, accepts them.

This may seem to be an REBT quibble. For if your therapist, who is presumably respectable and scientific, truly does accept you, isn't that good enough reason for you to accept yourself and think that you are really a "good person?" No, it isn't. For one thing, your therapist is prejudiced in your favor. He is being paid to accept you. He may be wrong, inept, or stupid. He has good therapeutic reasons for accepting you—because this plan will likely work—but he really may be pretending, and underneath may hardly accept you at all. He is only a single individual; and while he unconditionally accepts you, everyone else in the world may decide that you are a turd and may condemn you.

For many reasons, such as these, you are, to say the least, foolishly overgeneralizing when you say, "Because my therapist unconditionally accepts me, I can surely do the same for myself." Sure you can—with or without your therapist's approval. But you are still misled, and perhaps "crazy," when you take your therapist's word that you are really and truly a thoroughly "acceptable person."

Worse yet, you will almost certainly get "objective" disconfirmation of your therapist's showing you how "acceptable" you are. For as soon as you return to the world outside of therapy—which you soon will do and had better!—practically everyone else will often treat you as they previously did: rather shabbily and self-deprecatingly. At best, they will give you very conditional acceptance and, often, downright nonacceptance. Then where will you be? Practically nowhere.

Noting this, I, your REBT practitioner, not only give you what I honestly gave to Chana, unadulterated and unconditional acceptance, but, probably more importantly, I teach you how to consistently give it to yourself. For, in the final analysis, that is what self-acceptance is: *self-acceptance*. Even when I (or others) give it, you have to take it and make it your own. And since I, along with everyone else, am usually damned unreliable, you'd better not wait for us!

Accordingly, I showed and modeled unconditional acceptance for Chana. But I also carefully went over it with her a number of times and showed her why it was desirable, exactly what it was, and how to achieve it and keep achieving it on her own.[8] One of our conversations went like this:

AE: Do you see what I mean by your being able to uncondition-
        ally accept yourself, whether or not I or anyone else in the
        world accepts you?

Chana: Yes, I think I see it. But it looks like it's almost impossible to
        achieve that utopian state. It's almost unreal. After all, we
        live socially, in a community, and how can we possibly accept
        ourselves fully if and when many other people, sometimes
        almost all of them, reject us?

AE: It ain't easy! But it still can be done. Or, rather, you can do
        it.

Chana: Exactly how?

AE: Well, first a relatively easy way: by simply defining yourself,
        always defining yourself as a "good person."

Chana: Defining myself?

AE: Yes, because that's what we usually do, anyway, when we say,
        "I am a bad person." That statement is largely definitional. If
        we say, "I did a bad act," we are partly following consensus,
        because in our culture most people would probably agree that
        acts like stealing or murdering are "bad." But when we say,
        "Because I did a bad act, I am a bad individual," we are, first,
        overgeneralizing and, second, defining ourselves in this way."

Chana: What do you mean, again, by *defining*?

AE: Well, the term "bad person" doesn't just mean "a person who
        often or always acts badly." It also means "a person who is
        damnable and who doesn't deserve any real goodness in life
        because he or she *is* "bad." But the terms "deserve" and
        "damnable" are largely theological or definitional terms that
        millions of people would object to or disagree with. These
        words have individual meanings for almost all of us, ranging
        from "mildly damnable" for some of us to "totally damnable"
        for others. These terms usually refer to our essential being,
        or even to our "soul." Again, these are largely definitional
        items.

Chana: So I can say that I am a "good" or a "bad" person, but I
        cannot, even by consensus with other people, actually prove
        or disprove that I am. Therefore, I truly *define* myself in these
        ways.

AE: Exactly. Therefore, if you want to be a "good person," you

	merely can do what you usually do when you call yourself a "bad person"—define yourself as such.

Chana: You mean, *call* myself a good person? Simply that?

AE: Yes, simply that. So that solution will just about always work to *make you*, unconditionally, at least in your own eyes, a "good person." But can you see that it is inelegant and can be objected to by others?

Chana: Yes, I think so. Precisely for the reason that you just gave: It can be objected to by others. They can say, "You *think* that you are a good person and you are entitled to that view. But I think that you are a bad person, that you are damnable and undeserving of human happiness. And I am equally entitled to my view."

AE: Yes. So then what are you *really*—good or bad?

Chana: Quite a problem!

AE: Right. So REBT comes up with another, more elegant solution to your always and unconditionally accepting your self: To your gaining what we call USA—unconditional self-acceptance.

Chana: And that is?

AE: That is, you don't rate yourself, your being, your essence, your self, your personhood *at all*. You only, only, only rate what you *do*. You agree, usually with your social group, that practically all your thoughts, feelings, and behaviors are "good" when they lead to desirable results for you and for others. And agree, again with your social group, that other thoughts, feelings, and behaviors are "bad," "useless," or "unfortunate" because they lead to undesirable results. You can even rate each of your behaviors on a scale from one to 100. Thus, white lies that are done to save others from pain might be rated 10% bad, while black lies, done to harm others and to help yourself, might be rated as 90% bad.

Chana: And even those ratings would keep changing, in accordance with different circumstances?

AE: Right. But you still, at any one time and under any one set of conditions, have approximate ratings for your and other people's acts, emotions, and thoughts. The trick, however, is not to give you, your essence, or your personhood any global rating. Rate and measure only your behaviors, but refrain from ever rating your being, your self, or your personhood.

Chana: Can you really do that? Never give yourself a global or total rating?

AE: Yes, but not very easily. Yes, with difficulty, but you definitely can do so. If you really try and if you keep practicing to do so, you can avoid self-rating most of the time. As a human, you have innate and acquired tendencies—strong tendencies—to rate both your behaviors and your self. So you usually do both. But you clearly don't *have to* measure your selfhood. You can often stop doing so and rate only what you do. In time, you can automatically reduce self-rating and almost always stick to activity-rating.

Chana: If you do that, how does it make you a "good person"?

AE: Well, it really doesn't. It makes you a *person who* rates well in some of your activities some of the times—and who rates poorly in those same activities, as well as in other activities, at other times. You then can concentrate on what you *do*, and how to change it when it brings you poor results, and not on who you *are*, whether you *are* good or bad, nor on what to give as a rating for your personhood.

Chana: That sounds very neat—but awfully difficult to do!

AE: Right! But if you can't—or, rather, at times don't—do it, you can always fall back on the first solution we talked about: unconditionally accepting yourself just because you are human, just because you are alive and kicking, just because you decide that you are and define yourself as being a "good person."

Chana: Sounds fascinating!

AE: It is! Fascinating—and useful!

Chana was most intrigued by this conversation and seemed to get many of the concepts of self-worth that we were talking about. But we had to go over this ground many times before she strongly "got" it. When she did, she usually accepted herself as a "good person," even when she was failing at her tests and making herself needlessly panicked about them. But she sometimes was able to stop rating herself at all and rate only her "good" and "bad" behaviors. With both these solutions to her problems of abysmal self-downing, with which she originally came to therapy, she made herself considerably less anxious.

Chana took longer to achieve unconditional self-acceptance than to overcome her test-taking anxiety and her feelings of shame about her anxiety and about her poor test performances. But after seven months of therapy, she was well on her way to achieving it. At times, particularly when she did poorly in school or in dating, she fell back to conditional self-acceptance: She accepted herself because she was bright, attractive, and artistically talented. And, sometimes, because I, her therapist, fully accepted her with her failings. But she also learned, in our REBT discussions, that my acceptance of her came from a philosophy of not rating *humans* but only their *characteristics* and *behaviors.* She then began to apply this philosophy to herself, because *she* believed in it and not merely because *I* accepted her. So she kept trying for the philosophical change of unconditional self-acceptance (USA) and came close to fully achieving it. Close, but not entirely there. Does anyone, any human, 100% accept himself at all times? I doubt it. But it's a fascinating goal for your clients—and you!—to strive for.

THE USE OF OTHER REBT EMOTIVE AND VIVID METHODS

Many REBT practitioners have followed my lead in creating emotive and vivid methods of helping clients Dispute their irrational Beliefs (iB's) and arrive at the kind of profound philosophical changes that I have been advocating in this book. A number of these emotive methods are included in *The RET Resource Book for Practitioners,* edited by Michael E. Bernard and Janet L. Wolfe. I could quote many articles in this book, but to save space, recommend that you read the originals by I. F. Altrows, Robert H. Moore, K. M. Phadke, John R. Minor, I. J. Barrish, Ann Vernon, Clayton Shorkey, Windy Dryden, Donald Berch, Nicole Urdang, Stephen G. Weinrach, Paul J. Woods, Jeffrey M. Brandsma, and other contributors. You will see that these authors present a wide variety of effective REBT emotive techniques.[9]

Windy Dryden has been especially prolific in devising highly emotive methods of REBT. As I was about to send this book to the printer, his publisher, John Wiley & Sons, sent me a copy of the manuscript of his latest book, *Brief Rational Emotive Behavior Therapy.* Although written from a general REBT standpoint, and not stressing "elegant" brief therapy as my book does, Windy's manual is unusually comprehensive and includes some excellent points on brief therapy that add to those I have made here. By all means read it if effective brief therapy is your goal. Let me conclude this chapter with some emotive-evocative techniques from Windy's book.[10]

Forceful Arguments in Support of Clients' Rational Beliefs

Have your clients make a list of their persuasive arguments in support of their rational Beliefs. Example: "Now that I have lost my mate, I can find another one who is suited to me because there are so many potential partners to pick from and if I keep trying and experimenting, I am almost sure to find one or more who are good for me."

Review this list of rational arguments with your clients, to see if they seem to be good ones. But also have clients express their doubts, reservations, and objections about their own arguments and then vigorously Dispute their own doubts until they successfully resolve them. Example: "Yes, I'll *probably* find a suitable partner if I keep looking and experimenting. But suppose I am unlucky, and I never do find even a good one. What then?" Answer: "I'll still keep looking. But if I never do find one, I can *still* lead a happy life. Yes, even if I am *always* mateless. Tough!—but I'll *still* find some real happiness in life!"

See that your clients first devise and list good rational arguments to Dispute their irrational Beliefs. Second, check and possibly correct the rationality of these rB's. Third, let them write down their own doubts about their rB's. Fourth, have them write vigorous counterarguments to their doubts. Fifth, see that they convincingly surrender them.

Forceful Rational and Irrational Belief Zig-Zag Dialogue

Using another of Windy Dryden's emotive methods, you get your clients to write down a rational Belief (rB) and their degree of conviction in it, from zero (no conviction) to 100 (total conviction). Example: "I can unconditionally accept myself just because I'm alive and human, even if I do some real bad acts—such as lie to others. Degree of conviction: 75."

Second, have your clients irrationally *attack* their rational Beliefs in as many and as forceful ways as they can. Examples:

(a) "Even though I'm a fallible human, I don't *have to* lie to others. Therefore, I *should* not, and if I do what I *shouldn't* do, I'm a pretty bad person."

(b) "Even if I unconditionally accept myself when I lie to others, many or most people will put me down and hate me as a person for acting that rotten way. Maybe they're right and I *am* no good!"

Third, fully have your clients forcefully answer each of their irrational attacks on each of their rational Beliefs. Examples:

(a) "Even though I don't *have* to lie to others, there is no reason why I always *must* tell the truth. If I don't, that's bad, but my lie doesn't make *me* bad. It's only one *part* of the many things I do."

(b) "Yes, many or most people will put me down and hate me as a person for lying. But they then will be damning *me totally* for some of my poor *actions*. I never have to *agree* with them that I, a *whole person*, am no good."

Fourth, continue in this way until your clients answer all their irrational attacks on their rational Beliefs and are fully satisfied (and you are fully satisfied) with their answers.

Fifth, let your clients re-rate their level of conviction in their rational Belief to see if it has gone up to some considerable degree.

Forceful Two-Chair Rational and Irrational Dialogue

1. Let your clients sit in their regular chair and say a rational Belief (rB), as in the previous exercise, and say aloud how strongly (one to 100) they hold it.
2. Have them move to a second chair and orally attack this rB in a forceful way.
3. They go back to the first (rational) chair and strongly attack their irrational attack on their rB.
4. They keep voicing rational Beliefs (in the rational chair), moving to the irrational chair to attack these rB's, and then moving back to the rational chair to keep attacking their irrational attacks.
5. They use strong rB's, forceful irrational attacks on them, and vigorous rational attacks on the irrational attacks until they really believe their original rB and hold it more strongly than they first held it.

The foregoing forceful methods of Windy Dryden and a number of other cognitive and behavioral REBT methods that he describes in *Brief Rational Emotive Behavior Therapy* are well worth reading and using for regular brief therapy as well as for the kind of deep, intensive, and more enduring brief therapy that I am advocating in this book.

NOTES TO CHAPTER 10

1. Abelson, 1963; Bernard, 1991, 1993; Dryden, 1994a, 1994b; Ellis, 1965b, 1969, 1973a, 1985b, 1993j, 1993k, 1993m, 1994e; Ellis & Abrahms, 1978; Ellis & Abrams, 1994; Ellis & Dryden, 1987; Ellis & Velten, 1992; Greenberg & Safran, 1987; Greenberg, Elliott, & Litaer, 1994; Kellerman, 1992; Kiser, Piercy, & Lipchik, 1993; Mahrer, 1989; Moreno, 1990; Plutchik & Kellerman, 1990; Safran & Greenberg, 1991.
2. Ellis, 1993j.
3. Ellis, 1969, 1973a, 1985b, 1994e; Ellis & Abrahms, 1978; Ellis & Abrams, 1994; Ellis & Harper, 1975; Ellis & Velten, 1992; Walen, DiGiuseppe, & Dryden, 1992.
4. Ellis, 1977c, 1979d, 1981, 1987e; O'Hanlon & Beadle, 1994.
5. Ellis, 1977d, 1981.
6. Dryden, Backx, & Ellis, 1987.
7. Rogers, 1961.
8. Burns, 1993; Dengelegi, 1990; Dryden, 1994a, 1994b; Ellis, 1962, 1972d, 1973b, 1985a, 1988a, 1991g, 1992b, 1994e; Franklin, 1993; Hartman, 1967; Hauck, 1991; Lazarus, 1977; Miller, 1986; Mills, 1993; Tillich, 1953; Woods, 1993.
9. Bernard & Wolfe, 1993.
10. Dryden, 1995.

11

Behavioral Methods for
Effecting Brief and Intensive
Psychotherapy

Rational Emotive Behavior Therapy probably heads the list of all the other cognitive-behavioral therapies in encouraging the use of behavioral methods. This may well be because I employed these methods on myself to get over my phobias of public speaking and of approaching suitable females for dates. When I was 19, I followed the suggestions of some of the ancient philosophers—especially Democritus—and of John B. Watson and his early associates to do what I was terrified of doing. So I uncomfortably forced myself to speak in public, speak in public, speak in public—which I had always ruthlessly avoided for my first two decades—and within about two months time I completely overcame my phobia and (what do you know!) actually came to enjoy public speaking. As I often tell my workshop audiences, now you can't keep me away from the public speaking platform!

That experience was so salutary that, a little later that year, I again forced myself to do what I was previously terrified of doing. During the month of June, I made verbal overtures to 100 different women sitting on park benches in the Bronx Botanical Gardens, got rejected for dating by all of them (one woman kissed me in the park, and made a date for later that evening, but never showed up!)–and, once again, just about completely overcame my fear of talking to strange women and was easily able to do so for the rest of my life.

Great stuff! My adventures, in both these instances, were brief; they really worked; and they led to long-lasting, intensive change. Rarely, for the rest of my 80-plus years, have I had any anxiety about public speaking or encountering desirable women. I do so *easily* and *enjoyably*.[1]

This is not true with all of my phobic and other clients. They often resist courting discomfort and find a million excuses *not* to do so. Others try it a few times, then stop. Some even become more fearful. Why? Because they fail to do what I made myself do when I first terrifiedly forced myself to speak in public and to approach attractive women: They fail to *convince* themselves that it *isn't* horrible to fail and that they *don't* have to win their potential partners. Quite an omission!

Not so hundreds of my other REBT clients! They've seen their antiphobic duty and they've done it. I taught them what to do and encouraged them to do it. But, obviously, I didn't *make* them do anything.

IN VIVO DENSENSITIZATION

Observing my clients think *and* act against their irrational (self-defeating) fears, I (prejudicedly) "confirmed" my main hypotheses: The more strongly they Disputed their irrational Beliefs (iB's) that failure and discomfort are *terrible*, and that their *worth as humans* plummets to zero when they fail and get rejected, the more quickly and thoroughly they make themselves become less phobic. Good! So I keep using *in vivo* (and uncomfortable) desensitization, along with rational Disputing, to help my overly fearful clients.[2]

Peter, for example, was phobic about all kinds of public transportation–especially planes, which he always avoided. I couldn't very well get him to go on a number of air trips, as he couldn't afford to do so and wasn't going to take a chance on "sudden death," anyway. So I first suggested subway rides–short subway rides. Peter agreed, but managed to get up enough "nerve" to take only one ride a month.

That didn't work, because that gave Peter 29 or 30 days to reconvince himself that the train he was on would get stalled, that he would have a panic attack, that everyone on the subway car would look at him with disdain, that he would probably get mugged, that he would surely be trapped in a wrecked and burning train, etc. With all these "horrible" thoughts, Peter's subway and other transportation anxieties hardly diminished! On the contrary, with his continued horribilizing, he more *deeply* disturbed himself.

I explained to Peter that the infrequency of his subway trips was getting him nowhere and that, like so many other phobics I had successfully seen, he had better ride the blasted rails steadily—in fact, implosively. The more often he did so, I said, the more likely he was to quickly overcome his phobia instead of dragging it on interminably—and more painfully. Moreover—I fondly stated, using my own antiphobic experiences as an example—if he *really* wanted to become unafraid of the poor innocent subway trains, he preferably should take them implosively, one right after another: To prove to himself many times in a row that nothing even half "terrible" would happen.

Peter argued against this "frightening" assignment, but finally agreed to do it experimentally. He set himself the "gruesome" task of getting on a subway train every day, riding one stop at a time for five stops in a row, and then riding back to his original destination, also one stop at a time.

Peter's first "experiment" was most uncomfortable, and after going three stops he came within an inch of quitting. He reminded himself, however, that if he did quit, his antiphobic trip would take forever—or fail completely. That idea jolted him, so he continued on his unmerry way.

As you can well imagine—for I would hardly be telling you this story if Peter were still as phobic as ever—each of Peter's subsequent trips got easier. After two weeks, no sweat. He took longer and longer subway trips, began to actually enjoy them, and especially enjoyed his mastery over his phobia. On his own, he then tried city buses, long distance buses, and regular trains. A half year later, he took his first plane ride from New York to Washington and back. By the end of his first antiphobic year, he was taking longer air trips and suffering little anxiety and no panic. He started to date a well-traveled, on-the-go woman whom he previously would never have paired off with, and enjoyed several long trips with her.

If you and your clients can hack it, then the key term for *in vivo* desensitization is "preferably implosive." Not that gradual *in vivo* desensitization doesn't work. It does—sometimes fairly quickly. Gladys was afraid to ride in cars, because she might get queasy and vomit in front of other people. And that would really be *awful*! I tried to convince her that vomiting in front of others would be highly inconvenient, but hardly *unforgivable* and *awful!* No sale. I humorously suggested, to emphasize my point, that she deliberately take some rides, let herself vomit in the car, and see how downright helpful the other occupants would be. If not, who needed them as "friends." Still no sale.

Finally, because she was moving to New Jersey and would have to come by car to work in Manhattan, Gladys agreed to take one ride every weekend, to carry a barf bag with her, and ride only with people who knew about her phobia and would doubtless accept her if she did have an "accident." She kept to this program, at first very queasily, but after one car ride each week for 12 weeks she convinced herself that, one, she wouldn't vomit and, two, if she did it would be "embarrassing" but she could live with it. So she kept riding in cars, with some trepidation but no horror.

I tried to show Gladys that nothing is "shameful" except by somewhat arbitrary definition, and that even to call vomiting "embarrassing" was to be needy of others' approval—which she didn't have to make herself. No go. I also failed to convince her that if others saw her vomiting as "utterly shameful" and especially put her down as a "rotten person," *they* were bigoted and had an emotional problem.

So Gladys, through undertaking *in vivo*, and somewhat gradual desensitization, overcame her car phobia, but failed to make an intensive change in her "shameful" attitudes. I was content with this relatively brief but not-so-deep therapy. So was she.

What was the difference between Peter and Gladys in changing their phobic reactions? Two main differences: First, Peter tried going in subway trains more implosively than Gladys; he deliberately took on more pain *faster* and *saw* that Benjamin Franklin's statement "there are no gains without pains" had better be followed. Second, he convinced himself that he could go a lot further than he had gone in overcoming his phobia by deliberately taking more risks, graduating to additional kinds of transportation, and going with a woman who enjoyed travel. So Peter acquired a philosophy of increasing risk that led to less pain—and to greater enjoyment.

Gladys, on the other hand, took minimal chances, kept rigidly to one-goal desensitization, didn't try to see or advance further, and was interested only in overcoming her phobia, not in enhancing or fulfilling her life. She did well enough behaviorally, but shied away from making any profound (or even unprofound) philosophical change that I would have liked her (and similar phobics) to make. Not bad—but too bad she didn't try to go further. She could have, but I saw no reason why she absolutely *should* have.

STAYING IN DIFFICULT SITUATIONS

REBT often encourages people to stay in a fairly difficult situation—such as a poor marriage or a highly stressful job—until they work solidly at *not* unduly upsetting themselves about it. Only then should they decide to quit or stay with it. Why so? Because if people run away from an unpleasant situation in a huff, or if they stay in it in a disturbed manner, they are very likely to take their upsetness to almost any new situation that comes along.[3]

Morris, for example, hated his boss with a vengeance, and stewed about this boss's "unfairness" every day that he went to work—or stayed home with a stomachache. So he quit his well-paying, enjoyable job, found a much "nicer" boss, and then ranted and raved about the "unfair" working conditions and the "unjust" pay of his new job. I agreed with Morris that his first boss might have indeed been "unfair" and that the working conditions of his new job might well be "unjust." But his philosophy of horror about "unfairness" was still with him. Only "fairness," which rarely seems to exist in his world, would (temporarily!) stop his rage and low frustration tolerance.

So I tried to help Morris stay with his first job, give up his godlike demand that because justice is good it *absolutely must* exist, and *then* decide whether or not to quit the job. I failed. So I tried, once again, to help Morris unenrage himself about his second job—and its "unfairness." Failed again. Morris then made himself angry at me for my "unfairness" in not helping him find a "fairer" job. The last I heard of him, he was unemployed—and still ranting and raving.

Bill did better. He, too, hated his boss, his supervisor, and his co-workers—none of whom *really* appreciated how much good work he did. So for the first five weeks I saw him he kept threatening to quit and to go into business for himself. I thought that would be foolish—because, as far as I could see, he would soon hate his customers and put himself out of business.

As with Morris, I easily agreed with Bill that he probably wasn't too appreciated—as he presumably *should* be—but tried to show him that his *demand*, rather than the lack of appreciation itself, led to his upsetness.

Chances were, therefore, that he would keep this demand—and feel quite unappreciated on his next job. And his next. And his next.

Under my tutelage—and that of some REBT writings and cassettes—Bill convinced himself that he *should* be unappreciated (because he *was*); that his boss, supervisor, and co-workers were fallible, screwed up humans (and not rotten bastards); and that he could *stand* their lack of appreciation (but not *like* it). Whereupon Bill's rage became minimal. He still hated much of what his boss, supervisor, and co-workers did—and did not do. But he stopped damning them for their "delinquent" behavior, no longer obsessed about their "inequity" and "callousness," kept his job, and enjoyed it more than he had enjoyed any job before.

USING REINFORCEMENT METHODS

Because Rational Emotive Behavior Therapy is heavily behavioral, as well as cognitive and emotive, it often includes the technique of reinforcement. As B.F. Skinner and his followers have shown, people keep performing tasks for which they are reinforced or rewarded, and often drop behaviors for which they are not reinforced. Thus, if they agree with themselves and with their therapists to do certain kinds of homework projects in order to change their thoughts and feelings, they had often better arrange to reward themselves soon after they have completed these projects and to omit these rewards when they do not perform them. They can allow themselves some pleasurable activity, such as reading or listening to music, only after they have finished a number of REBT Self-Help Forms or after they have used Rational Emotive Imagery to change an unhealthy negative feeling to a healthy one. This is particularly true when they find doing their homework "too hard" or "unbearable" and when they therefore avoid doing it.[4]

If your clients reinforce themselves for doing difficult homework assignments, that in itself may by no means help them change their basic self-defeating philosophies. As I note in a recent paper with Hank Robb, "Acceptance in Rational Emotive Behavior Therapy," when you are faced with a difficult situation—such as a "bad" job or marriage—you can follow Paul Hauck's practical suggestions of staying with it, leaving it, or changing it. But, as Hank and I point out in our article, you can do any of these things and still upset yourself about the situation.[5]

Take Joseph, for example. He had a practically sexless marriage and didn't like it at all. So he first tried to change it by inducing his wife to have more sex. So she did. That worked much better, but he still strongly believed that she *should* enjoy sex more than she did and was "irresponsibly goofing" because she didn't even attempt to enjoy it. Then Joseph tried putting up with practically no sex and still staying with his wife. That attempt failed because he had extreme low frustration tolerance and, despite the fact that his marriage included many good things, he "couldn't bear" not having more sex and was often angry at his wife and the world. He finally tried separating from his wife and having sex with other women. But that didn't work out because many other women wouldn't go to bed with him until he was actually divorced. He also had to spend too much time convincing a woman that he really loved her before she would have sex with him; and the few women that he finally got to bed with were not great sex partners. So he was quite upset—or rather, he upset himself—about that. None of Joseph's three plans worked, mainly because all of them included problems and because his low frustration tolerance kept him overly frustrated and depressed about those problems.

But reinforcements can sometimes work. Joseph, with my help, continued to live apart from his wife, but decided to allow himself to have an enjoyable Sunday with their two young children only after he had worked a few times a week to counter his low frustration tolerance. So he kept using the REBT Self-Help Form, forceful rational coping self-statements, and Rational Emotive Imagery each week until he concluded that his sexual situation and the other difficulties of his life were truly frustrating, but that they were not *too* obnoxious and that he definitely *could* stand them. When, with the use of these methods, he changed some of his basic attitudes, he began to enjoy his separation from his wife, his regular visits with his children, and the adventure of looking for suitable sex partners and companions even when he found it difficult to locate them. His reinforcing himself for doing the REBT cognitive and emotive homework didn't exactly *make* him change his basic low frustration tolerance, but it distinctly *helped* him to do so and to make a philosophical as well as a behavioral change.

Joseph's various plans to improve, stay with, and finally leave his marriage took nine months and, as noted above, gave him some useful information. But they were not really very successful. When he began reinforcing himself to help change his low frustration tolerance attitudes and feelings, he was able to do so in another four months and to feel much better about the progress he had made.

USING PUNISHMENTS AND PENALTIES

Although B. F. Skinner and his followers usually take a dim view of using penalties and punishments to help clients change their behaviors and their thinking, I have found that this is often desirable in the case of difficult customers (DC's).[6] Don't forget, in this connection, that of the millions of people who give up a heavy addiction—such as being addicted to alcohol, drugs, or nicotine—most of them do so under their own power, with little support from self-help groups, therapy groups, or individual therapists. How come? Probably because the addiction itself finally becomes so onerous—leading to losses of job, marriage, and physical health—that they decide that the punishments and deprivations of keeping it outweigh the immediate gratification of indulging in it. So they quit.

Similarly, some people who are "addicted" to emotional disturbances will not quit bothering themselves until they convince themselves that the penalties of their self-defeating behaviors outweigh the rewards of their indulging in these behaviors. So you can encourage some of these recalcitrant individuals to use punishments and penalties to increase the likelihood that they will work to give up their emotional "addictions." As I often tell my workshop audiences, how many smokers would continue smoking if every time they took a puff they immediately put the lit end of the cigarette in their mouth?

A case in point was Julia, who never was able to fulfill a long-term relationship with a man during her 39 years of dating. Her main dysfunctional or irrational Beliefs (iB's) that we discovered during her first few sessions of REBT were: (1) "I *absolutely must* have a permanent relationship or else I am an inadequate partner and a no-goodnik!" (2) "When I am in a relationship, my partner must not do *anything* that really upsets me, and is a louse if he is even moderately inconsiderate and unloving." (3) "My steady relationships *must not* include major frustrations, such as too much or too little sex, and I *can't stand* staying in them if they do!"

Well, what do you know: Julia had all three of the basic musts that people seriously upset themselves with. Then, when these arrant demands led to her or her partners ending their relationships, she also *couldn't stand* being mateless, even for a short while, and tended to stay home and drink too much to drown her "horrible sorrows."

With my help, Julia quickly saw her iB's, and also saw how self-defeating they were. But she did practically nothing to think, feel, or act against

them. Cognitively, she rarely Disputed her musts, especially in any persistent or forceful manner. She only mildly believed that her mating
behaviors were stupid but that she was not a stupid, inadequate person
for engaging in them. She powerfully believed that she was a "real idiot"
and a "hopeless clod."

Emotively, Julia felt angry and depressed much of the time and only
occasionally felt just frustrated and disappointed with what was happening in her life. When she worked at feeling disappointed rather than
depressed and angry, she soon went back to indulging in the "horror"
of it all and to honestly enjoying her anger against her "impossible"
partners.

Behaviorally, Julia told herself a hundred times that she would soon
go out socially and look for a new partner, now that the former one was
gone. But she stayed at home for months at a time, usually drinking
steadily, and then berated herself savagely for not going out and looking.

Using reinforcements, such as allowing herself to visit her sister and
nieces only after she had done some of her cognitive, emotive, or behavioral homework, did not work for Julia. She really, in a way, "enjoyed"
her hibernation, including staying away from her sister and her nieces,
so her "reinforcements" were not powerful enough. She also didn't want
to try any punishments, because she said that, first, she would not enact
them; and, second, if she did she would rebel against them, and insist
that she shouldn't *have to* do them to get herself going.

I unangrily and acceptingly kept showing Julia that she was at an impasse, and that in the long run she would get more pain than gain from
her resisting change. She moderately agreed, but still would do nothing
differently. I kept after her and finally persuaded her to agree that she'd
better use some punishments to help her effect a real change. But what
penalty? She couldn't think of one herself and she quickly rejected all
that I suggested.

I showed Julia that, because of her low frustration tolerance, she was
insisting on *easy* and *comfortable* ways of changing, when there didn't seem
to be any. Whether she liked it or not, she would most likely have to
choose an *un*comfortable way—such as, again, enacting a stiff punishment every time she promised herself to modify her behavior and then
refused to do so. Agreed. But, again, what punishment?

I finally found a "good" one—"good" because it seemed to break the
vicious circle that she usually got herself into. Once any relationship was
"bad," she soon broke it up—and then stayed at home by herself for awhile.
Finally, she got so fed up with inactivity that she ran out pell-mell and

quickly arranged to get into another, and equally bad, relationship. To stop this vicious circle, I suggested, she could make herself stay in the next bad relationship, refuse to break it up until she gave some real time and effort to simultaneously date someone else, and then replace it with a better relationship. Why not look for a new and better one, take her time in finding it—and still stay with the "bad" one?

Julia was at first revolted at the very thought of trying this punishing tactic, because it seemed so obnoxious that she couldn't possibly carry it out. But she realized that it would probably work. After weeks of coming to this "miserable" conclusion, she finally decided to try it. She easily got herself into a relationship with another "wrong" and "bad" partner, but this time she stayed in it and refused to run away even when she felt strongly impelled to do so. Then, to make things more difficult, she dated on the side of this relationship, which she had never done before, because she considered herself to be "strictly monogamous." But she forced herself to do this additional dating and got into a few minor relationships, which she quickly ended, convincing herself that she didn't *have to* stay in them.

After a few months, she found what seemed to be a "decent" second relationship, and then worked on putting up with its hassles—which it definitely had. Her new lover was "nice" and "undifficult," but was low-sexed and avoided having intercourse with her. She at first seethed about this and hated him for his avoidance. But, working on her low frustration tolerance, she explained to him what he could do, aside from intercourse, to satisfy her sexually, got him to see that it would be fine, and worked out noncoital relations that were among the best she had ever had in her life. Things got so good between the two of them after awhile that she actually, for the first time in her life, got engaged.

All this wasn't easy for Julia. She found that staying with Lover Number One, after she had decided he was not for her, was most difficult, but she bore it for two months while she was looking for Number Two. With this second lover, she at first found staying with him without "proper" sex satisfaction very unrewarding. She also found it "terribly hard" to talk with him about changing their sex patterns. But she accepted these conditions in order to work toward achieving her long-range goals. And, for once, she did.

As in so many cases like Julia's, the Catch-22 is that they usually have to tolerate real discomfort in order to work on their low frustration tolerance—that is, to work on their intolerance of discomfort. Often, they simply won't do this, so they are left with their original LFT—and with failure to solve their basic problems. The advantage of REBT is that it keeps showing them there really is no other way—no gain without pain—and that accepting a real pain for a relatively short period of time is practically the only way for them to get what they "truly" want. Too bad—but that's it!

Helping clients, as in Julia's case, to accept punishments (or penalties) involves not merely suggesting them but also getting them to accept the punishments—for their own ultimate good. REBT, therefore, uses this behavioral technique, which is quite simple and direct, along with the more complicated method of helping them to accept philosophically the desirability and, at times, the near necessity of actually using this method and accepting its "terrible" inconveniences.

Of course, the punishments that clients choose are often not actually levied. The mere thought of how obnoxious it would be if the client did levy them helps them to change their ways without actually enacting them. Thus, in Julia's case, she could have *decided* to stay with her first lover, while looking for a second and better lover, and actually not have done so because it was too uncomfortable. Or she could have quickly thought about staying with the first lover, have seen how "awful" that would be, therefore quickly left him, and therefore forced herself to keep looking for her second lover, instead of spending months at home hibernating and drinking. Or she could have kept the first lover, looked for the second one, found him, thought that staying with him and not having great intercourse *too* obnoxious, and therefore kept looking for a third and better lover.

Paradoxically, therefore, thinking about giving yourself punishments (or penalties) if you do not do something that you consider "too hard" may make that thing "much easier" to do—and you may actually do it, to your distinct benefit. But actually arranging to accept a punishment, as in Julia's case, may, first, prod you into forcing yourself to do something "less" punishing (changing your behavior). Or, second, it may help you work on your low frustration tolerance, and see that bearing "intolerable" pain is not "awful," and that you can bear it better than you first thought that you could and still use it (since it is painful) to prod you to work on some more basic aspect of your problems.

In using behavioral methods, then, REBT does not employ them by themselves—nor does practically anybody. Clients had better get and *accept* the idea that behavioral methods will actually work. They often can be helped, meaning persuaded, to use them by an active-directive therapist. You can therefore encourage them to *check* and *think* about how well they really work–and to *think* about revising them or even giving them up.

Behavioral methods, therefore, go with cognitive and emotive methods. When some of the radical behaviorists, like Michael Dougher, Neil Jacobson, and Stephen Hayes, say or imply that they rarely help people to change their thinking in order to help them change their feelings and their behaviors, this is doubtful.[7] This also applies to the problem-solving and solution-oriented therapists, such as Milton Erickson, Jay Haley, Jeffrey Zeig, Steve de Shazer, and Bill O'Hanlon. When they point out that unless people change their behavior, no real therapy is likely to occur, they are often on the right track. But when they state or imply that deliberately changing one's behavior is the secret of therapeutic success, they are omitting a great deal of the thinking and emoting that not only accompanies behavioral change but often precedes it.[8] Along with the behavioral changes that lead to "deep" therapy seem to go a work-oriented *philosophy* of growth. When clients acquire this kind of *attitude*, it works synergistically with their *actions* to instigate change and to keep *perpetuating* it.

REBT, as this chapter shows, greatly emphasizes and encourages several behavioral methods, and is in some respects the most behaviorally oriented of all the popular cognitive-behavior therapies. But it consciously uses behavioral methods along with important cognitive and emotive ones. It does so to try to effect not only briefer but also more intensive, pervasive, and long-lasting change.[9]

POSSIBLE DISADVANTAGES OF BEHAVIORAL METHODS

As usual, I had better point out that behavioral methods of therapy, as used in REBT and in other kinds of psychological treatment, are likely to have distinct disadvantages, and sometimes to even lead to more harm than good. Here are some of their possible disadvantages:

1. As noted before in this chapter, *in vivo* and implosive desensitization may prove harmful to some clients. Thomas Stampfl, in the 1960's, advocated implosive imaginal desensitization for clients who, among other things, had profound and irrational fear of snakes. He had them imagine a whole barrel of writhing snakes, putting their hand in the barrel, and letting the snakes writhe around it. Although this form of imaginal desensitization seems to be the opposite of that advocated by Joseph Wolpe, reciprocal inhibition–where clients afraid of snakes imagine them at a

distance, then relax, then keep getting closer and closer to them in their imagination, and keep relaxing each time–Stampfl's method sometimes works more quickly and better than Wolpe's.[10]

But not so fast! While Wolpe's clients rarely became more upset as they did his form of imaginal desensitization, a larger number of Stampfl's clients grew more fearful; some even had panic attacks. So, both implosive imaginal therapy and *in vivo* desensitization frequently work. Moreover, they may well usually work more quickly than gradual desensitization. But they also have their hazards and had better be used carefully with certain clients!

2. As noted above, behavioral changes are almost invariably made along with cognitive changes, and "cause" the latter as well as being "caused" by them. But clients have a wide choice of cognitions to use with their new actions, and may easily pick wrong, self-sabotaging ones. Thus, when they make themselves change from doing something pleasant, such as smoking, to not doing this harmful act, they may rebel against giving it up by thinking things like, "Yes, I can stop smoking, but it's much *too hard* to do so and I *shouldn't have to* do this. How horrible to deprive myself!" With such cognitions, they may easily go back to smoking. Even if they keep away from doing so, they may suffer, suffer, suffer, and increase their low frustration tolerance.

Other clients who stop smoking may tell themselves much different things, such as: "It's really not that hard to stop. Look how good it is that I have mastered this obnoxious habit! I feel deprived of smoking, but I'm also depriving myself of emphysema and lung cancer!" With these kinds of thoughts they will produce higher frustration tolerance, a sense of mastery, and fewer feelings of great deprivation.

As a safeguard, therefore, you had better *look at what your clients are thinking as they use* "good" behavioral methods, and thereby help them to have useful instead of sabotaging thoughts. Consciously try to help them employ a changed, often a radically changed, philosophy along with their modified actions.

3. Behavioral changes are frequently the fastest methods of helping clients to change, but not necessarily the deepest or best. I sometimes quote, in this connection, Maimonides, who in the twelfth century pointed out that if parents force their children to read they may well drive them away from the intrinsic pleasures of reading they may otherwise acquire if they were not forced. Similarly, if you push your clients too quickly to stop destructive habits like drinking too much or avoiding writing reports, you may help them to function better in important respects. But

their drinking and their avoiding writing reports may have been defenses against their feeling very anxious about doing things imperfectly. If you help them to change their behaviors, and not at the same time work on their anxiety-creating cognitions, they may actually be worse off than they were before. Therefore, as I keep emphasizing in this book, behavioral methods had better usually be employed in conjunction with effective cognitive and emotive methods of therapy, so that your therapy is brief, but with deep and intensive improvement resulting.[11]

4. Behavioral improvements may, of course, be taken to iatrogenic extremes. Helping a client to overcome his serious procrastination about writing term papers may help him turn into a grind who does very well at school but who now compulsively turns out paper after paper, neglects his social life, and perhaps takes only those subjects that he knows he will succeed at and not those subjects that lead to his long-term career goals.

Changing behaviors, then, may lead to profound philosophical change. But it also may not. It usually *includes* an element of cognitive change because it involves self-discipline, which in itself means that clients have *decided* to attempt long-range gains instead of merely going for short-range ones. But working hard to change behaviors *plus* pushing ahead to more sensible philosophies is (I think!) more likely to result in brief therapy *with deep and intensive* results.

NOTES TO CHAPTER 11

1. Ellis & Dryden, 1991; Palmer & Ellis, 1994; Warga, 1988; Watson, 1919; Watson & Rayner, 1920; Weinrach, 1980; Wiener, 1988.
2. Baldon & Ellis, 1993; Corsini, 1979; Ellis, 1971, 1972a, 1972c, 1973c, 1975a, 1977a, 1977b, 1978, 1979b, 1979c, 1980b, 1983c, 1985b, 1988a, 1990a, 1990f, 1991f, 1992a, 1993d, 1994d, 1994e, 1995a; Gelber, 1993; Kanfer & Goldstein, 1986; Kanfer & Schefft, 1988; Marks, 1994; Maultsby, 1971b; Skinner, 1971; Wolpe, 1990.
3. Ellis & Abrahms, 1978; Ellis & Abrams, 1994; Ellis & Harper, 1975; Ellis & Knaus, 1977; Ellis & Velten, 1992.
4. Ellis, 1979a, 1980a, 1983b, 1985b, 1988a, 1990a; Ellis & Velten, 1992; Ellis & Whiteley, 1979; Sichel & Ellis, 1984; Walen, DiGiuseppe, & Dryden, 1992.
5. Ellis & Robb, 1994.

6. Bjork, 1993; Ellis, 1979c, 1985b; Ellis & Abrahms, 1978; Skinner, 1971; Woods, 1974, 1983, 1985.
7. Dougher, 1993, 1994; Ellis, 1994c, 1994e; Hayes & Hayes, 1992; Hayes, McCurry, et al., 1991; Jacobson, 1992.
8. Bandler & Grinder, 1978; de Shazer, 1985, 1990; Erickson, 1980; Erickson & Rossi, 1979; Haley, 1963, 1973, 1990; O'Hanlon & Beadle, 1994; O'Hanlon & Wilk, 1987; Zeig, 1992.
9. Ellis, 1990f, 1991d, 1991f, 1991h, 1991m, 1992a, 1992d, 1993b, 1993d, 1993h, 1995a, 1995b; Ellis & Velten, 1992.
10. Stampfl & Levis, 1967; Wolpe, 1990.
11. Ellis & Abrahms, 1978; Ellis & Abrams, 1994; Ellis, Abrams, & Dengelegi, 1992; Ellis & Whiteley, 1979.

12

Methods of Brief but Less Deep and Intensive Therapy

Almost innumerable methods of brief therapy exist. In fact, even the conventional methods—such as psychoanalysis—can be specially adapted to briefer form or can occasionally, almost by accident, lead to significant improvement after only a few sessions.

In this chapter I shall deal with many of the usual brief therapy methods, but shall try to show why they rarely are designed for or lead to intensive change, even accidentally. You may find this not too surprising because, in my not so humble estimation, long-term therapy, too, often brings "good" results, but not what I (prejudicedly) deem "elegant" or "great" outcomes. Not as I call them!

Anyway, here is a fairly long list of brief therapies, all of which *at times* produce good (but not equally good) outcomes for many clients. Let me review them.

USING CLIENTS' RESOURCES AND TALENTS

Milton Erickson pioneered in helping clients solve some of their "emotional" and "practical" problems by quickly discovering that they had some good and sometimes unusual resources and talents, and instructing or encouraging them to use these resources to solve presenting problems that they at first failed to solve. A number of his students and followers—including Jay Haley, Ernest Rossi, Jeffrey Zeig, Steve de Shazer, and Bill O'Hanlon—have used and modified his methods.[1]

Using clients' resources and talents often quickly works, for clients either have "hidden" problem-solving resources of which they are only dimly aware or can use their known talents in ways they previously didn't realize. Or, they can—especially with the help of clever and creative therapists like Erickson—be persuaded that they have problem-solving skills that they barely, if at all, really have. In the latter case, they can be subtly taught to have new talents or they can be led to think they have "rare" capabilities, thus gaining so much false confidence that they actually work harder and better to solve some of their presenting difficulties.

Nonnie came to see me because she kept making herself anxious at job interviews and therefore failing at a good many of them. I soon convinced her that she was anxious only in job settings but that she handled other situations very well. Thus, she spoke very unanxiously to me, had an unusually beautiful voice, answered questions intelligently, and was quite fluent verbally even when she felt anxious. Bolstered by these "facts," which I tried hard not to exaggerate, she quickly started to do better in job interviews, felt she *could* continue to do so, conditionally accepted herself because of her increased competency, got the best job she had ever had—and quit therapy after eight sessions.

Nonnie was very happy about her improvement, but I thought she had made gains that were "great" but superficial. She was still basically anxious and easily made herself anxious about her anxiety. She especially felt anxious when she dated "good" males and felt depressed when her relationships didn't work out. So her "cure" was quick—and partial. As therapy ended, I encouraged her to keep using REBT, through our books, cassettes, workshops, and other media, but as far as I can tell she did so only to a limited extent.

I have other clients, fortunately, that I quickly help by showing them they have, and can ably use, resources and talents of which they are only dimly aware. But they also learn to accept themselves more fully when they are not acting too competently. So, this let's-look-at-your-resources method can be used as a prelude to or in addition to employing other more intensive REBT techniques. By itself, it has real limitations. These especially include:

1. Clients (like Nonnie) like themselves mainly *for* their newly discovered resources, and therefore achieve only *conditional* self-acceptance. Not *un*conditional!

2. They may use these resources for practical purposes and pleasures, but not to change their disturbed thinking.

3. They may feel so satisfied with new successes that they quit therapy too soon, before they deal with other important problems.

4. They may strive for competence in one area, neglecting achievement that they might be capable of in other areas, and lead a happier but still not very fulfilling life.

5. They may delude themselves that they have "better" resources than they actually have, may strive unrealistically, and may disillusion themselves when they fail.

Even when it "works," therefore, pushing clients to use their "natural" resources and talents can have distinct limitations. By all means, use it at times. But often try to help your clients go well beyond it.

SOLUTION-FOCUSED THERAPY

Partly inspired by the *utilization* tactics I just discussed, but particularly—and rather brilliantly—started by Steve de Shazer in the 1980's, solution-focused therapy has become something of a rage among brief therapies. During this brief method, the therapist listens attentively and empathically to the client's main problems, picks an important one, and then asks several pertinent questions aimed at showing clients that they had already partially solved these problems previously, obviously knew how to solve them, and therefore can once again figure out, with the therapist's collaboration, "good" solutions again.[2]

Using solution-focused therapy, you ask your clients pertinent questions like these: What kinds of problems did you previously solve? When you had a problem like this present one, what good solutions did you work out? What changes did you make that were better than those you are now making? What were the times when you expected to have this anxiety or related problem and you didn't actually have it or you dealt very well with it? What solutions to your upsetness worked at times and what didn't work for you? Under what conditions do your disturbances occur and not occur? When you stopped feeling upset, what had you done to make yourself stop? What interrupted your problem and made it better or more tolerable? What made it worse? Did you put yourself down for being disturbed? If not, what did you do to prevent your self-downing? Did you stay with the problem or run away from it? How did you make yourself stay and cope with it?

Questions like these will frequently help your clients see past solutions, and potential present ones, to their "emotional" and other problems. Fine—and rapid! But not, I would say, usually "best" or "intensive."

Frank got along well with new women partners for a few weeks or months but then, "They found me out, discovered that I was negative and critical, and left. I've suffered greatly several times from these rejections and now feel depressed and hopeless. I'm sure I'll never make it in a permanent relationship with a good woman who will always find me out."

I at first tried to help Frank see what he was irrationally thinking to create, and to express, his negative and critical feelings. He irrationally believed that he *absolutely had to* express all his negative feelings to others, or else he was a *dishonest, hypocritical person*. I tried to rationally show him that honesty was *preferable* but not always *completely necessary*. But he stuck to his "realistic" guns and said that he was negative and critical only when people, including his temporary partners, *were* acting badly, and he was only trying to help them change—for themselves as well as for others. And he expressed his criticism because he was trying to be quite honest about his feelings, especially in a close relationship. So he was obviously "right," and it was pointless to make him responsible, first, for his feelings and, second, for expressing them. So I got nowhere in trying to show Frank that he needlessly felt and expressed negativism and undue criticism.

Thwarted, I gracefully retreated and tried solution-focused therapy with Frank. "Did you ever manage to go with a woman for any length of time who didn't find you out and who didn't leave you?"

"Oh, yes. Once," Frank answered.

"For how long?"

"Oh, well, two and a half years. She stayed, but I finally left her."

"What did you do, that one time, to help the relationship continue?"

"Oh, I could see that she was such a basket case—she couldn't take *any* criticism, of herself or of practically anybody else—that I decided to keep my mouth shut. I—well, frankly, I lied and told her only good things about herself. I hated to be so dishonest, but I saw that there just was no other way to keep the relationship going."

"And you wanted to keep it going because?"

"She was the best damned sex partner I *ever* had. Absolutely terrific. But terribly weak in all other respects. That's why I finally left her."

"But you did manage to stay with her—and get her to stay with you—for two and a half years?"

"Yes. She would have stayed forever. But, aside from the great sex, she had little else to offer."

"Doesn't your success in staying with her show you something you could do to stay with another woman—one who would be more satisfying?"

"You mean—keep my big mouth shut?"

"Right. Be as negative and critical as you want to be in your head. Be as honest as you can be with *yourself* in that regard, so that you don't lose any integrity. You still think and feel what *you* think and feel. But watch how you express your feelings to your partners! As you have already seen, practically none of them can take it."

"Not *practically* none. None!"

"Okay. So what can you do when you try relating to your next woman?"

"Mmm. Shut my big mouth!"

We agreed, Frank and I, that he would experimentally try this, and he did with a "terrific" woman whom he next dated. It worked. After he had been going with her for three months, she got more and more involved with him and kept talking about their possibly marrying. Frank was convinced that shutting his mouth worked. In fact, it worked so well that after dating his partner for a while, and having her respond so well to him, he *felt* less negative and critical of her than he had ever felt about a woman before—so he didn't have too much to shut his big mouth about!

Though his relationship with this woman finally ended because she wanted to marry and have at least two children and Frank was unenthusiastic about having even one child, Frank had learned his lesson and acted less negatively with subsequent partners until he finally married one. Marvelous! But after I had seen him in individual and group therapy for five months, he still took no real responsibility for his overly negative and critical attitudes.

In fact, he took less. Because he was now nicer to women and they, in return, treated him better, he convinced himself that previously he had picked the "wrong" women, that they "deserved" his honest criticism, that women *as a rule* were "naturally difficult," and that only a rare one was not. So, although he succeeded in solving his presenting problem of being rejected by suitable women, he never acknowledged, and therefore never really solved, his emotional problems. Frank was satisfied and I accepted, but was not enthusiastic about, his "marvelous" progress. He still had underlying absolutistic demands for "real" honesty, which might well create trouble in his future relationships.

Solution-focused therapy, however, can work more elegantly if you and your clients focus on their achieving philosophical-emotional change. Thus, Jeff miserably excoriated himself when he failed at any aspect of his bookkeeping job and was frowned upon by his boss for failing. He strongly believed and felt that it was *his* error and that therefore *he* was a rotten bookkeeper and a total nincompoop.

I naturally, following REBT, tried to talk Jeff out of his self-castigation, but at first failed. Then I asked him, "Did you ever really fail badly at your work and *not* demolish yourself for doing so?"

"Only once that I can remember," Jeff replied.

"And that was?"

"Once, when I did very badly, but my assistant did much worse. I saw how hard she tried and how she just couldn't make it. So I felt pity for her, realized that she was doing the best she could, accepted her with her limitations, and kept her on till she got pregnant and left the job. I then realized that I, too, was doing the best I could. So I, for once, stopped blaming myself and even felt pretty good about some of my work."

"Fine!" I said. "Good job—at least, of working on yourself. Now, why not do the same thing again, have some pity on *you*, accept *you* with your limitations, and stop telling yourself that you are a rotten bookkeeper and a total nincompoop? You did it with her, your assistant. Why not do it now with *you*?"

Jeff had a hard time accepting himself as he had once accepted his assistant when she was doing her best but still was failing. Finally, he was able to do so. So his previously working on an *emotional* problem (accepting his assistant with her flaws) helped him to partially solve another problem (self-acceptance). Solution-focused therapy worked.

I keep stubbornly trying to help my clients achieve an *elegant* improvement—which Jeff failed to achieve as he mainly started to accept himself *because* he was doing his best at his work. So I tried to orient him toward unconditionally accepting himself (and others) even if he (and they) were *not* doing their best to perform well. I pointed out that, even then, they were still fallible humans, hardly subhuman, and didn't deserve damnation. No go. Frank wouldn't take it *that* far. But his surrendering *some* of his self-rating was good enough. So we left it at that and the particular kind of solution-focused therapy we achieved was at least partly effective.

However, the usual kind of solution-focused therapy often deals with *practical* rather than with *emotional* problems, and has these limitations:

1. Many clients can't come up with *how* they previously solved their presenting problems—even when they actually did so.
2. Their severe anxiety, depression, and/or rage stops them from remembering prior solutions or using them now if they do remember them.
3. Their previous "solutions" were better than nothing, but were not really that good.
4. Their previous "solutions" worked temporarily, but didn't have good lasting effects.
5. Their previous "solutions" worked in a way—but actually *kept them* from much better solutions. Thus, they avoided job-seeking anxiety by failing to look for new and better jobs, and their avoidance *kept them* from dealing adequately with their anxiety. Or they "conquered" their elevator phobia by always renting an apartment and office on the first floor of the building. Some solutions!
6. Even when they solved an important aspect of one of their emotional problems—such as their irrational phobia of using elevators—they failed to solve other aspects of it, such as their anxiety about plane trips, public speaking, and letter writing.

For many reasons, such as the foregoing ones, solution-focused therapy often doesn't work or works poorly. By all means try it at times. But also often try to go beyond it.

SHOW CLIENTS THEIR SUCCESSES AND ASSETS

One of the most common techniques of brief (and longer) therapy is to show clients that, yes, they have failures and failings, but they also have successes and assets. Therefore, you point out they can't be *all* bad, can't be *inadequate persons*, and—considering that they have so *many* good points—they may see themselves as "good individuals."[3]

True—but weak. For several reasons:

1. Your clients may really act poorly or inadequately in *many* (occasionally *most*) ways. Are they *then* inadequate persons? No. But, using your own arguments, they may easily *see* themselves as such.
2. Almost everyone has *some* good traits. Even Hitler was kind to his mother, his mistress, and his dog. Did that make him a good person? Not exactly.
3. If you point out to your clients their successes and assets, they will often give themselves *conditional acceptance*—because of these good points. But that is light years removed from their according themselves *un*conditional self-acceptance (USA).

Frances hated herself because she was largely disorganized and therefore failed badly at school, at work, at keeping her apartment in order, and in intimate relationships. I showed her that she was still not a "no goodnik" because she was excellent at tennis and at baby-sitting. She finally agreed that she was not a *total* incompetent or a *complete* slob. So some of her feeling of being "nothing" ameliorated. But she still insisted that school, work, keeping house, and intimate relationships were *very* important, but tennis and baby-sitting were not. So she was less self-hating, but still depressed. She never bought the REBT philosophy that human worth can be accepted independently of one's good and bad performances. But she did make some real gains.

POSITIVE VISUALIZATIONS AND AFFIRMATIONS

Emile Coué, who in many ways was quite pioneering, was one of the main modern inventors of both positive visualizations and positive thinking or affirmations. He realized that disturbed people used autosuggestion to create negative images and views and, instead, they could replace these with positive images and ideas. He was followed, with and without due credit, by Norman Vincent Peale, Napoleon Hill, Dale Carnegie, Maxwell Maltz, and a host of other positive affirmers.[4]

All this kind of stuff works—and often quickly. REBT's rational coping self-statements and Effective New Philosophy include positive thoughts that can be quite helpful. Doreen, with her parents' "help," was depressed largely because she strongly told herself, "I can't do any important things well. I never will. Because I'll always fail, I'll have no joy whatever. I'm obviously no good!"

When I showed her these negative self-statements that led to her feelings of hopelessness and depression, she quickly agreed that they "caused" her misery, and she collaborated with me to substitute positive affirmations, including: "I can, with some effort, do important things well. I definitely *can* improve. Even though I often fail, I can find enjoyable aspects of life."

These positive affirmations significantly helped Doreen, and she did do several things much better and did find enjoyable pursuits (including writing poetry, which she was not very good at). She also imagined herself doing better at sports and at reciting her poems, and actually improved in both these areas. Thus, her positive thinking and imagining were both productive.

Positive thinking and visualization is often used in REBT, as well as in Aaron Beck's Cognitive Therapy, Maxie Maultsby's Rational Behavior Therapy, Donald Meichenbaum's Self Instructional Training, William Glasser's Reality Therapy, Richard Lazarus' Stress Coping Therapy, and other kinds of cognitive-behavior therapy.[5] In REBT, as noted above, you usually help clients to Dispute (D) their irrational Beliefs and arrive at an Effective New Philosophy (E), which can be written or recorded and then used many times as a rational coping self-statement. This is especially useful with children and with unsophisticated individuals, who are not likely to do much Disputing on their own, but who you can help to arrive at E and then use it many times until they really believe and feel its "truth" and usefulness. Thus, in one of my cases in the 1950's I helped an eight-year-old bedwetter, who was terribly ashamed of her siblings and friends teasing her for her problem, to keep saying to herself, "I'm okay even if I do wet my bed and people tease me for it. Having this problem is *not* shameful, only unfortunate." Within four sessions, she was remarkably improved by internalizing these self-helping, rational Beliefs (rB's).

As noted previously, rB's are more effective when they include philosophical statements such as, "Even if I fail in this course, I'm *never* a failure or a stupid person," rather than only realistic statements such as, "If I keep trying, I really *can* pass this course." But sensible coping self-statements have their distinct limitations as well as their clear-cut benefits. For example:

1. People can easily "parrot" rational Beliefs without really *believing* them. They can tell themselves a hundred times, "I'm okay if I lose this game," and believe, "No, I have to *finally* win." "At least I must do my *very best* to win," or "If I were really a competent and good person, I would keep winning." As many thinkers have pointed out for centuries, *saying* something and *truly believing* it are hardly the same!

2. The nature of humans, REBT hypothesizes, is to often simultaneously hold *both* rB's and iB's. Thus, your clients can *easily* believe "*It's best* for me to write this report right now and I can easily do it and get it out of the way," *and* "It's *too hard* for me to write this report right now and therefore *it's better* if I do it later." Without realizing it, they can hold *both* these Beliefs and hold the irrational one *more frequently* and *strongly* than the rational one. Hence, their rational self-statement won't help them too much.

3. Rational coping statements can be created and held sloppily and inelegantly. For example: "I can study hard and get good marks," instead of "I can, *but only with much effort*, study hard and get good marks. But even if I don't, I'm never a *rotten person.*"

4. Many clients have a profound and basic negative attitude about themselves and others, and they return to this attitude even when they temporarily change it. Thus, they think that they basically *can't stand* not being loved by significant others, *temporarily* tell themselves that they *can* stand it and that it *isn't awful,* and after awhile go right back to "It's *too hard* to be loveless. I *can't tolerate it* for *so* long!" Unless they *thoroughly and strongly* surrender their basic *need* for love (or almost anything else), and unless they keep powerfully *proving* to themselves that frustration of this "*need*" still permits them to have a reasonably enjoyable life, they will often fall back to reinstating it. This kind of self-proof of their rational coping statements requires *more than* merely affirming them. So, to achieve a more intensive and elegant solution to their self-defeating thinking, they had better (a) fully acknowledge their remaining and underlying irrational ideas and (b) keep proving to themselves the "truth" and "effectiveness" of their rational coping Beliefs.

5. Positive visualizations are usually empirical rather than philosophic statements. Thus, you can help your clients vividly imagine themselves succeeding rather than failing at school, at work, or at sports; and this kind of imaging may indeed help them to improve their performances. But it is harder—though not impossible—to show them how to imagine their failing and still unconditionally accepting themselves. This latter procedure would tend to require them to see themselves failing and *also* to give themselves a strong coping statement—for example, "Yes, I failed but I'm *still* always an okay person!"—or to work at *figuring out* an unconditionally self-accepting *philosophy*.

As can be seen from the above points, positive visualization and self-statements can be quite useful—and quickly effective. But note their limitations and often use them *together with* other more elegant cognitive, emotive, and behavioral methods.

HAVE MANY DIFFERENT TECHNIQUES AVAILABLE

Some therapies—such as solution-focused and multimodal therapy—advocate your having available many different techniques, so that if your main ones don't work too well with some clients you can switch to other, more useful ones. Why not? You have little to lose, particularly if you have a good theory of therapy and many techniques to back it up. As I keep emphasizing in this book, if none of your "good" methods work, why not experiment with a "worse" one?[6]

REBT, of course, includes many cognitive, emotive, and behavioral methods, many of which are often used and some less frequently. So it provides many possibilities. Gina, a 37-year-old engineer, used REBT Disputing of her irrational Belief that she *absolutely must* marry and have a child by the time she reached 40, but stubbornly held to this iB and was often panicked. Also, to little avail, she used strong coping statements, Rational Emotive Imagery, and reverse role-playing, penalizing herself when she refused to do her dating homework, and other REBT methods. Nothing helped too much.

I finally, almost against my will, used hypnosis, which she kept asking for. I usually avoid using hypnosis because I prefer my clients to do their forceful Disputing on their own, without relying too much on me as their hypnotist-persuader. But I acquiesced in Gina's case when nothing else seemed to be working well.

I helped Gina to go into a light hypnotic state and told her that, posthypnotically, she would very strongly convince herself, at least five times every day, "Even if I *never* marry and have a child of my own, I can *definitely* lead a happy life and spend several fine hours every week taking care of infants at an orphans home. I *can*, I *can*, I *can!*"

I made a tape recording of our one and only hypnotic session and gave it to Gina to keep playing over at least once a day. She did so, followed the post-hypnotic instructions on the tape, and within the month gave up her absolutistic dire need to have a child soon. She kept dating unfrantically, married a couple of years later, and was comfortably resigned to most likely never becoming pregnant.

Thus, this hypnotic technique, which I only rarely use, seemed to work very well; so may other "odd" or "poor" methods that you may occasionally use. But the availability of multimodal methods, while often effective for brief therapy, may not bring about elegant, philosophical change for several reasons:

1. They may encourage you to go lightly with or give up on the few elegant, intensive methods that you and your clients may otherwise employ. In Gina's case, for example, she used forceful coping statements to good effect in overcoming her terror of remaining childless. But she never really "saw" that she could have a good degree of happiness *no matter what* deprivation she suffered. She was able to fall back on spending time every week visiting children at an orphans home, and she enjoyed doing so. But she never overcame her shame about being a single person without a husband; she wasn't able to work out this kind of "shameless" solution to her problem. So her solution was "good"—but not quite elegant.

2. Having a number of techniques, and especially using them eclectically, often leads to quick but not deep solutions to emotional problems. Unless you, the therapist, have a theory and practice that look for and deliberately try to achieve *intensive* change, you are not likely to help your clients achieve it.

3. Some methods of therapy—such as shamanism, New Age cultism, and other "magical" methods—work with some people some of the time, but for the average client they include real dangers, may do more harm than good, and may well help you and your clients to give up on better, less dangerous methods.[7] "Magical" solutions are contradicted by social reality and often lead to disillusionment and to the false conviction that *nothing* will work if the magic doesn't.

4. This is also true of pollyannaish solutions. Emile Coué's famous

formula, "Day by day in every way I'm getting better and better!" helped innumerable people temporarily overcome physical and emotional ills. But it promised too much and led to such disillusionment that Coué, by far the most famous therapist of his day, practically went out of business.

EMPHASIZING RELATIONSHIP METHODS

A great many authors emphasize the effectiveness of arranging a warm and/or close relationship with clients in brief (and in regular) therapy. Considerable research has tended to show that when such a relationship exists clients seem to improve significantly—or, at least, to *feel* better.[8] So it definitely has its benefits.

There are, in fact, several ways in which achieving a warm, close, and collaborative relationship may work well. First, if clients think that you are attentive, are personally interested in helping them, and really like them as individuals, they are likely to listen better, respect you, see you as quite competent, and ignore the fact that your theory and practice may not really be as effective as the relationship with you makes them think that they are.

Second, many clients intend to come only for a few sessions, but if they think you are reacting warmly and personally to them they will be "hooked" into coming longer; their doing so may help them even in brief therapy.

Third, many clients have real problems in relating closely to almost everyone; if they are able to achieve a trusting, warm relationship with you, their therapist, they will get good experience and practice at relating.

Fourth, therapists often do well to show clients how they are functioning poorly and thinking crookedly; these clients are likely to resist hearing and benefiting from this kind of "grim" feedback if they do not have a good relationship with their therapist.

Fifth, much of what is called a transference or interpersonal relationship in therapy consists of therapists instructing or training their clients to successfully manage their relationships, first, in the therapy sessions themselves and, second, in their outside lives. If these clients dislike their therapist, are indifferent to him or her, or are distrustful of the therapist, this kind of interpersonal training during therapy is likely to be interfered with.

Sixth, whether we like it or not, innumerable clients come to therapy mainly to be understood, to gain a friend, and to have a relationship in the course of which they can be open and free about their feelings (including their feelings for the therapist). Unless their relationship with the therapist gives them what they want in this respect, they are very likely to quit therapy in short order.

Seventh, therapy, especially REBT, often requires clients to do difficult homework assignments, and because they want and "need" approval so much, including that of the therapist, they may do these assignments for the "wrong" reasons—to please the therapist. In any event, their doing so may help them considerably.

Thomasina came to see me "as a last resort" because she had five previous therapists during the past nine years, had not been helped by any of them in her view, and was quite sure that she could not be helped at all. But her best friend, Nan, whom I had seen a few years before, was so insistent that Thomasina come to see me that she decided to try it a few times.

Although I often do not really like my clients personally and sometimes even inform them honestly, when they ask about my feelings for them, that because of their frequent obnoxious behavior I would boycott them socially if they were not clients, the opposite was true of Thomasina. I found her to be an exceptionally nice individual, with exceptionally warm feelings for other people and not merely with a dire need for their love. So I not only tried to give her unconditional acceptance—which I do with just about all my clients—but I also felt genuinely friendly toward her and showed this in my therapeutic relationship with her. When she was ill at home, I even called to find out how she was and showed real interest in her regaining her health.

Though still abysmally self-downing and pessimistic about her ability to overcome her long-term feelings of depression, Thomasina became attached to me, genuinely seemed to enjoy our sessions, and worked harder in between sessions than she had ever worked with other therapists. She first achieved conditional self-acceptance—liked herself because I liked her and had faith in her. That was an improvement, but I showed her that it was a relatively small success—for what would happen after our therapy ended? Back to self-loathing she might well go!

I used the security of our therapeutic relationship, however, to work out with her several assignments in which she tried to relate with a few men who were clearly more educated and successful than she was, and to risk rejection by them. When these rejections actually occurred, she seemed to be able to take them—partly because she knew that she still had the relationship with me to fall back upon. After a few months, however, she began to see that she didn't really *need* others' approval in order to contingently accept herself and she settled, for the first time in her life, for a regular lover who, like herself, was only a high-school graduate and who worked for a delivery service. When her friends pointed out that he was not too bright or competent, she made herself feel unashamed, even when he visited them with her.

After I showed Thomasina what great progress she was making in this respect and how she could continue to give herself unconditional self-acceptance (USA), she admitted that she still depended on my acceptance of her. We kept talking about this kind of conditional acceptance, and she finally deliberately joined one of my therapy groups, instead of seeing me individually, knowing that as one of the group members she would no longer have that close a relationship with me. After four months of group therapy, she actually weaned herself away from relying on my personal approval of her and achieved a much greater degree of accepting herself unconditionally. Even when two of the group members expressed real dislike for her, she strongly maintained her USA.

Dick was a socially inept man of 43, although he was a successful attorney and had some toady friends who liked him for his great generosity to them. But he was quite narcissistic, often inconsiderate of others, and obviously not interested in them and their doings. He came to see me when he was depressed about not being made a senior partner in his large law firm, mainly because he did not socialize well with business people and, therefore, for all his great work as an attorney, didn't bring in enough clients to his firm. In talking with him, I never really found him very likeable and did not pretend that I did. But I kept showing him how his ways of dealing with me—including his coming late to our sessions, falling behind in paying his bills to the Institute, and harsh criticisms of my "coldness"—were probably indicative of the ways in which he commonly acted with people outside my office. At first he resented the feedback and skill training that I tried to give him in these respects, but then found it quite helpful in his outside affairs. He started not only to act much better with me but also to show a real liking for me that was absent from most of his other relationships. Later, he forced himself to attend to and relate to other people much more interestedly, and his social life improved considerably.

Because Dick was getting better socially and began to attract more clients to his firm, his depression alleviated. But he never became less disturbable, only currently calmer and better functioning. So in my eyes his therapy was a limited "success."

This happens, as I have discovered, with much "successful" relationship therapy. Clients definitely *feel* better after relating well to their therapist, but in my estimation they do not really *get* better. Sometimes, as in Dick's case, their presenting symptoms are alleviated and their functioning improves. So that is excellent. But they still depend very much on fairly good relationships, on material success, and on environmental support. And when things go wrong—and especially quite wrong—in any of these respects, they are again very likely to make themselves anxious and/or depressed all over again.

Some of them, of course, even become *more* disturbed as a result of their therapeutic relationships. Thus, they make their therapist practically their only friend. Or they depend on him or her as a guru. Or they model their lives so closely after what they think their therapist's life is like that they neglect their own individuality. Not so good!

Some dependent clients, again, stay in therapy literally for many years, and do not allow themselves—nor do their therapists allow them—to go free. But even in short-term therapy, if you emphasize the relationship aspect too much and tie your clients too warmly or too closely to you, you may "help" them in a brief period of time but not help them free themselves of what psychoanalysts call their "positive transference," but what I often call their basic neurosis. The desire for love and approval is practically the human condition and helps foment much pleasure and achievement. But the *dire need* for approval can be a sad saboteur of healthy self-direction. Especially when working with severe neurotics and people with personality disorders, watch out!

SHOWING CLIENTS THAT THEY CAN CHANGE

One of the main methods of Rational Emotive Behavior Therapy and most of the other forms of cognitive-behavior therapy is to show clients, usually in the first few sessions, that they themselves are partly or mainly responsible for their neurotic problems, and that because they largely *constructed* these problems they can also *de*construct them and significantly change. Thus, I frequently show unsophisticated clients, in their very first session, that they consciously and unconsciously choose to take some of their important goals and values and make them into neurotic musts and demands. Therefore, they always have the possibility of changing them back into unneurotic preferences.

This often works very well—and quickly. Thus, Jim was utterly convinced that because he was quite bright and had a history of mostly getting A's in his graduate program in Business Administration, he absolutely *had to* do so and was really quite stupid, and potentially a great failure, if he got any B's—or heavens forbid!—C's. Naturally, he had severe test anxiety, as well as anxiety about his anxiety.

When I quickly showed Jim that his strong desire for A's was fine but that his frantic musturbation about achieving them almost inevitably created his severe states of panic, he saw this right away and acknowledged that he was unwittingly doing himself in with his demandingness. He then felt much better, because he knew that he could do something about his test-taking anxiety and could possibly control it.

Unfortunately, he did not work very hard at giving up his absolutistic musts, but did so only at special times—when the test that he was taking was not too important. So he quickly made considerable improvement—but not enough. Only after several months of REBT, in the course of which I showed Jim that he not only could deconstruct his dogmatic shoulds, oughts, and musts, but that he had better work quite hard at doing so, did he finally do this work and largely gave them up. His taking responsibility for creating his demands was fine; but at first his working to change them was not. Only later did he decide to do this work and actually do it.

Constructivism is an excellent form of therapy—as Epictetus showed some two thousand years ago. But many of our best constructivist therapists—such as Michael Mahoney, Vittoria Guidano, and Greg and Robert Neimeyer—believe that because clients are natural constructivists, they somehow have to naturally take quite awhile, with sympathetic and not too active-directive therapists, to do their own reconstruction.[9] This will sometimes actually work—but they rarely will be able to quickly change themselves. In REBT we tend to take a more realistic stand and to assume that even though most clients have the ability to change, they had better be active-directively taught that, first, they really do have this ability and, second, they can learn specific techniques of using this ability. Only then are they likely to change quickly and deeply.[10]

Showing people that they are largely responsible for their own neurotic constructions and that they can change these constructions also has dangers and disadvantages. Such as these:

1. Many clients would much rather blame their parents, their culture,

and their rotten environment for their disturbances and not assume responsibility themselves for partly creating them. Being self-downers, they blame themselves when they do assume some responsibility for creating their neuroses; their self-damnation then tends to make them much more neurotic. Unless they quickly assume responsibility and also give themselves unconditional self-acceptance along with this responsibility—that is, blame their self-defeating *behaviors* without blaming *themselves* for these behaviors—they may depress themselves even more. Active-directive education by their therapists in this respect is often required for the nondamning acknowledgement of their own responsibility.

2. Even clients who do not particularly damn themselves when they accept responsibility for their disturbances really do not know exactly *how* to recognize the musts and commands they use to upset themselves and therefore had better often be clearly educated in this respect. Letting them stew in their own neurotic juices until they spontaneously reconstruct their disturbed behaviors can often, again, do more therapeutic harm than good.

3. The homework in between sessions that most clients can do in order to constructively reduce their disturbances had better not be simply left to their own devices to work out. Instead, it had best be collaboratively arranged, in most cases, with an experienced active-directive therapist. This is particularly true when they are more than merely neurotic, which is the case with a large percentage of clients, and when they are naturally, even biologically, in the personality disorder range.

4. Constructivist therapists of the nondirective school—which seems to me to be something of a contradiction, but that definitely exists in some instances—seem to forget that many clients are suffering immensely when they come to therapy, and are making themselves more inefficient and self-damaging because of their suffering. Therefore, it is usually wise to help them alleviate their suffering as soon as feasible and to get on with reconstructing their lives. Again, especially in brief therapy, this can often best be done if the therapist—meaning you—is active-directive.

NORMALIZE CLIENTS' DISTURBED FEELINGS AND ACTIONS

A number of therapists, without necessarily trying for brief therapy, attempt to show their clients that some of the thoughts, feelings, and actions that they view as being distinctly disturbed are really "normal" or "healthy." This method often works very well since even when clients are distinctly disturbed they frequently, as I keep showing in this book, disturb themselves about their original disturbances, and thereby make themselves much more upset than they originally are. Consequently, if you show them that some aspects of their original "disturbances" are really much healthier than they view them as being, they may be considerably helped by your doing so—and helped quickly.[11]

Occasionally, this is an elegant method of therapy because your client may actually not be very disturbed, but may view himself as being so and thereby disrupt his life. Also, some of your clients who have secondary disturbances, and who give them up when you show them that their primary upsetness is really "normal," may also see, in the course of your talking with them, that even if they have serious primary problems they never have to put themselves down for having them. This kind of self-acceptance may be crucial for their accepting themselves unconditionally in other respects, too, and it may therefore lead to deep and intensive improvement.

A curious case occurred when I gave live demonstrations in Los Angeles several years ago. One of my demonstratees, who has identified himself in his book, *Life 102*, and whom I can therefore mention by name, was the well-known poet and writer of self-help books, Peter McWilliams. He came to one of my popular workshops on "How to Stubbornly Refuse to Make Yourself Miserable About Anything—Yes, Anything!" and presented the "problem" of being treated for eight months for his "sex addiction," but still being plagued by it.

I quickly showed Peter that his so-called "sex addiction" was largely a fiction of his therapist's imagination and of his agreeing with his therapist that he was truly "addicted." He seemed to see this in only a few minutes of our talking together in this public demonstration, and since that time he has been quite unobsessed with his "sex obsession!" However, as he also notes in unusual honest detail in *Life 102*, at that time he still remained a member of a dogmatic cult and swore allegiance to the leader of that cult. So I didn't quite cure him of all his emotional problems![12]

Anyway, showing people that their supposed "disturbances" really consist of pretty "normal" and healthy behaviors has its distinct virtues—even, as I said above, when they are more disturbed than you are letting them know that they are. On the other hand, this method of therapy, as you may well imagine, has some distinct disadvantages, too. Such as these:

1. If people really are disturbed, you may well help them to feel better,

but hardly to get better. For their serious emotional problems may truly exist and hardly will disappear just because they no longer view them as problems. Therefore, to show them that they are not disturbed when they really are will only rarely help them to face their upsetness and to deal with it therapeutically.

2. Even if you show your clients that they are not *as* seriously disturbed as they think they are, you may encourage them to get themselves off the hook and refuse to face the extent to which they truly *are* behaving neurotically. Again, they may feel much better than they felt before, but still live with their self-defeating behavior instead of acknowledging it and minimizing it. So you had better help them to give up their self-downing about being disturbed but then go back to their actual upsetness and encourage them to work on minimizing that.

3. Both your own and your clients' view of what is "normal," "good," or "moral" may be prejudiced and one-sided. It is therefore usually preferable to show this to clients, to help them see that there are *many* social views of "normality," and to leave them with better informed choices of what behaviors will and will not probably get them into trouble in their community.

4. Antisocial and narcissistic clients may cleverly use your view of "normality" to perpetuate their unethical exploitation of others.

5. Many irrational thoughts and actions are common human failings, and statistically "normal." Thus, your clients will often "normally" overgeneralize, musturbate, and be perfectionistic. So you had better point this out to clients and help them to "abnormally" minimize these "normal" self-harming and socially-harming behaviors. In fact, "deep" and "elegant" brief therapy may well involve your helping many of your clients to make themselves "abnormally" healthy!

DISTRACTION METHODS

Perhaps the most popular of the palliative inelegant methods of (brief and prolonged) psychotherapy are those involving distraction. For centuries, people who are anxious and depressed have used meditation, yoga, ritualistic exercises, and enjoyments for distraction purposes. They strongly focus on a mantra, on observing their thoughts, on doing bodily exercises, and on closely following various kinds of rituals or enjoyable pursuits. All these kinds of concentration work, at least temporarily, to take their minds off their primary symptoms of anxiety and depression, as well as off their secondary symptoms, such as their anxiety about their anxiety and their depression about their depression.

In modern times, these ancient distraction methods have been supplemented by newer ones, such as relaxation techniques and biofeedback. Hundreds of articles and books have been written on these methods, including those by Herbert Benson, C. R. Carlson, R. H. Hoyle, Robert Fried, Daniel Coleman, Edmund Jacobson, Maurits Klee, S. Moore, D. H. Shapiro, and R. N. Walsh.[13]

Most of these distraction techniques work quite well—at least temporarily. For when your anxious or depressed clients powerfully focus on almost anything *except* the Activating Events to which they are overreacting, they find it almost impossible to demand that these events *must not* occur and that it is *awful* if they do happen. After a period of meditating, relaxing, or using other distraction methods, they no longer feel very upset and may solve some of their problems or engage in enjoyable pursuits about which they do not awfulize.

Distraction techniques, if you use them with your clients (and with yourself), have several advantages:

1. They can be quickly learned and adapted—or even spontaneously invented by your clients themselves.
2. They often immediately block disturbed feelings and replace them with enjoyable or neutral emotions.
3. They interfere with your clients engaging in harmful compulsions—such as overeating and smoking.
4. They are often enjoyable in their own right. Yoga and reading, for example, may be quite absorbing and pleasurable.
5. They sometimes lead to beneficial philosophical changes. Thus, meditators may watch their anxious thoughts and conclude that the "terrible" things they include will most probably never actually happen and that, even if they do occur, the meditator can actually cope with them.

Because of these frequent advantages, distraction methods, as noted above, have been popular for many centuries and the newer ones—like Jacobson's progressive relaxation techniques and biofeedback—have been used by thousands of therapists and millions of clients. Why, nonetheless, do distraction procedures almost always produce palliative, inelegant results? For several reasons:

1. If relaxation is done only for distracting purposes, as is usually the

case, it does only what it is asked to do—taking your clients' anxiety-producing thoughts, such as, "I *absolutely must* do a perfect report and never be criticized for doing it poorly," and turning these thoughts to other things, such as meditation, Yoga, breathing exercises, or whatever they will. But the underlying *message* or *philosophy* of their thoughts still remains. They still strongly think and feel, "It is *absolutely necessary* for me to do this report perfectly well—or else it is *awful* and I am an *incompetent person!*" Temporarily, while focusing on the distraction method, they do not think this thought. But it is still there—and it will almost inevitably return. Therefore, once their diversion technique calms them down and they go on with their lives, they will keep returning, usually again and again, to their panicky philosophy and will keep upsetting themselves when they are participating in, or even thinking about participating in, an important task like doing a "fine" report.

2. Because various distraction methods work very well and for the nonce divert people from panic and depression, they actually include a pernicious aspect: They don't allow seriously upset people to see what they are doing to create their disturbed feelings and behaviors, and therefore they are distracted—ironically enough!—from truly understanding and more beneficially dealing with their basic problem. Thus, if I do deep meditation or Yoga every time I panic about writing an imperfect report, I quickly make myself unpanicked and perhaps even later finish a reasonably good report. But I still will often think that my panic comes from being assigned the report to do, rather than from my telling myself that I *absolutely must* do it perfectly well and *completely have to* be approved by others for doing it. Therefore, I rarely see this "real" cause of my panicking, practically never contradict the irrational Beliefs (iB's) that create it, and keep living with this destructive philosophy for perhaps the entire rest of my life. So my distraction technique works, all right, but not very permanently or elegantly; very often, it actually *stops* me from devising a better and deeper method of dealing with, and perhaps basically stopping, my strong tendency to panic.

3. The steady use of distraction methods may actually increase your clients' low frustration tolerance. As I keep pointing out in this book, in order to make a more intensive and more enduring change in their disturbability, your clients, you, and practically everyone else had better clearly see exactly what they are thinking, feeling, and doing to needlessly upset themselves, until they finally become significantly less disturb*able*. However, because your clients (and other people) frequently are afflicted with low frustration tolerance (LFT), they often do almost

anything possible to avoid the hard work of self-reparation. They consequently tend to look for magical solutions—e.g., faith in God or in their therapist—or for easy ones. If they zero in on distraction methods that work, they feel comfortable and unstressed while using them. They may, therefore, actually addict themselves to these methods—e.g., meditate for two or three hours every day—because (like drinking and drugging) they are (in the short) run "easy ways out" of their difficulties. Their addiction to distraction may thereby increase their LFT!

4. Therapists, including possibly yourself, have their own distinct degrees of low frustration tolerance and, therefore, often find palliative and inelegant ways of helping their clients—particularly their most difficult ones. This happened in my own case with Celia, who got little sleep at night because she frequently had a nightmare about being physically attacked while her friends, relatives, and lover refused to come to her aid, so that she was maimed or killed in the course of her nightmare. Once she had awakened in a state of terror, she then worried about having another "horrible" nightmare, and she kept herself awake for the next hour or two.

I naturally tried to show Celia what were her core musts and demands, and how to challenge and minimize them. Thus, she strongly believed, "I *must* win the complete love of my friends, relatives, and lover so that I can have a *guarantee* that they will always help me when I am in trouble!" "If my support people do not really love me and go to my aid when I need their help, they don't really love me at all, are rotten hypocrites for saying that they do, and deserve to be punished and damned!" "My terrible nightmares *must* stop and *must not* interrupt my sleep! I *can't stand them* at all! When I have one of them, I can't calm down for quite awhile and *must* keep feeling panicked about having another one. How awful my poor life is when I am so beset with horrors like this!"

To help Celia calm down and get some more sleep each night, I taught her Herbert Benson's relaxation response method as well as focusing, whenever she couldn't start sleeping or go back to sleep, on monotonous counting. Thus, using the Articulatory Suppression technique of A. B. Levey and his associates in Cambridge, England, she would force herself to say to herself, three times a second, "One, two, three. One, two, three," and persist at doing so, no matter how upset she felt, until she went to sleep.[14]

Celia used these two distraction methods very successfully. Within a few weeks after I first saw her, she taught herself to go right back to sleep after she woke from her "terrible" nightmares. She got so expert at doing so that she rarely stayed awake for more than 10 minutes at a time. Also, seeing that she could control her sleep so well, she stopped thinking that it was "awful" to wake with a nightmare, that she *couldn't* do anything about sleeping again after she had one, and that her life really was as uncontrollable and "horrible" as she had been making it out to be.

In other words, Celia first reduced her secondary anxiety—her horror of having nightmares and of being sleepless. Doing so, she started having much fewer nightmares, which was her primary symptom for which she first came to therapy. So she was doing quite well. Unfortunately, however, she was doing so well with her distraction techniques and with her realistic belief that whenever she woke from a nightmare she now had an almost sure-fire way of putting herself back to sleep, that she quit therapy after three months and seemed to be very happy with the results she had achieved with my help.

I only mildly tried to talk Celia into staying in therapy longer to work on her basic problem of *needing* her friends' and relatives' complete support and putting herself down when it looked like she wasn't getting it. In being so mild, I may well have given in to some extent to my own low frustration tolerance—because Celia was a difficult customer (DC) for elegant REBT, and she was highly pleased and already much better functioning with the inelegant methods I was using with her. So I let her quit therapy and only mildly reminded her that she could come back for more sessions if she reverted to her previous panic states.

Fortunately, you might say, Celia's current lover, with whom she had been involved for two years, suddenly left her a half year later; she felt so depressed about this that she did return to therapy. She was still on top of her nightmare and her sleeping problems. She now, however, was obsessed during her waking hours with how "horrible" it was to lose her lover and how "worthless" she was for having lost him. She also went back to her basic insistence that she *absolutely must be completely loved and supported by significant others* and that they *utterly must* give in to her demands or else they were unmitigated scoundrels. It took Celia and me several more months of REBT hard work to help her face these demands and to ameliorate them. This was good and I was much more satisfied with her ultimate and basic philosophical and emotional improvement than I had been when she first overcame her horror of nightmares and of not sleeping.

So watch your own possible low frustration tolerance! By all means be prepared to use several methods of distraction with your clients, because doing so will often appreciably interrupt their worst states of panic, depression, rage, and self-hatred. But watch out for some of them using these "effective" methods to "solve" their emotional problems in "too good" a manner, so that they arrange having palliative or inelegant "solutions" for them. If necessary, look at your own LFT when you let them off the hook too easily in this respect!

THE USE OF RELIGIOUS AND SPIRITUAL METHODS OF PSYCHOTHERAPY

Psychotherapists and counselors used to mainly shy away from using religious and spiritual methods in their treatment because these were often considered to be unscientific and even harmful. These methods involve clients (and other people) firmly, and often devoutly, believing in hypotheses that could never be, if we are to believe philosophers of science like Bertrand Russell and Karl Popper, empirically proven or disproven, that therefore can be uselessly argued about forever, and whose discussion can sidetrack us from the important question of whether belief or nonbelief actually works. Do, for example, religionists and spiritual believers actually turn out to be more or less neurotic and otherwise disordered than nonreligionists and antispiritualists?[15]

Actually, no one knows nor is likely to know in the near future. As I have pointed out in some of my writings, the "scientific" literature studies of the value and disvalue of religious and spiritual beliefs on mental health is quite suspect and prejudiced. The investigators in these studies are most likely to be biased in one way or another and, therefore, to set up their "experiments" to "validate" their own slanted points of view. The subjects of these studies are also usually prejudiced and, therefore, not too likely to give "honest" answers to the questionnaires they are usually asked to answer.

If, for example, you are a strong believer in God, the Church, or powerful Spiritual Forces in the universe, and you are asked to answer a set of questions about how happy, mentally well balanced, and successfully married you are, your assessment of your "personality" in these respects is very likely to be biased by the "help" you are sure that you are getting from these religious and/or spiritual resources. If, on the other hand, you are skeptical about such sources, you will probably much more honestly assess how "emotionally disturbed" you "are." So the increasing number of studies that recently tend to show that religious and spiritual people are "happier" and "healthier" than nonreligious and nonspiritual individuals are not to be taken too seriously.

In any event, it can hardly be doubted that people's religious and spiritual views often do affect their disturbances: In some cases, these views tend to spark unhealthy feelings and actions, while sparking healthy feelings and actions in others. Their views, moreover, can sometimes very quickly lead to emotional changes, and not infrequently to profound ones. Thus, millions of individuals seriously addicted to alcohol, smoking, gambling, and other harmful activities have "got religion" or "seen the spiritual light," stopped their addiction, and remained unaddicted for awhile or forever. The adoption of—or devotion to—religious and spiritual ideas and practices, then, often has distinct advantages. Such as these:

1. Religious and spiritual creeds often include characterological and moral rules which, if followed, bring about good individual and/or social results. Thus, various religions and sects urge their members (or even command them) to give up their anger, to stop their harmful habits, to help other people, to give serious thought to changing their lives, and to do various other things that many societies consider "beneficial" and "healthy."

2. Faith in religious and spiritual notions helps many people to be less anxious than they otherwise would be—even if that faith is unrealistic and utopian. If your clients believe that "God will provide" or that there is some Central Spirit or Spiritual Force in the universe that will help them overcome their troubles, they will tend to make themselves less anxious and depressed than they otherwise might be.

3. Religious and spiritual practices, including many rituals, often give believers interests and goals that are constructive. By going to church regularly, saying their prayers, or conducting spiritual incantations, people can often distract themselves from their disturbances, engage in constructive pursuits, and sometimes give themselves a vital, absorbing interest, such as I discuss in more detail later in this book. As Viktor Frankl and many other existentialists point out, humans are usually healthier and happier when they have a central meaning or purpose in their life. Religion and spirituality, even when based on highly dubious allegations and suppositions, may offer such a basic meaning or purpose.[16]

Although these ideas are today more popular than they have been in the past and although you may carefully listen to your clients' religious and spiritual views and may at times refer them for counseling in these areas by qualified religious and spiritual advisors, the inclusion of "spirituality" in therapy can also be hazardous. Note its possible disadvantages:

1. If your clients are moderately or undevoutly religious and/or spiritual, believe that there is probably some kind of Higher Power, and think that this Power can help them in their hours of need, their Beliefs are "normal" and "preferential," will probably do them little harm, and may actually be helpful. But if they devoutly believe that there *absolutely has to be* a Higher Power or some kind of Higher Spiritual Force and that they are powerless without it and without a belief in it, they may then be in serious trouble. For they really are saying, in that case, that they are utterly powerless to help themselves, and that without the existence of the Higher Power in which they believe, they cannot significantly change their thoughts, feelings, or actions. Their religious or spiritual Belief is then non-constructive because it takes away their *own* power to understand and to change themselves and gives it to the tender mercies of the Supernatural Power in which they believe.

2. As emphasized in this book, the core of what we call neurosis and, even more so, of some of the severe personality disturbances usually lies in strong, dogmatic, one-sided, musturbatory thinking. Moderate religionists may have little of this absolutistic ideation, but devout religionists will tend to have much more of it. Thus, if your clients tend to forcefully believe, "There is only one powerful, all-seeing God, who utterly controls me and the universe, and to be happy and healthy I *absolutely must* follow His or Her sacred commandments and devote myself to His or Her Church, else I am in great risk of eternal damnation," these clients are much more likely to have other dogmatic disturbed ideas than if they were moderate religionists or nonbelievers.

3. Although you may encourage some of your clients to adopt more religious or spiritual pursuits—and, especially, to follow some of the ethical and moral codes of the Judeo-Christian and other religions—you had better watch your being too specific in this respect. If you push any one form of religion, you are presenting your own biases and may be discouraging your clients from thinking for themselves and developing their own religious—or nonreligious—philosophies and practices. Your psychotherapy had better be releasing rather than constricting in this, and in other important, areas.

4. Certain kinds of religion and spiritual teachings are prone to attract followers who may be obsessive-compulsive to begin with, and who may become more so as they follow these teachings. Many of the popular spiritual groups, organizations, and religions—such as the New Age cults,

transpersonalists, Rajneeshists, Theosophists, Moonies, Christian Fundamentalists, and other assemblies—have a high percentage of pietistic, scrupulous followers who are addicted to the "divine" and "sacred" teachings of their groups and their leaders. Members of such groups may be happy, or even at times ecstatic, but they are not necessarily in any usual sense of this term, "well adjusted." Hardly! A case could easily be made that immoderate religionists and spiritual devotees are encouraged by the teachings and practices of their groups to be fanatical, obsessive-compulsive, and hence disturbed. But even though cultish beliefs of this sort do not always lead to this kind of obsessive disturbance, they often enhance it.[17]

For these reasons, pietistic religious and spiritual learnings may mix poorly with mental health. Inflexible, one-track-minded devotees of these notions may sabotage rather than augment their adjustment to themselves, to others, and to their environment. Any benefits that they are likely to get from making their point of view sacred may well be ephemeral. Even when they benefit from religious and spiritual teachings—which I again emphasize may happen and does often—they rarely if ever seem to achieve the deep, intensive, "elegant" type of personality change that I am favoring in this book. So give careful thought before presenting your clients with religious and spiritual "solutions" to their presenting problems.

The points I have just made about religion and spirituality, when taken to devout extremes, including many antiscientific, superstitious, pollyannaish, perfectionistic, and obsessive-compulsive ideas and practices, do not lead to the conclusion that all spiritual attitudes are "sick." Many theologians—such as Paul Tillich and Martin Buber—hold religio-spiritual views in an open-minded, humanistic manner; they and their followers thereby retain its benefits and reduce its potential dangers.

If you wish to do so, you can use the term "spiritual" in a humanistic way that separates it from religion, God, supernaturalism, and other occult connotations. Today, many advocates of what is "spiritual" really are endorsing the idea that people should preferably put a "real meaning" in their lives, such as devoting themselves to "unselfish" social interests. In REBT, as I noted previously, we frequently encourage our clients to acquire a "vital absorbing" interest in long-range goals, such as building a business, rearing a family, or committing themselves to a political or other cause.

This process of acquiring a heartfelt meaning and purpose in life and devoting themselves to community and social rather than purely individualistic interests may be exceptionally helpful to your clients—as well as to the people with whom they live and to the human race as a whole. The question arises: Shall we call this kind of goal and purpose a "spiritual" quest, and thereby confuse it with a quest for superhuman, mystical, sacred, godlike meanings?

If you encourage your clients to create almost any kind of strong, lasting meaning—or meanings—to their lives, they will tend to automatically give *spirit* (that is, enthusiasm, verve, élan, and passion) to their thoughts, feelings, and actions. This kind of "spirituality" may be highly motivating and enjoyable. But it can be, and probably usually is, far removed from any faith or reliance that your clients have on other kinds of *spirits*, such as wraiths, Higher Powers, demons, or Supernatural Forces of the universe.

So by all means consider helping your clients to achieve the "spirit" and "spirituality" of heightened *human* consciousness, intelligence, passion, and vital absorbing interests. If they choose to be "spiritual" in a superhuman or divine sense, you can still acknowledge their choices and the possible benefits they may receive from these choices and avowals. But you'd better be wary about pushing your clients into any devout dependence on "miraculous" kinds of "spirituality." Their moderate beliefs in omnipotent spirits and omniscient spirituality may be harmless, but their pious reliance in their worldly entities has some emotional dangers!

NOTES TO CHAPTER 12

1. See Note 8 to Chapter 11.
2. de Shazer, 1985, 1990; O'Hanlon & Wilk, 1987; O'Hanlon & Beadle, 1994.
3. O'Hanlon & Beadle, 1994.
4. Carnegie, 1942; Coué, 1923; Maltz, 1965; Peale, 1952.
5. Beck, 1976; Ellis, 1957a, 1962; Ellis & Dryden, 1987; Ellis & Harper, 1975; Glasser, 1965; Lazarus & Folkman, 1984; Maultsby, 1984; Meichenbaum, 1977.
6. Brammer & Shostrom, 1968; Corsini, 1989; Corsini & Wedding, 1995; Ellis, 1984a, 1985b, 1989b, 1993c, 1993d, 1993i; Goldfried & Davison, 1991; Hammond & Stanfield, 1977; Lazarus, 1989, 1992; Thorne, 1950; Walen, DiGiuseppe, & Dryden, 1992.

7. Ellis & Yeager, 1989; Kurtz, 1986; May, 1986; Randi, 1987; Schneider, 1987.

8. Alexander & French, 1946; Balint, et al., 1972; Bordin, 1979; DiGiuseppe, Leaf, & Linscott, 1993; Dryden, 1994a, 1994b; Ellis, 1986c; Ellis & Dryden, 1985, 1987; Friedman, 1993; Horvath & Luborsky, 1993; Kottler, 1991; Orlinsky, Grawe, & Parks, 1994; Schofield, 1964; Whitaker, 1992.

9. Guidano, 1991; Guterman, 1994; Kelly, 1955; Mahoney, 1991, 1995; G. Neimeyer, 1993; R. Neimeyer, 1993.

10. Baldon & Ellis, 1993; Dryden, 1995; Ellis, 1962, 1991j, 1991m, 1992a, 1992d, 1993c, 1993i, 1993k, 1993m, 1994e, 1995a, 1995b; Yankura & Dryden, 1990.

11. O'Hanlon & Beadle, 1994.

12. McWilliams, 1994.

13. Benson, 1975; Carlson & Hoyle, 1993; Fried, 1993; Goleman, 1993a; Jacobson, 1938; Kwee, 1991a, 1991b; S. Moore, 1994; Shapiro & Walsh, 1984.

14. Benson, 1975; Levey, Aldaz, et al., 1991.

15. Ellis, 1995b; Popper, 1985; Russell, 1965.

16. Frankl, 1959.

17. Ellis, 1994e, 1994f; Ellis & Yeager, 1989; Kaminer, 1993; Kurtz, 1986; Maslow, 1973; May, 1986; T. Moore, 1992; Stace, 1960; Tart, 1992; Underhill, 1974; Walsh & Vaughan, 1994; Wilber, 1990.

13

More Methods of Brief but Less Deep and Intensive Therapy

PRACTICAL PROBLEM SOLVING

A number of therapists, and notably those who are interested in brief therapy, specialize in problem solving. We may honestly acknowledge that practically all of us therapists–yes, even "deep" psychoanalysts who mainly attempt to uncover their clients' unconscious processes and aim for an intensive personality change–actually participate in a great deal of problem solving. Clients come to therapy because they have important problems which they are not solving well; even if they come for other reasons, practically all of them bring up practical issues about which they are disturbed and ask for help in making themselves less disturbed *and also* in solving these issues.[1]

REBT makes problem solving one of the main aspects of therapy—but preferably the second rather than the first aspect to be worked at. If people are in real trouble—are living with an abusive family member, are drinking heavily, or are in danger of becoming or remaining unemployed— I may well choose to try to help them work out this dire problem first. Otherwise, they may have few resources to work with and may be so upset about unsolved dilemmas that their therapy is seriously interfered with.

Practical problems, moreover, usually require a good deal of decision making and planning and scheming. Clients are not usually in a good position to deal with them well—or even to figure out what some of them are—when they are exceptionally anxious, depressed, enraged, or self-hating. In such instances—which are, of course, everyday occurrences in psychotherapy—clients will frequently pick the "wrong" practical problem to work on, will select goals that are questionable, and will, even with the best of help, be so inept that they will sabotage almost any problem solving they do. Therefore, I usually encourage them to work on their serious emotional disturbances first and, while we are doing so, I help them get to their important goals and motives and to figure out what practical issues they want to work on and how to best do this.

So REBT stresses practical problem solving, as well as self-actualization, in addition to the minimizing of serious disturbances. Sometimes this works very well—and quickly. But sometimes problem solving works too well!

Ted was very upset about his program in graduate school, had already switched from taking an MBA course to studying law, and then, a few months before I started to see him, switched to education. He had interests in all three of these areas, but was not sure which one would serve him best for the next 20 years of his life and was very anxious about making the "right" choice. Because time was passing and because most of his college friends had definitely decided on their careers and were busily engaged in working at them, Ted felt left behind and depressed himself about this.

As usual, I quickly tried to show Ted some of his main irrational Beliefs—especially the idea that he *absolutely had to* make the right choice, *had to* make it very soon, and *had to* pick a field in which he would greatly succeed and with which he would never get bored. We started working on his clearly seeing and minimizing these irrational demands and on turning them back to realistic preferences. Meanwhile, I suggested that Ted really throw himself into his graduate work in education, temporarily pick a goal like winding up as a school administrator, and talk to his professors about the possibilities in that area. He took to my suggestions very well, especially because they gave him something practical to do immediately and distracted him from his anxiety about decision making.

Within six weeks, Ted was doing better at school than he had ever done before, gained a great deal of information about what a school administrator does, became fired with the idea of eventually building a college that would be much more career-oriented than research-oriented (which his own school was not), and was no longer undecided about what he would do for the rest of his life. No more anxiety about that. Problem solved!

Unfortunately, Ted sidetracked his Disputing of his perfectionistic, anxiety-creating Beliefs, and applied his musturbatory ideas to his newfound career goals. Now that he had firmly decided on the goal of educational administration, he insisted that he *had to* get A's in all his courses, that he absolutely *must* win the enthusiastic approval of all his main professors, and that he *must* get a new mate who would be an enormous asset in his newly chosen career and who would not merely have the fine wifely and child-raising talents his present wife had.

Although in several ways Ted was now better off than when he first came to therapy, he had hardly overcome his basic problems of easily and entrenchedly making himself anxious and depressed. These disturbances were still interfering with his newfound goals; they were helping to create so much emotional turmoil that he was both sabotaging some of these goals and remaining miserable while working for them. So I stressed Ted's striving for his educational goals as an incentive to encourage him to go back to Disputing his overwhelming musts. It took him almost a year and a half to return to active Disputing, because his obsession with his goals blocked him from turning them back from arrant demands to strong preferences. Finally, when he changed some of his basic perfectionistic philosophies, Ted was able to relieve his obsessive panic states and work for his new goals in a determined but unfrantic manner.

Thus, too much of an emphasis on practical decision making and problem solving has its therapeutic disadvantages. This may be especially true if you, as a therapist, work too hard to collaborate on solving specific problems with your clients rather than on teaching them to be better problem solvers in their own right. One of the elegant goals of therapy is to show clients how to think for themselves and come to their own conclusions in the many years of their lives subsequent to therapy. Therefore, being a partner to them in their problem solving, even making a number of suggestions that they find useful to implement, has its great virtues, but you can also run this sort of thing into the ground–as I think I partially did in Ted's case.

Other disadvantages of overemphasizing problem-solving methods of therapy and of focusing on this aspect prior to helping your clients work on alleviating their basic disturbances include these:

1. It is easy for many clients to pick relatively unimportant problems, or even the "wrong" ones, to work on. Thus, they may push you to help them make a lot of money to prove how "great" they are as persons, rather than because they truly want the advantages that money may bring. Or they may insist that you help them on their goal of being outstanding in some area that they really have no talent for. Or they may "successfully," with your help, make fine material achievements but neglect social-sex relationships that might well have brought them greater life satisfactions. Thus, focus with them, if you will, on what they say they really want to achieve in life, but also raise the possibility of their striving for many-sidedness instead of mainly one-sidedness.

2. Some of your clients' practical goals may, in your own estimation, be unrealistic. If a male or female client has only a high school degree, is 40 years old, and has three young children and few financial resources, it may not be realistic for him or her to determine to be a physician or an opera singer. Noble goals, but won't it be better to show such clients the impracticality of achieving them?

This may be a ticklish issue. Your "unrealistic" client may actually have an outside chance to succeed at an "impossible" goal. Or may never succeed at it, but still find it worthwhile to keep unfrantically working at possibly doing so. REBT, fortunately, has an answer that may sometimes work in regard to these "ridiculous" strivings. Seymour, one of my 42-year-old college graduates, always had wanted to be a physician. As we worked at helping him to stop denigrating himself because he was not one, but was only a fairly low-paid draftsman, with a nonworking wife and two young children, he made himself much less self-denigrating, but still wanted to get through medical school. I "responsibly" showed him that this goal in all probability was impractical, but I was able to offer him a philosophical solution to his problem. I showed him that he could take the outside chance of applying to medical schools, but at the same time work on his low frustration tolerance ("I *absolutely must* get the kind of work I really want to do!") and his anxiety ("Wouldn't it be *awful* if I managed to get into medical school and then flunked out! I *must* be a good student to make it or else I am an inadequate person!").

I showed Seymour that if he worked to overcome his LFT and his *dire need* to succeed in medicine, he could still honestly try to achieve his "impractical" goal while working on unconditional acceptance of himself and his frustrating life in case he did not get into medical school. He agreed to keep working in these cognitive-emotional respects and finally accepted the fact that no regular medical school would take him. So he compromised by becoming an unorthodox chiropractor who used as much regular medicine in his work as he could possibly integrate with it. He wasn't deliriously happy with his choice, but he was able to live with the restrictions of his new field of work and derive great satisfaction from helping his patients. Seymour's case shows that practical problem solving can be combined with philosophical restructuring, so that your clients may achieve good, though hardly perfect, results.

3. Practical problem solving may become something of an obsession in its own right. This, as I note below, has its advantages because it can be made into an absorbing, vital, self-actualizing interest. But it can also lead to obscuring the forest by concentrating on the individual trees. Working at the details of problem solving may become so intriguing and time-consuming that it blocks out "better" long-range goals. Thus, Marie, one of my clients who had an excellent business, became so absorbed in making money in the stock market that she neglected the business, almost ruined it, and antagonized her two sisters who partly owned the business with her. I first tried to help her manage her days so that she could spend sufficient time at her business, at her stock market transactions, and at getting along with her sisters and other family members. But these time-management procedures did not work because Marie wouldn't give up her irrational dire need to make a million dollars fast in the stock market and thereby show everyone what a "real genius" she was. As a result, my at first neglecting her obsession for more "practical" time-management procedures wasn't really too practical!

When I induced Marie to question her dire need for instant stock market success and to give up her trading desperation—which was actually helping her to make poor, overimpulsive transactions—she reassessed her life goals, decided that her relationship with her sisters and her nephews and nieces was more important than trying to convince everyone what a genius she was, and went back to her previous nonobsessive interest in her business. Even though she found stock trading more exciting and potentially more money-making, she compromised on business security and on family relating and began to lead a more satisfying life.

In spite of the cases I have just outlined, problem solving is an important part of anxiety and stress management and may help untangle, either temporarily or permanently, some emotional difficulties. For it largely involves changing the Activating Events or Adversities of life that cognitive-emotive-behavioral problems are usually about. Thus, by helping your clients to solve their practical issues, you may help them achieve economic betterment, change their work and living situations, improve their love and sex relationships, upgrade their educational, vocational, and recreational satisfactions, and achieve other benefits. In doing so, they may feel much more optimism, pleasure, involvement, and other emotional fulfillments. They may take more kindly to working on their disturbances; may have more resources for doing so; may lead a more purposive existence; may find notable meaning in their changed conditions; may feel more relaxed; may acquire more interesting friends and intimates; and may make their problem solving a vital absorbing interest in their life and acquire an experimental, self-changing and environment-changing attitude. Resolving everyday problems may lead to–and may actually *be*–profound emotional experiences. And so may emotional changes lead to–and *be*–solutions to severe practical impasses.

For reasons such as these, and because you observe that the good life of your clients (and yourself) can well include both practical problem solving *and* philosophical reconstruction, you can use many of the useful methods advocated by Jay Haley, Arthur Nezu, Marvin Goldfried, T. D'Zurilla, G. Spivack, M.D. Shure, Irvin Janis, Donald Meichenbaum, and other advocates of resolving dilemmas. As noted above, you can not only directly help your clients achieve better practical solutions but also teach them some techniques of enhancing their own problem-fathoming abilities and using them long after they have completed their therapy. This often involves their acquiring an experimental trouble-shooting attitude and, at the same time, being realistic about what difficulties they take on and work to sort out and overcome.[2]

Some of the problem-solving attitudes that you can help your clients (and yourself) achieve have been nicely outlined by Donald Meichenbaum and his associates, including the following points[3]:

- Analyze the important situations to be solved.
- Don't take on too much to be solved too quickly.
- Consider best solutions as well as alternative solutions.
- Try a number of solutions even when, at first blush, one may seem to be the most suitable.
- Check your solutions to see how well they produce the results you want.

- Assume that good solutions are possible; but do not insist that they *have to* be achieved.
- Help yourself set realistic goals by stating the problem and also stating some steps to solve it behaviorally.
- Try to generate a good many potential solutions.
- When you feel anxiety or stress about your problem solving, imagine how other people might respond to similar dilemmas and might resolve their stress about doing so.
- Evaluate the pros and cons of each solution and rank order them for their practicality and their possible results.
- Rehearse some of your strategies and likely behaviors before actually trying them out. As you work on them, continue constructively imagining better answers to them and following them through in your head.
- Expect some failures and do not insist that they must not occur.
- Reward yourself for trying even when your plans do not work out well.
- Convince yourself that you can still keep doing well once you are on the road to solving the problem.
- When you are blocked, see what you are telling yourself to possibly create the blocking. Suspect that you are sneaking in some absolutistic shoulds, musts, and demands. Find them if they exist and actively and forcefully Dispute them.
- Discover some positive, hope-oriented ideas that can help you, such as, "I really can do this," "Now that I'm doing well, I can even do better."
- Convince yourself that if the worst things happen and you cannot solve a problem well, or even at all, no disaster will ensue and you can still find several things to be happy about.
- Try to see the problem situation, even when you are doing poorly with it, as a real challenge. You can almost always help yourself learn by attempting to solve it, learn by failing, and enjoy the process of trying to find good and better solutions.

USING ENCOURAGEMENT AND SUPPORT

Almost all therapists at times use considerable encouragement and support, as Alfred Adler advocated in the early part of the twentieth century, and as many other therapists have endorsed, including Leopold Bellak, Leonard Small, and Lewis Wolberg.[4] REBT largely goes along with Adler and holds that many clients are so self-doubting and self-downing, and therefore likely to do relatively little to actively help themselves, that they had better have an active-directive therapist who is clearly on their side, who encourages them to change and who sometimes forcefully persuades them to push themselves.[5] Some of the advantages of this method include:

1. It can quickly help clients to get going and to use talents and capacities that they actually have but think they don't have and that they do not push themselves to actualize.

2. Many clients wrongly believe that they cannot change without solid direction from a therapist; therefore, they will not try to do so unless they see that this kind of help is coming. Even though seeking support may be a basic disturbance—because they have a dire *need* instead of a strong *desire* for it—they may refuse to work to overcome it until they first actually get what they "need." Therefore, it may be somewhat "wrong" but still effective to give them this support. Later, they can presumably be helped to overcome their disturbed "need."

3. When clients are pushed by a supportive therapist into helping themselves, they frequently push themselves to do things they otherwise would not do, thereby gain evidence that they really can do them well, and then gain achievement-confidence or self-efficacy (as Albert Bandura has particularly shown).[6] Having this self-efficacy, REBT holds, may not be an elegant solution to people's problems, because they then usually accept themselves conditionally—only because they now see that they can perform well. But self-efficacy is better than self-inefficacy and conditional self-acceptance is inferior to unconditional self-acceptance (USA), but it still may benefit many clients (as I show again below).

4. Giving your clients reassurance that they can do better than they think they can and that they can change themselves when they think they are able to do so is usually to some degree quite realistic because they are often much more pessimistic in these regards than they need be. So if you show them that they can do what they actually can, they may

get reinforced for their behavior and may become more realistically self-efficacious.

Giving your clients reassurance, support, and encouragement naturally can have distinct disadvantages, as a number of writers on therapy have pointed out.[7] For instance:

1. It may, as noted above, reinforce their notion that they absolutely *need* your (and other people's) support and that they can't do many things on their own that they really are capable of doing. They may thereby reinforce or aggravate their lack of self-direction.
2. Clients may let you do their thinking for them and, even when they have benefited from your advice and support, may refuse to think things through in their own right. They may, with your help, do the right things now but still be incapable of figuring out how to do them when you and other helpers are not around.
3. Clients may easily be sold on practical solutions that are not really suited for them and that will give them less satisfaction than they otherwise could work out for themselves. They may adopt your goals and values rather than their own. Even when they succeed in achieving some of these taken-on goals, they may derive relatively little pleasure or creativeness in pursuing them.
4. Clients may feel, as a result of your giving them support and reassurance, that they are *more* efficacious than they really are. They may therefore attempt to achieve goals, particularly performance goals, that are beyond their capacities and that will lead them nowhere.
5. As a result of the false sense of efficacy just mentioned, your reassured clients may easily acquire conditional self-acceptance, or self-esteem, which is far from their achieving unconditional self-acceptance. I shall get back to considering this in the next section of this chapter.

Because of the above disadvantages, giving clients support, reassurance, and encouragement surely has its questionable aspects. However, as also noted above, it has distinct advantages, especially when you want to do brief therapy. So use it with caution, don't take it to exaggerated

extremes, and mix it in liberally with the concepts and practices of unconditional self-acceptance that I stress in this book.

ENHANCING CLIENTS' SELF-ESTEEM

As I keep pointing out, the technique of helping your clients to
enhance their self-esteem is one of the most commonly employed by
regular and brief therapists. Almost innumerable theorists and practitioners have endorsed it, including Leopold Bellak, Leonard Small,
Nathaniel Branden, Sandor Ferenczi, Peter Sifneos, Ayn Rand, and Charles
Soccarides.[8]

Enhancing clients' self-esteem may be abetted in several major ways:
first, by your showing them that you really like them and think that they
are more capable than they generally think they are; second, by your
showing them that even though they often perform badly and are rejected by others, they also have a number of good behaviors and traits
and they are therefore quite capable of succeeding in the present and
future; third, as I have mentioned above, by your demonstrating that
they have some outstanding assets and are even above average in various ways.

All these methods of helping clients to enhance their self-esteem boil
down to helping them to achieve what I call highly *conditional* self-acceptance. For you encourage them, or actively teach them, to accept, like, or
respect themselves because they are capable of doing well and being
acceptable to others and not because they are unconditionally okay in
their own right, just because they are alive and kicking. This kind of
qualified self acceptance is just about universal, and probably most humans have an innate tendency to think this way on their own, without
any special teaching from others. Once they decide that certain ways are
"correct" and "proper," and once they see that they actually are able to
achieve them by their own efforts, they use their successes as "proof"
that they are "good" people, and they quite conditionally accept themselves on that basis. Unfortunately, once they fail and get rejected by
significant others, they also tend, because of their innate tendencies and
their social learning, to despise themselves and to think themselves unworthy of goodness and happiness.

Obviously, this kind of "self-esteem" is variable and insecure. All
humans seem to be exceptionally fallible and will fairly often fail at important tasks and relationships. They will easily, therefore, tend to deni-

grate themselves for their "poor" behaviors; even when they are doing well, they will make themselves anxious about doing equally well—or better!—next time. So self-esteem is a very enjoyable feeling and it helps people to persist at trying to accomplish "important" things. But it has great disadvantages, especially for so many of us who are not too competent or attractive, but also for many of us who are favored in these respects. For we are always in danger of not doing *well enough*!

Let me review, once again, some of the specific dangers of your helping your clients to achieve self-esteem or conditional self-acceptance:

1. If they achieve it because they know that you, as their therapist, like them and/or fully accept them, they also know that you are an exceptional person in their lives, one who is peculiarly on their side and who is even paid to favor them. Therefore, they may discount your approval, thinking you are pretending or are biased, or they may strive mightily to please you and accept themselves only when they do so. Even if they become convinced that you really do like them and accept them, they still live in a world where others do not favor them or greatly reject them. Thus, the self-esteem they have achieved in your presence is soon likely to erode. Or, once again, because you fully accept them, they may actually convince themselves that others *absolutely should* equally favor them. They may desperately try harder than ever to win these others' approval, but may fall on their faces in these attempts. None of these pernicious effects may occur, but all of them may!

2. By showing your clients that they are not worthless because they have some very good traits, and that their having these traits makes them a "good person," you often encourage them to *need* to maintain these good traits. Also, if they simultaneously have "bad" aspects and behaviors, they may easily "find" that these outweigh their "good" ones and may put themselves down again. Some of them, who tend to be perfectionistic, may even insist that their "good" traits must always be "good" or be "perfectly good." And where will that get them?

If the clients view themselves as good because of their good traits, they may, as Emmett Velten (personal communication, 1995) points out, deny or hide bad traits, refuse to work to change them, and down themselves for them. If they see themselves as "good persons" because of their good traits, they may refuse to take risks to try new endeavors— because they might, and often would, do poorly.

3. If you demonstrate to your clients that they have some excellent resources and are even "especially good" or "superior" in those respects, they will usually conditionally accept themselves—but, again, often insist

that others have to agree with you and them, that they must maintain these "excellent" behaviors, and that they must keep improving in these respects. When these things do not happen, they are once again prone to denigrating themselves.

For reasons such as these, self-esteem is a seesaw that almost always tends to lead clients (and nonclients) to serious mood swings. They *now* appraise themselves as "fine" and "excellent" and *then* appraise themselves—or remain fearful that they are going to appraise themselves—as "bad" and "unworthy." Only perfect humans and those who are always accepted by other significant people can live securely with this kind of "self-esteem." Try it and see for yourself! Insist that, in order to like yourself, you *have to be* a perfect therapist. Well...?

Trying to help clients enhance their self-esteem, however, also has its advantages, especially for many of them who will not give up conditional self-rating and who abysmally denigrate themselves. With them, you can use the various methods I have been discussing in this book that often work well temporarily. These include: (1) showing clients that they have good resources and traits; (2) showing them that their poor behaviors are just a *part* and not the whole of their actions; (3) showing them that you fully accept them with their "reprehensible" thoughts, feelings, and actions; (4) reassuring them that they can do better in the present and future; (5) helping them to actually improve some of their performances and skills; (6) encouraging them to change their home or work environment to one where they will meet less competition and be less rejected by others.

The "real" solution to this problem of "self-esteem," however, is probably the one I keep presenting in this book: Give your clients unconditional acceptance (or what Carl Rogers called "unconditional positive regard") no matter how they perform inside and outside of therapy. At the same time, actively teach them to give it to themselves by defining themselves as "good" just because they are alive and human and/or by learning to rate only the effectiveness of their behaviors while not rating their self, their being, or their essence.

HELPING CLIENTS GAIN INSIGHT INTO THEIR DISTURBANCES AND INADEQUACIES

Sigmund Freud and many of his psychoanalytic followers have stressed the point for the last century that giving clients insight into their disturbances and their inadequate behaviors is the most effective way to help them, and that this can sometimes be done within a few weeks or months of therapy. Psychoanalytic insight usually involves the clients understanding, especially historically, some of the main reasons why they became disturbed and the important mental and emotional mechanisms that they use to keep disturbing themselves.[9]

Many nonpsychoanalytic therapists do not go along with the Freudian and other analytic explanations, but do agree that helping clients achieve "good" explanations of how they got disturbed, and especially how they are now creating and recreating their disturbances, can help them quickly and even intensively. Thus, in REBT and most of the other cognitive-behavior therapies, clients are given "suitable" explanations of what happened to "make" them the way they now are and what they can specifically do to "unmake" their disturbances. Experiential, bodywork-oriented, and other kinds of therapists also instruct their clients about what they can do to change, but also explicitly or implicitly teach them "reasons" why they became upset and "explanations" why certain therapeutic procedures will help them.

It often doesn't matter too much whether the therapist's explanations and the "insight" that they help their clients achieve with these explanations are accurate or realistic. As long as the clients believe they are valid, these "explanations" often work because the clients then "know" why they are ailing and "know" that there is something they can do to make themselves "better."

Rona, for example, was convinced by the analyst she saw for three years that she picked the wrong men to date and to have relationships with because she was afraid to relate permanently with anyone. Why so? Well, obviously, her analyst explained, she lusted after her very attractive father, was quite neglected by him, and was terribly afraid to get involved with any other attractive man who might (a) have "incest-involved" sex with her and (b) then tend to his business and almost completely reject her. This "good" explanation of her failure to have a permanent relationship with an attractive man and her "deliberately," though "unconsciously," always picking unattractive men to go to bed with satisfied Rona because it helped her to stop blaming herself for her relationship failures and to largely blame them on her "horrible" history with her father.

Unfortunately, Rona's "insight" didn't help her to pick better partners or to form a lasting relationship. She came to see me after her analysis dismally ended because she was still picking unattractive men, whom she ultimately rejected, and was exceptionally panicked before and during her dates with attractive and seemingly suitable men.

I quickly ascertained that during her entire life, and up to the present, Rona absolutely believed, "I *must* succeed in all my important relationships, especially with a suitable man; if I don't, my whole life is useless and worthless, even though I am doing well and thoroughly enjoying my professorship in mathematics." Quite possibly, this arrant demand had been influenced by Rona's relationship with her father, which was now excellent but had not been during her early life. Oddly enough, however, her sister, who was seven years younger than Rona, always had a much better relationship with their father, and she had almost the same "horrible" fears of failing with a suitable man as Rona did.

In any event, when I quickly showed Rona that whether, in spite of or because of her upbringing, she now insisted and commanded that she *must have*, instead of only strongly *wanted*, a suitable partner, and that her present demands were most probably sparking her panic states about dating and mating, she accepted this REBT-oriented explanation, started working on ameliorating her demandingness, and within 11 sessions of therapy was able to date some very attractive men without any feelings of panic. As she said during one of our last sessions, "I now see that even though my father was very neglectful of me when I was young, I apparently convinced myself that I absolutely *needed* his love and that I also completely *needed* the acceptance of other males, especially attractive ones. Now that I am giving up this *need*, I am no longer panicked about dating attractive men. Peculiarly, I also find that less attractive men are much more to my liking than I used to find them and I think I can relate to one of them without quickly breaking off with him."

Even when you help your clients to achieve "good" or "true" or "proper" insight into the sources of their disturbances, and even when they are pleased about this, insight is often not enough to help them surrender their symptoms. This goes for "efficient" cognitive behavior therapy, as well as for other "inefficient" modes of psychological treatment—as I, Aaron Beck, David Burns, David Barlow, and a number of other cognitive behaviorists have shown.[10] Here are some of the reasons:

1. When clients like Rona zero in on the "true" explanation for their disturbances, they largely see what they have done in the past and what they are still doing to needlessly upset themselves. But, unlike Rona, they frequently do not work very hard to change their unhealthy thoughts, feelings, and actions. Rona's sister, Sharon, whom I also saw for therapy after Rona had finished with her sessions, acknowledged that she had

demands similar to those of her sister and that she, too, was insisting that men whom she found "attractive," "nice," and "suitable" give her a guarantee that they return her feelings for them and put her in no danger of rejection. Like her sister, she mainly dated "much less suitable" men and had several passionate affairs with them, but soon rejected them as marital partners.

After talking awhile with me (and with Rona), Sharon clearly saw her demandingness, realized that it was interfering with her risking rejection by partners who might really be good mates for her—but for many months refused to change these demands into preferences. Although younger and better looking than Rona, Sharon was even more basically insecure and was anxious, and often panicked, about her work as a teacher, too. She was, as far as I could see, more avoidant than Rona and had a severe personality disorder. After two years of steady REBT therapy with me, she finally gave up some of her perfectionistic demands of herself, of others, and of the world, and made herself significantly less panicked. Still, at the end of our sessions she was more disturbed than was Rona at the end of her sessions and she eventually compromised by marrying a man who was not as bright and talented as she was, just as she had compromised by becoming a high school teacher rather than trying to be a professor of English. Thus, intensive, prolonged therapy partially worked with her—or, rather, she worked at using it—even though early in the game she saw what her main irrational Beliefs were and saw how she was harming herself with them.

2. There probably is rarely one "true" explanation of or insight into clients' disturbances. Your clients may, with your help, zero in on their core ego-driven must, "I *absolutely must* perform well at love (or school or work) or I am worthless!" They then have insight into the "cause" of their anxiety and depression. But, seeing this, they may neglect their core hostility-creating must, "You *absolutely must* treat me considerately and fairly or else you are no good!" and fail to have insight into the main "cause" of their rage. They may also neglect discovering their core low frustration must, "Life *completely must* be easy and enjoyable!" and fail to have insight into their horror of the world in which they live.

In Sharon's case (unlike her sister, Rona), she also believed, "The attractive men that I may choose to go out with *absolutely have to* return my feeling for them or else they are bastards, who don't deserve to have me!" And she also believed, "The conditions under which I date *absolutely should be* better than they are! I *must* not have so many hassles and problems put in my way by the dating system! It *should be* arranged so that things are much easier for me than they often turn out to be! How awful that this lousy dating system exists!" So she was angry and had low frustration tolerance (LFT), in addition to her self-denigration. At first, as in Rona's case, we revealed and worked on her self-damnation. But as she started to give that up, her other two main irrational Beliefs emerged and she worked on them, too—at least, after awhile. In her case, her original insight into the creation of her disturbances was only partial; therefore, it was good that she had it and worked with it. But this was not enough for a more comprehensive improvement in her thinking, feeling, and behaving.

One solution to achieving and using insight is to help your client acquire the three main kinds of insight that REBT posits: (1) insight that they largely create their own neuroses, with one, two, or three basic absolutistic musts; (2) insight that no matter how and when they started to devoutly hold these musts, they still importantly have them today if they are still neurotic; (3) insight into the social reality that there is usually no way but hard work and practice to Dispute their neurotic Beliefs in order to ameliorate them. Yes, persistently and forcefully Dispute them with a number of cognitive, emotive, and behavioral methods. These three kinds of insight will help many of your clients to achieve a fairly quick change, and some of them to achieve a profound, lasting change.

Recognize, however: The usual kinds of psychological insight, and particularly the "understanding" that their past experiences made your clients as neurotic as they are today, are not enough. More action-oriented "insight" is also required. And much more hard work to implement this insight!

EXPERIENTIAL THERAPY

There are a number of therapies that emphasize experiential processes and that also claim to be brief and intensive. They encourage clients to experience felt bodily reactions, including those that go with emotional shock. Through these reactions and the feelings, body sensations, and experiences they learn from them, they make philosophical and emotional changes, and sometimes radical personality changes. Some of the theories behind experiential therapy may be found in the writings of Freud, Otto Rank, Sandor Ferenczi, Wilhelm Reich, and other early psychoanalysts; among more recent therapists they have been promoted by Carl Rogers, Eugene Gendlin, Alvin Mahrer, J. D. Safran and Leslie Greenberg, and others.[11]

The theory behind experiential therapy seems to have something of a solid basis, because in the course of human history perhaps more people have changed significantly by undergoing unusual experiences, including extreme physical and near-death experiences, than may have changed in other ways. Thus, people have a gruesome experience by almost drowning or almost suffocating in a fire and they are so shaken up and so profoundly affected for awhile that they think about their previous, present, and past life and decide to behave radically differently from before.

The encounter movement in psychotherapy, which started in the 1960's, particularly used experiential methods, including quite a bit of physical contact among members of experiential groups. But somewhat similar methods have been used for centuries by religious groups and cults. And at the present time, the New Age movement endorses a good many experiential exercises. Considerable research by various psychologists, such as Leslie Greenberg and J. D. Safran, has also shown that in the course of regular psychotherapy, clients who are given emotionally arousing exercises like those used in Gestalt therapy may focus more attentively on what is transpiring in the therapy process and may help themselves to change more quickly and better.[12]

REBT has always used some forms of experiential therapy in that it has encouraged clients, right from its start, to take risks of failure and rejection *in vivo*, to face their physical and emotional fears and thereby help themselves overcome their irrational phobias. I also saw, when I read the material of Will Schutz and Fritz Perls in the late 1960's, that experiential methods can productively be included in the REBT armamentarium. So, since 1968, REBT practitioners and I have been giving marathons, workshops, and intensives that include experiential exercises and we have incorporated many of these into our regular individual and group psychotherapy sessions. I would say that this experiential aspect of REBT has an emotive-evocative quality that often works very well. I would also say that even by itself experiential therapy produces some good results, frequently in a brief period of time. It introduces a novel, forceful, vigorous element into therapy; and most of the exercises that are used are also behavioral and encourage a pronounced active-directive change.[13]

However, when used by itself, without adequate cognitive Disputing and other techniques, experiential therapy has its distinct limitations and disadvantages, such as:

1. Almost 30 years of experience, particularly on the part of people who participate in encounter groups and intensives, has shown that the

startling improvement that often takes place when clients and nonclients participate in these experiences is dramatic but temporary. The participants often feel high for a few weeks after their new experiences and sometimes make, or at least determine to make, real changes in their lives. But come around a few months later and almost all of them seem to have reverted to most of their old dysfunctional thoughts and habits. A few of them make fairly profound changes and stick with these changes—or even grow beyond them—but most of them don't.

Four couples, for example, were in one of my 14-hour marathons at the Institute for Rational-Emotive Therapy in 1975 and all of them started to have improved marital relationships. Unlike most members of marathon groups, they kept in touch with each other and had regular yearly reunions every year over the next five years. One couple began to do poorly in their marriage, and ultimately separated. However, the other three couples continued to do well and traced their improvement to the initial marathon, to the reunions, and to their continuing to read and listen to REBT materials. Without the reunions and without the use of these materials, their continued success might not have been ensured.

Several hundred participants in one of the REBT intensives were studied a couple of months after they had participated, and the group on the whole showed significant improvement over their irrational Beliefs and dysfunctional feelings. However, the special research funds that were made available for this study were never renewed, so later investigation of this group of intensive participants could not be pursued.[14]

2. The changes that people make as a result of their having experiential exercises in individual and group therapy, as well as by participating in workshops and intensives, are not always "healthy." Some individuals dramatically change, all right, but both they and other observers question how "good" some of their changes are. I have heard almost a hundred instances where participants in experiential marathons and intensives have wrecked their marriages, quit satisfying jobs, and become addicted to alcohol and hard drugs soon after they had "ecstatic" experiences. Others have "seen" the light of growth and development, never pushed themselves to follow it, and remained more depressed than ever with their "undeveloped" lives.

3. Practically all the organizations and groups that specialize in dramatically experiential procedures are run not by mental health professionals but by individuals whose only training is in the organization itself. People are not screened before participating in these experiential groups and some of them are highly disturbed and disorganized indi-

viduals who cannot take the regular group processes. They may become seriously aberrated during or soon after their experiences and may have to be medicated or hospitalized. Where reputable therapists will refuse to treat severely disturbed individuals with dramatic let's-let-it-all-hang-out exercises, nonprofessional leaders will do so at great risks for some individuals. Also, reputable therapists will often refer clients for psychotropic medication, while nonprofessional organizations and leaders will rarely do so.

4. Well-designed experiential exercises help some people some of the time to see how they are reacting self-defeatingly and give them notions of how to change themselves, which they then healthfully follow. But many people on their own, when they mainly or only engage in these exercises, do not adequately think through their newly arrived ideas about changing themselves. Consequently, they had better have a combination of experiential procedures and a good amount of cognitive understanding of how they are disturbing themselves and what to do about this. The theory of experiential focusing and changing, as enunciated by Carl Rogers and Eugene Gendlin, is largely an existential theory that assumes that people are quite capable of experiencing something new and then spontaneously changing themselves for the better. This is sometimes true, but probably more often false, because most people, and especially most clients, have limited capacities to come to therapeutic conclusions on their own. Experiential procedures, therefore, had better be mixed with a liberal amount of cognitive procedures, and both processes had better be shown and illustrated to clients by an active-directive, competent, well-trained therapist. That, at least, is my prejudiced view!

PARADOXICAL INTERVENTIONS

Humans are indeed paradoxical, probably the more so in their disturbances and how they attempt to deal with them. Thus, when they try very hard to overcome an emotional problem, they frequently tend to exacerbate it. As I point out to my clients, if they make themselves phobic about, let us say, elevators, they then feel most uncomfortable about entering them. So to rid themselves of this discomfort, they refuse to go in elevators—and thereby they increase their phobias! If they keep telling themselves, "I *must not* be anxious! I *must not* be anxious!" that will usually tend to increase rather than decrease their anxiety!

Many therapists, consequently, try to help people by using paradoxical interventions. Thus, they may prescribe a paradoxical task–as Paul Watzlawick and his associates and Jay Haley often do–such as telling their clients to deliberately make themselves anxious, knowing that they may then actually relax and make themselves less anxious. Or they may deliberately reframe what clients are doing. Thus, Maria Selvini-Palazzoli and her associates may convince people that their family members are being noble and are trying to help them when actually these members may be trying to harm them. Or the therapists may do paradoxical positioning by defining clients' situations as more dismal than they originally saw it in order to induce them to work harder against it. Both Knight Dunlap and Victor Frankl began prescribing paradoxical acts to clients in the 1920's and presumably helped them get good results by doing so. Milton Erickson used similar paradoxical prescriptions in the 1950's, as did many other therapists in recent years, even though the results they achieved have been–paradoxically!–both good and bad.[15]

Anecdotal reports by Erickson, Frankl, Watzlawick, Luciano L'Abate, G. R. Weeks, and others indicate that paradoxical interventions can sometimes lead to remarkable changes in one or a few sessions. Even though clients perceive their therapists' paradoxical prescriptions as being irrational, they sometimes follow them and make startling and quick changes and sometimes these changes even seem to last. As A. Seltzer points out in his comprehensive review of paradoxical strategies in therapy, "A paradoxical strategy refers to a therapist directive or attitude that is perceived by the client, at least initially, as contrary to therapeutic goals, but which is rationally understandable and specifically devised by the therapist to achieve these goals."[16]

Many therapists use paradoxical interventions in a startling manner, while giving their clients no explanations of them. This technique has the advantage of novelty and of breaking up the clients' stuckness, especially when they have been in a rut for a long period of time and when their behavior, as noted above, seems to make them worse rather than better. But it also has the disadvantage of being inexplicable and confusing to the clients. We read about the cases of Erickson and Frankl, where the clients accepted the paradoxical prescriptions of their therapists and soon improved remarkably, but we rarely read of the cases, which may well be more frequent, where the clients did not accept these assignments or accepted them and became worse.

In REBT and other cognitive-behavior therapies, there is a tendency of the therapist to use paradoxical interventions quite selectively, mainly when regular methods do not seem to be working, and to explain to the clients some of the rationale for using them. Thus, I sometimes advise my clients who are afraid to encounter other people who might reject them to deliberately try, this week, to get at least three or four rejections. In doing so, they may well get some acceptances; and usually they will find that they survive any rejections they receive, observe that they are really able to take great "risks," get practice at encountering others, and give themselves an opportunity to change their irrational Belief that being rejected is "horrible" and makes them worthless individuals. So I often persuade them to do what they are most fearful of doing and show them the advantages of doing so, including the paradoxical advantage of helping themselves in the course of "failing" when they make approaches.

Therefore, by all means consider using paradoxical methods, as long as you do so selectively, with some rational explanations to your clients and with your own clear therapeutic rationale for why you are using them. Some advantages of using various kinds of paradoxical interventions include these:

1. As noted above, clients often paradoxically avoid many situations, such as encountering others, while telling themselves, "If I risked this encounter and failed in it, that would really be horrible and would prove that I am a dismal failure! Therefore, I'd better help myself by staying away from it." They thereby increase rather than decrease their phobic behavior. When they are urged to deliberately fail in their approaches, or to try to succeed but to view their failures as helpful learning experiences, they soon may overcome their phobic reactions, see their approaches as much less "dangerous," become comfortable in doing them, and even learn to enjoy participating in them.

2. Clients who paradoxically take great "risks," and who make themselves feel very uncomfortable in so doing, discover through their actions that the risks they imagined are much less dangerous than they *defined* them as being. Their paradoxical action gives them evidence to Dispute their irrational beliefs about "enormous dangers."

3. Clients who are encouraged to risk failing are able to actually fail and cope with their dysfunctional ideas about being *a failure*. Their failings give them opportunities to work on their self-defeating philosophies.

4. When you help clients to reframe what is happening to them in a paradoxical manner, they often see the "truth" of the reframed situation. If you convince someone that her husband divorced her in order to show her that she could independently run her own life, rather than because

he wanted to punish her, she may see that whether or not this was his main reason for divorcing, she now has the opportunity to run her own life and to make herself happier than she had previously been.

You'd better recognize, however, that using paradoxical interventions also has its disadvantages and its therapeutic dangers. Such as:

1. Reframing situations to your clients may actually be helping them to adopt a lie. If you convince a wife that her husband divorced her in order to help rather than hinder her and she later has evidence that he really was trying to punish her, she may lose trust in you for lying to her, lose faith in herself for believing your fabrication, and more than ever distrust her husband and other men.

2. As in the case of implosive desensitization, paradoxical strategies may lead to harmful results. Thus, if you encourage a man who is exceptionally afraid to make mistakes at work to deliberately be somewhat sloppy and make errors in order to prove to himself that nothing terrible will happen when he makes them, he may actually lose an excellent job that he is not able to replace. Or he may become more anxious, while deliberately making mistakes, than he ever was before. Or he may go to the other extreme and not care at all about his making mistakes, and therefore become a less competent worker.

3. Clients may temporarily change as a result of their doing some paradoxical assignments, but they may not simultaneously change their basic philosophy of self-downing and/or their low frustration tolerance. Thus, one of my clients, Jim, took the homework assignment of deliberately getting three rejections from women each week for a month, and actually succeeded in three of the 13 times that he tried to be rejected. He falsely concluded that he was "terrific" at getting dates with women and that therefore he was a competent and "good" person. I had a difficult time showing him that, yes, he was more competent at getting dates than he had ever thought he was, but that his newly discovered competence hardly made him a "good" or noble individual.

4. While paradoxical intervention may have good shock value for some people, it is too shocking and disruptive for others. Even when the technique works, it is confusing to them. For they are not sure why it actually did work; they may learn very little about what to do to help themselves in the future; and they may view their therapist as a magician whose help they now "need" to produce other "magical" interventions. Therefore, the watchword is caution.

5. V. Shoham and M. Rohrbaugh, in their article on "Paradoxical In-

terventions" in Raymond Corsini's *Encyclopedia of Psychology,* recommend these precautions for using the paradoxical techniques: Define behaviors positively and when prescribing a symptom do not attribute negative motives to people—such as needing to control, resist, or defeat themselves or others. Be especially cautious with challenging or provocative interventions: "Have a clear idea of how the problem is being maintained and how the paradoxical intervention you select may help to change it."[17]

In particular, in going along with the theme of this book, when you use paradoxical interventions consider not only the short-term but the long-term effects they may have on your clients. Even when you think they will work quickly and be helpful, consider how they will or will not help your clients to make a deep and lasting change. Think in terms of the intervention leading to their becoming less disturbed not only right now, but also in the future.

TIME-LIMITED THERAPY

A few therapists have gone so far as to set definite time limits for the number of their therapy sessions and have insisted that doing so helps clients to do better in therapy. Otto Rank was one of the first therapists to suggest that the client and the therapist set a definite limit to the number of sessions, at least after therapy had gone on for awhile. D. H. Malan, J. Mann, Paul Watzlawick, and others have advocated this kind of procedure and have reported good results in using it. R. Rosenbaum, Michael Hoyt, and M. Talmon have also presented evidence that single session therapy works very well in some instances and that clients may prefer it to multiple sessions.

I have never deliberately forced my clients to have a limited number of sessions, but have gone along with this procedure hundreds of times when my clients were going to be in New York for only a specific number of weeks or months. When that occurred, I found that we frequently had the same kind of sessions that I generally had with other clients who had no time constraints and with whom I never discussed having a specific number of sessions.

I have also done a great deal of therapy over the phone. Sometimes, I first see clients in regular face-to-face sessions; then, when they move out of town, we mainly continue their sessions over the phone. At other times, I have never or rarely met my out-of-town clients and see them exclusively over the phone, with perhaps a few additional sessions when they come to New York or when I give an out-of-town presentation in their region. My phone sessions with clients are not exactly time-limited, but they often turn out to take only a small number of sessions, partly because clients do not want to run up large telephone bills. Or perhaps because my speaking to them over the phone encourages them to work harder on their problems in between sessions and therefore to have fewer sessions than they might well have if I saw them regularly in my New York office. Once again, I find that my phone sessions with clients do not differ too much from my face-to-face therapy sessions.

Over the years, particularly since I started using REBT in 1955, I have had literally hundreds of clients who came to see me for only a single session or two. Often, they came from out of town, and even from out of the country, and merely wanted to have a one-hour or even a half-hour session. At other times, they came from New York but had a specific problem, such as a sexual hangup, had heard that I am an authority in that area, and therefore planned to have only a session or two to talk to me about their problem. Again, I find that these one-time or two-time sessions can be quite effective. Sometimes I see these clients several years later, often about an entirely different problem, and they tell me that the original session they had with me worked wonders and that it showed them how to deal effectively with an important disturbance.

Finally, I have had over a thousand one-shot sessions with people at my regular Friday Night Workshop: Problems of Everyday Living, at the Institute for Rational-Emotive Therapy in New York, and have also had over a thousand similar one-time sessions at hundreds of workshops that I have given all over the world. These sessions usually last from about 15 minutes to 45 minutes, and often I record them and give the demonstratee a copy of the recording. I have had hundreds of feedback conversations and letters from the people who have presented their emotional problems in the course of these single sessions and I have no doubt that a great many of them have benefited greatly as a result of their therapy and that some of them have clearly solved some of the main problems that they talked about in public. A follow-up study of scores of people with whom I had a single session at my Friday Night Workshop also shows that many of them feel that they have significantly benefited from this kind of very brief therapy.[18]

From all this personal experience, you can see that I am rather enthu-siastic about the possibility of helping people in one or a few therapy sessions. I also feel that the great majority of them would have been helped even more if we had, say, five or 10 additional sessions. But one never knows!

Time-limited psychotherapy sessions have some advantages because, first, they encourage the clients to focus in the few sessions that they have and to use them, presumably to the best effect. When they know that they are going to see a therapist, say, 10 times, they may realize that they had better bring up their main problems fast, instead of gradually getting around to them. They also had better do their homework, do supplementary reading and listening to therapeutic materials, ask the therapist pointed questions about what specifically to do next, talk to other people about what is happening to them in their therapy, and the like. Studies have not been made to see whether clients actually use these kinds of aids, but we can guess that at least some of them do.

Second, the therapist may well be on his or her toes when it is known that the sessions will last only a limited length of time. Presumably, the most important points had better soon be covered and clients be checked on to see if they understand the therapy and are working to implement it. Clients preferably should also be given a good understanding of their emotional problems and what they can do about coping with them during the therapy period and, probably, long after it ends. Again, the therapist had better urge clients to do their homework, to get to their supplementary reading, to take adjunct workshops and courses, and to do other things that might not be so important if they had unlimited sessions of therapy.

As usual, the technique of having time-limited sessions of therapy may well have its disadvantages. Thus, too much emphasis may be given to immediate problems and not enough to clients' underlying disturbances. Some important issues may not be tackled at all, both by the therapist and by the clients, because a rush-rush attitude is taken and it is assumed that these important problems can wait or that they will automatically be solved by the client after the time-limited sessions have ended. Superficial problems may be tackled because the client and the therapist become pressured about getting somewhere in a short period of time. Important disturbances may be considered, but elegant, long-lasting solutions to them may never be considered.

Despite these potential limitations of time-limited therapy, I don't think that you have to eliminate it completely. Often, whether you like it or not, circumstances will restrict you to using it. So you had better inquire as to whether new clients really intend to stay for the number of sessions that you would prefer to have with them, and whether it is economically and otherwise feasible for them to do so. If it looks like time-limited therapy actually will occur, whether because of managed care or other reasons, it is usually better to agree on it from the start and for both you and your clients to consider undertaking a modified form of what you usually do or would prefer to do. Don't think that time-limited therapy means that you necessarily have to go for superficial solutions; and don't convince yourself that just about nothing can be done in fewer sessions than you would like to see arranged. Also, you and your clients can consider having time-limited therapy at first, and later, if it is then feasible, arranging for another less limited series of sessions. Once again, you can emphasize the desirability of homework, and of continuing it after your time-limited sessions have ended, so that you can see whether your clients are really following up on some of the things that you encouraged them to do during your initial sessions.

STAYING IN THE PRESENT

As you would expect in brief therapy, a number of authorities in the field recommend focusing primarily on the present rather than on the client's past history, and focusing particularly, as we have noted, on her or his main current problems. This goes well with the theory and practice of REBT, which holds that it was not merely your clients' past experiences that caused their present disturbances, but also how they tended to react, for a number of reasons, to their past and how they are still reacting to it now. You therefore had better learn something about their history and their present life circumstances and reactions. But you can get by without much historical information; of course, if you insist on an extensive history, therapy will hardly be brief. Oddly enough, it may also be relatively ineffective!

In rereading some of the therapeutic literature recently, I was surprised to see what Carl Jung said to Richard Evans as reported in Evans' book, *Conversations with Carl Jung*. Here are some direct quotes from Jung: "Well, obviously I always insist that even a chronic neurosis has its true cause in the moment now. You see, the neurosis is made every day by the wrong attitude the individual has. It wouldn't exist today any more if there were not immediate causes and immediate purposes to keep it alive today. Because of this, a neurosis can be finished suddenly on a certain day, despite all causes. There is no one-and-only system in therapy. In therapy you treat the patient as he is in the present moment, irrespectively of causes and such things" (pp. 82, 90).[19]

I suspect that Jung anticipated REBT's Insight No.1 and Insight No.2 (that people create their disturbances in the past and re-create them in the present) partly because he had (just as I have had) a good many time-limited sessions with clients who came from all over the world to see him. Therefore, he realized that going at great length into their past just wouldn't work. So he probably got a relatively brief history and then pretty much stuck to his clients' present dilemmas. That is what brief therapists almost always have to do, whether they like it or not. The advantages of staying largely in the present, to summarize some of the things we have been saying in this book, include the following:

1. Clients come because they are suffering. If you are to quickly help them to lessen this suffering, you just haven't the time to explore and deal with the past in detail.
2. As Jung noted, and as REBT theory postulates, it wasn't merely their past history, but the attitude they took toward it that mainly helped them upset themselves—and they are still retaining their dysfunctional attitudes today. Therefore, you and they had better see what these attitudes currently are, how strongly and rigidly they hang on to them, and what you can do to encourage clients to change them.

As several therapists and other social thinkers have pointed out in recent years, humans particularly relate to other humans and almost always tend to do so in a narrative way. Even what we call problem solving includes a great deal of narrative—both in creating the problem and in presumably fixing it. So we cannot really dispense with narrative, especially in therapy.

However, not all aspects of narrative are equally important for therapeutic purposes. And the "stories" that people now tell themselves about what happened to them in the past and about what is happening to them today are often more important narratives than what "actually" happened. So therapy that focuses on the present can still be highly narrative and can considerably help clients when some other aspects of the narration are minimized. Don't forget, in this connection, that even a thousand-page novel tells only about certain aspects—normally, dramatic and supposedly important aspects—of the main characters' lives. It hardly includes everything! So therapeutic narratives, while sometimes of real importance, had better be realistically limited to certain, and not all, aspects of a client's life. Otherwise, therapy becomes endless![20]

For reasons such as these, it is wise for you to get at least a brief history of your clients' problems and unusual life events. But, again, don't get hung up on their past, even when it has been highly dramatic; and don't think that your and their understanding it will necessarily help your clients to change. When doing brief therapy, you had better largely stay with present thoughts, feelings, and actions. But largely doesn't mean completely!

As can be seen in the material in the last two chapters, indeed many roads lead to Rome. A list of all the different methods that are sometimes successful for brief and effective therapy would be endless. Many of them have not yet been invented or reported–but eventually they will be! The moral of these two chapters is that many "sensible" *and* "irrational" methods work–at least, some of the time. There doesn't seem to be any method that works all of the time. But, obviously, those that work best include those that frequently are effective with most clients. They also include those that work well for many clients–but not for many others.

The main point that I want to make again is that some techniques that you use with some of your clients can take a long time or a short time. Those described in this chapter and the previous one can often bring good results quickly. But not necessarily "deeply" or "elegantly." As I keep pointing out, "elegant" solutions to people's emotional problems usually have to be looked for and specifically implemented. I shall devote the next chapter to summing up some of the main ways that you can accomplish this.

NOTES TO CHAPTER 13

1. Baldon & Ellis, 1993; de Shazer, 1985; D'Zurilla, 1986; Ellis, 1991e, 1991k, 1992f, 1993l, 1994e; Ellis & Abrams, 1994; Ellis & Velten, 1992; Guterman, 1994; Haley, 1963, 1973, 1990; Janis, 1983; Meichenbaum, 1977; Nezu, 1985, 1986; Spivack, Platt, & Shure, 1976; Spivack & Shure, 1974; Walen, DiGiuseppe, & Dryden, 1992; Watzlawick, Beaven, & Jackson, 1967; Watzlawick, Weakland, & Fisch, 1974.
2. See Note 1.
3. Meichenbaum, 1977; Meichenbaum & Cameron, 1983.

4. Adler, 1927, 1958; Ansbacher & Ansbacher, 1956; Bellak & Small, 1977; Small, 1979; Wolberg, 1965.
5. Ellis, 1962, 1971, 1985b, 1994e, 1995a, 1995b.
6. Bandura, 1986.
7. Dryden, 1994a, 1994b, 1995; Dryden & DiGiuseppe, 1990; Dryden & Hill, 1993; Ellis, 1971; Ellis & Dryden, 1987, 1991; Ellis, Krasner, & Wilson, 1960; Walen, DiGiuseppe, & Dryden, 1992; Yankura & Dryden, 1990.
8. Bellak & Small, 1977; Branden, 1970; Ferenczi, 1952; Rand, 1961; Small, 1979.
9. Berne, 1961, 1972; Ellis, 1962, 1968, 1994e; Eysenck, 1985; Ferenczi, 1952; Freud, 1965; Sullivan, 1953.
10. Barlow, 1989; Beck, 1976; Burns, 1980, 1989; Ellis, 1962, 1994e.
11. Crawford & Ellis, 1989; Ellis, 1991c; Ferenczi, 1952; Freud, 1965; Gendlin, 1981; Rank, 1945; Reich, 1960; Rogers, 1961; Safran & Greenberg, 1991.
12. Greenberg & Safran, 1987; Safran & Greenberg, 1991.
13. Ellis, 1969, 1985b, 1994e, 1995a; Ellis & Abrahms, 1978; Ellis & Abrams, 1994; Ellis & Velten, 1992; Perls, 1969; Schutz, 1967.
14. Ellis, Sichel, Leaf, & Mass, 1989.
15. Ascher, 1989; Dunlap, 1932; Erickson, 1980; Frankl, 1959; Haley, 1990; Hayes & Melancon, 1989; Olkin, 1994; Watzlawick, 1978; Watzlawick, Beaven, & Jackson, 1967; Watzlawick, Weakland, & Fisch, 1974.
16. Seltzer, 1986.
17. Shoham & Rohrbaugh, 1994.
18. Ellis, study on Friday Night Workshop demonstrations, in progress.
19. Evans, 1978.
20. Ellis, 1962, 1968, 1989c, 1994e; Eysenck, 1985; Grunbaum, 1993; Guterman, 1994; Horney, 1937; Hornstein, 1992; Marmor, 1962; Salter, 1952; Skinner, 1954.

14

Better, Deeper, and More Intensive Methods of Brief Therapy

This—I hope!—will be one of the most important chapters of this book. In the previous chapters, I have mentioned many methods of helping your clients with brief therapy and several ways of encouraging them to institute fairly quickly a more profound, more lasting change that will possibly lead to their making themselves significantly less disturbable. I shall now summarize, and in some ways add to these "elegant" methods, show how REBT specializes in them, and demonstrate how you can help your clients—or at least *some* of your clients—to use these techniques.

DISPUTING ABSOLUTISTIC, RIGID, IRRATIONAL, DYSFUNCTIONAL BELIEFS

According to the theory of Rational Emotive Behavior Therapy (REBT), one of the main reasons for or "causes" of human disturbance, and especially of what we often call neurosis, is the way people firmly and rigidly hold on to important dysfunctional, irrational Beliefs (iB's). They easily adopt these Beliefs from their family and culture—and they are really talented at creating their own!

As I showed in my first article on REBT in 1956 and as scores of other cognitive behavior theorists and therapists have agreed since, people often have a good many neurosis-creating irrationalities—such as awfulizing, I-can't-stand-it-itis, damnation of self and others, allness and neverness, and rationalizing. But accompanying, and to some extent usually "causing," these iB's, they have three basic grandiose *musts* and *demands*: (1) "*I absolutely must* perform well and be approved of by significant others—or I am an inadequate and worthless person." (2) "Other people *absolutely must* treat me fairly and considerately—or they're rotten individuals!" (3) "Conditions under which I live *absolutely must* be comfortable and *must not* be painful or frustrating—and it's *awful* when they're not comfortable, I *can't stand* it, and the world's a rotten place!"

When your clients hold one, two, or all three of these dysfunctional demands, they won't necessarily feel anxious, depressed, or enraged. But there's a very good chance that they will—and that they will also make themselves feel anxious about their anxiety, depressed about their depression, and guilty about their rage. As I keep noting, they're very efficient at driving themselves crazy![1]

Assuming that I am reasonably correct about your clients' irrational Beliefs (iB's), how can they profoundly and elegantly minimize them, keep them minimal, and get to the point where they rarely re-create them or manufacture other iB's? In these ways:

1. They can acknowledge that whenever they feel or act dysfunctionally they most probably have one, two, or three of the grandiose musts described above, that they should keep looking for them until they find them, and that they then should actively, forcefully, and persistently Dispute them until they change them to distinct—and nothing but—preferences.
2. They can Dispute their demands and commands *empirically* and *realistically* by showing themselves that no matter how preferable it may be for them to do well, be treated fairly, and live comfortably, there is *no* reason why these preferences *must* be fulfilled—and considerable evidence exists that they actually will *not* be. Social reality very often blocks their desires and affords them *no* guarantees that their demands *have to be* achieved.

3. Your clients had better "logically," strongly Dispute their *musts*. They'd better avoid mere *unthinking parroting* and instead vigorously *prove* to themselves, again and again, that whenever they powerfully *want* something and whenever it would be *most desirable* that they get it, *it never follows* that they therefore *must* have it. You can show them the vast differences between sensible *conditional* musts—e.g., "If I want to get a college degree, I *must* take certain courses and pass them"—and *absolutistic* musts—e.g., "Because I want a college degree *so much*, no matter what courses I fail to take or take and fail, the college *must* give it to me!" They had better heed sensible conditional musts and give up crazy absolutistic ones.

4. Your clients can keep asking themselves, *pragmatically* and *practically*, "If I keep believing my musts and other irrational Beliefs (iB's), what results will I almost surely get? How will that help me? What harm will they lead to? How would changing them to preferences and other healthy Beliefs help me to create a more productive and enjoyable life?

5. You can encourage your clients to actively and persistently Dispute their other important iB's that accompany, derive from, and add to their grandiose and perfectionistic musts. They can, again, Dispute these iB's empirically, logically, and pragmatically. For example, here is how they can Dispute their awfulizing, their self-deprecation, and their I-can't-stand-it-itis:

Empirical Disputing: "Where is the evidence that it's *awful* and *horrible* if I lose my job?"

Effective New Philosophy: "Nowhere! If it were *awful* it would be *totally bad* or *as bad as it could be*. But, obviously, it could be worse. If it were *terrible*, it would be *more than bad*. But it can't be 101% bad. Therefore, it may be, in my view, *exceptionally bad*—but still not *awful* or *terrible*."

Logical Disputing: "How does it follow that if I keep failing at several jobs, as well as in my important relationships, I am an *inadequate, inept person*?"

Effective New Philosophy: "It doesn't follow! From these data I can conclude only that I am *a person who* keeps failing at jobs and relationships. My *behavior* in these areas is poor or inadequate, but it never follows that I, my whole personhood, is bad. If *I were* inadequate, I would *only and always* fail at important tasks and would be *undeserving* of succeeding. But I can logically rate only my thoughts, feelings, and behaviors, and not give a *single, global* rating to my being, my essence, or my self."

Pragmatic Disputing: "If I irrationally believe that I *can't stand* being deprived of things that I really want, where will my Belief get me?"

Effective New Philosophy: "In the soup! The feelings of low frustration tolerance and self-pity that I then produce will make me *more* frustrated than I now feel; will hardly help me work to change my deprivation; will make me so disturbed that I will be less able to cope with and ameliorate my frustration; will encourage me to give up, cop out, and refuse to try to change unpleasant things in my life; and will stop me from looking for and arranging other enjoyments. Et cetera! So I'd better work to change what I can change, gracefully accept (not like) what I can't change, and have the wisdom to know the difference!"[2]

You can show your clients these methods of Disputing their irrational Beliefs (iB's) in regular therapy and in brief therapy so as to help them arrive at profound, deep, long-lasting, and "elegant" Effective New Philosophies that will serve them well in regard to their present and future emotional-behavioral problems. To accomplish this, they had better do their Disputing frequently, forcefully, and persistently and arrive at Effective New Philosophies that they strongly believe and do not merely parrot. Moreover, they had better keep acting against their iB's and using some of the emotive-evocative techniques described in this book to change their unhealthy negative feelings to healthy, self-helpful ones. Effective Disputing, as I keep repeating, is done not only cognitively but emotively and behaviorally as well. Otherwise it can easily lead to "good" insights, but superficial and short-lived changes.[3]

REALISTIC EXPECTATIONS OF CHANGE

Unless your clients firmly believe that they *can* change and *can* stay improved, they are not too likely to work for even inelegant improvement. But if they pollyannaishly believe that they can profoundly change themselves effortlessly and magically, and that once they improve they will never be in danger of falling back, they may also resist ameliorating their disturbances. First, when your and their "magic" fails, they will tend to feel hopeless, succumb to their low frustration tolerance, and give up. Second, they may first help themselves considerably, feel horrified when they fall back, become disillusioned about *all* change possibilities, and again give in to hopelessness and lack of effort to change.

How, then, can your clients have realistic, down-to-earth expectations that help them push for change, push again if they revert to former disturbance, and keep working to make themselves less disturbable in the future? Here are some points you can help them with in this connection:

If clients largely accept REBT's basic ABC theory of human neurosis, as well as the theory of most other cognitive-behavior therapies, they will see that, although their disturbance has many contributing factors or "causes," one important contribution is their Belief system (B) about the unfortunate Activating Events or Adversities (A's) of their lives. Human Beliefs, however, are changeable. People can observe, analyze, Dispute, and modify them.

Your helping to convince your clients, therefore, that they partly *create* their Belief-incited emotional and behavioral problems and that they consequently can uncreate and recreate their own neurotic ideas is one of the crucial aspects of brief—as well as longer-lasting—therapy.

Lisa, for example, was sure that her panic about riding buses stemmed from the time when she was nine, when the school bus in which she was riding was hijacked for half an hour by a gang of teenagers, driven wildly in traffic for 10 minutes, and finally crashed into a tree, killing one of her classmates and injuring three other children. She blamed this traumatic incident, as well as her mother's subsequent constant reminders that "Buses are dangerous! Always avoid them!" for her phobia about buses and for her panic states when she thought she might have to ride in one.

I quickly convinced Lisa that most children who are in "terrifying" bus rides soon overcome their anxiety and ride in them without too much trouble. I also showed her that millions of mothers tell their children that buses—or autos, trains, or planes—are dangerous and are always to be avoided. But, again, these children usually learn to ride such forms of transportation without much fear after awhile—and often greatly enjoy doing so.

We quickly zeroed in on Lisa's main panic-inciting iB's: (1) "I must not be panicked if I ride in a bus. People will see what a weakling I am and will despise me! I must *never* show them how easily I panic!" (2) "My mother was right! Buses are very dangerous! I *absolutely must* avoid them if I am to survive!" (3) "What an idiot I am for avoiding riding in buses when they are one of the safest forms of transportation—and far safer than cars, which I keep using!" (4) "My mother was a terrible worry wart and I look like her and have several of her other traits. So I *can't* stop panicking about buses and about many other minor dangers! I'm doomed to panic!"

Lisa soon saw that she herself had adopted and kept maintaining her mother's phobic ideas—and that she had added several of her own, which her mother never had. Within eight sessions, she tackled these ideas, especially the notion that she was a total idiot for panicking about buses and the idea that, like her mother, she was doomed to keep panicking. She forced herself, at first uncomfortably, to ride a bus to and from work every day, soon *saw* that it was safer than driving a car, and began to enjoy riding in it, particularly after she found that she could read most of the time she was in the bus.

Lisa's knowledge that *she* took over her mother's horror of buses, that *she* kept recreating this horror for herself, and that therefore she could change her *own* irrational Beliefs about bus riding importantly helped her to change. I then made the second antiphobic point in her case that helped her even more profoundly. For as soon as she began to go in buses despite her discomfort, to stop putting herself down for being panicked, to overcome her panic, and to enjoy bus riding, she reported, "I never felt so good about myself in my whole life as I do about these great accomplishments! Now instead of seeing myself as a *weak person,* I see that I am really a *strong person.* And I really *like myself* for that."

"I hope not," I said to Lisa's surprise.

"Why? What's wrong with *that?*"

"Liking what you now *do* and liking your *new thinking* is great!" I said. "But liking *yourself* for those good *behaviors* is continuing to make the same mistake you have been making all your life—rating *you,* for what you *do* or do *not* do."

"You're right!" Lisa exclaimed. "Thanks for reminding me about that. After all, if I failed to improve and hated my *self, me,* for that, I would be doing the same thing I've always done about my phobia—put *me* down as *a weakling.* But now you're saying—and I'm sure you're right about that— I'm not a *'strongling'* for acting strongly any more than I was a *weakling* for acting weakly. That's very important. I'd better see that more clearly."

"And more *often.* Yes, *very* important!"

So Lisa, more elegantly, began to accept her *self, whether or not* she saw that she largely created—and therefore had the power to *un*create—her phobic reactions and her self-deprecation about those reactions.

Later, Lisa got to the third point that you can sometimes help your clients see when they acknowledge that they largely create, and can therefore disembowel, their neurotic reactions (and their neurosis about their neurosis!). As we worked together on analyzing and changing her dysfunctional Beliefs, she began to see that she *just about always* had some of them and that therefore she *just about always* could discover them and correct them.

As Lisa noted after 11 sessions of REBT, "Hell, look how I continually musturbate! Not only, 'I must not be phobic!' Not only, 'I must not turn off others with my panic!' Almost every damned thing! I *steadily* must, must, must! I really do!"

"Yes," I agreed. "You and the whole human race!"

"Indeed, yes! All my friends—and relatives. Every damned one of us."

"And you can conclude from that?"

"I really have a chance. Seeing this, I can keep finding my musts when I'm upset, track them down, and push myself to give them up. Instead of letting them control me, damn it, I can now find and control them!"

I could see that Lisa was on her way to *elegant* change: (1) Acknowledging her irrational Beliefs. (2) Not rating herself for having—or for reducing—them. (3) Seeing that she could *practically always* change them by Disputing and acting against them. (4) Eagerly, confidently *looking forward* to a lifetime of continuing this self-therapizing process. (5) Getting to a point where she automatically created and held on to fewer iB's; and whenever she did hold them again, quickly working at Disputing and acting against them again.

I still see Lisa from time to time when she invites me to speak on Rational Effectiveness Training to the social service organization she directs. She now *expects* to have some irrational Beliefs, *expects* to be able to revise them, and *expects* to thereby largely be in control of her emotional destiny.

To summarize: A number of therapists advocate that you help your clients, especially in the course of brief therapy, to have realistic expectations of change. These include Roberto Assaglioli, Simon Budman, Steven Friedman, Russell Grieger, Michael Hoyt, Mary Koss, Julia Shiang, Jack Trimpey, Otto Rank, and Paul Woods. I agree. But to encourage your clients to make even deeper and more lasting changes, you can try to help them acknowledge their neurosis-inciting dysfunctional Beliefs, unconditionally accept themselves with them, realize that they can definitely find and change them, confidently look forward to being able to do this in the future, and forcefully Dispute and act against them until they semiautomatically bring fewer iB's to new Adversities. They can, and often will without your help, try all kinds of magical, mystical, and transpersonal methods of "miraculous" self-change. But teach them the unmiraculous, realistic philosophies described in this book to see how effective they can be. If not, you can then (at their risk!) try some New Age revelations.[4]

ACCEPTING THE WORST POSSIBILITIES

A number of brief (and not-so-brief) therapists help their clients anti-castastrophize and anti-awfulize by asking them, when they are imagining some "disaster," "What's the worst thing that could happen, if you lost your job? Or if you failed to get a single hit during the game? Or if your lover left you?" They hope that their clients will then give an anti-awfulizing answer, such as "I'll be unemployed for awhile—and then get another job." Or: "I might be without a lover for awhile, but hardly forever."[5]

This technique of questioning the "awfulness" of possible failures and rejections often works quite well—and swiftly. But it is far from elegant, because the clients you use it with could reply, "Yes, I'll get another job—but suppose I don't and am unemployed forever!" Or: "Yes, I'll survive if my teammates laugh at me. But suppose they refuse to let me play again! And suppose no other team will have me!" Or: "Yes, I could get along without having a lover for awhile. But I suppose I *never* wind up with a suitable mate and am always alone!"

Anti-awfulizing, to be truly effective, had better consider these *really* worst possibilities and show clients that *even then* they can still survive and lead reasonably happy lives.

Roberta was seen by one of my supervisees, Gail, at the psychological clinic of the Institute for Rational-Emotive Therapy in New York because she was terrified that she might get a sexually transmitted disease, including even AIDS, from petting with her and her partner's clothes on—or even by shaking hands with someone who might possibly have a disease. So she led a very restricted, panic-stricken, and hypochondriacal life. Gail worked with Roberta but had a difficult time convincing her that the probability was exceptionally low that any sexual disease, especially AIDS, could be communicated to her through petting with her clothes on or through handshaking. She kept telling her that only the common cold, the flu, and a few other diseases could likely be caught in those ways, but they would hardly kill her.

Because of Gail's persistence, Roberta became less panicked and phobic and even risked petting with a very safe man, who had had no sexual contact with anyone else for 10 years, who kept all his clothes on during their petting, and who additionally appeased her by wearing a condom. When Roberta saw that even this kind of heavily restricted petting was quite enjoyable and resulted in mutual orgasm, she became less fearful, planned on having more sex with the same partner, and was about to terminate her therapy.

Gail and I agreed that this was pretty good progress for Roberta after only 12 therapy sessions. I pointed out, however, that as the end of her therapy approached, Roberta was still squeamish about shaking hands with people and was still hypochondriacal about any slight aches or pains with which she was afflicted. A stomachache surely meant that she had cancer of the colon and a pain in her side signified appendicitis or a heart attack.

So I suggested that the next time Gail had a client like Roberta she go for the elegant solution and try to get her to see that, yes, the probability of her acquiring a truly deadly disease was low—indeed very low—but that if she did acquire it, death would be final but not quite *awful.* Why was it not awful? Because it wasn't 100% bad—she could always die younger and more painfully. It certainly wasn't 101% bad—nothing could be. And it wasn't *so* bad that it *absolutely should not* ever transpire. No matter *how* bad it was—or she *viewed* it as being—it *should* be that bad—because that's the way it *was:* very bad!

So Roberta, I said to Gail, was indeed helped by her therapy. However, she could still worrisomely tell herself, "But suppose the outside chance *does* happen and I *do* get a sexual disease. Suppose I *do* get AIDS. Oh, my god! How terrible!" Then she would be panicked again.

Gail agreed that Roberta's problem of severe anxiety would probably best be resolved if she adopted the elegant solution that I presented. But she was sure that Roberta would never go that far and go along with this solution. I said, "You're probably right, since you know Roberta. But now that she is terminating, why not experimentally try it, to see if she will accept it."

Gail decided to experiment and spent a good part of the next session with Roberta trying to convince her that nothing was awful, including death. She used with Roberta the point that REBT practitioners often use with clients who are exceptionally afraid of death: the idea that death, to the best of our knowledge, is exactly the same state as people are in before they are conceived—zero. No pain, no hassles, no worries. Nothing. Why, therefore, bother yourself about it, when you will ultimately face it, anyway, and when worrying about it while you are still very much alive may well cause—until the age of 95!—enormous pain?

During the session in which Gail presented this argument, Roberta refused to buy it. She acknowledged that death itself might not be so horrible, but that dying painfully might well be. But she thought about it more after this session and saw that Gail was almost certainly right. Death itself, she concluded, was nothing to worry about too much; and even dying would normally be pretty quick and painless. If it were prolonged, moreover, she felt that she could figure out some way to painlessly kill herself.

After Roberta came to this conclusion, she was less afraid of contracting a sexual or other disease, began to take more risks, and during her last therapy session thanked Gail for helping her conquer her anxiety. "Now that you've helped me think this thing through to the bitter end," she said, "and even see my death as *damned undesirable* but still not *awful,* I feel really freed up. I'm sure I'll have some worries for the rest of my life. But not that many and not that severe!"

When Roberta arrived at this more elegant solution to her lifelong panics and phobias, her delight in getting there was rivaled only by Gail's pleasure in helping her become so worry-free.

The advantage of the *"Suppose-the-worst-thing-does-actually-happen"* approach is that, if you are successful in using it with your clients, it tends to end their awfulizing not only about relatively minor "disasters" but about the possibility of major ones as well. For if you can help them see that even the worst possibility, if it ever does occur, is *only* highly frustrating and *not* more than bad, they may thereafter resist making themselves disturbed about practically anything. They can still be *concerned* but not *horrified* about possible, or even actual, Adversities.

Clients who adopt this solution to their franticness will also usually stop exaggerating the probability of "dire" things actually happening. Thus, Harry was afraid to go to a baseball game for fear that a baseball would fly into the stand in which he was sitting, hit him in the eye, and blind him for life. When he finally accepted the fact that even if this did happen he would certainly suffer but still could survive and lead a decent life, he was able to fairly easily see that he could choose a safe position to sit in the stands, that he could catch or ward off any ball that was coming his way, and that there really was a very low probability of his being struck and blinded. He then lost his fear of attending ball games and went to many of them without qualms.

Another form of accepting the worst possibilities that may occur is to accept the reality that we humans have little or no control over what we call "fate" and over innumerable occurrences and accidents that may happen and that we can apply pseudo-control only by greatly limiting our freedom and our lives. Thus, if we avoid traveling by "dangerous" planes, we may be killed in a car crash. If we "safely" stay in our apartment or house, we may get trapped in a fire. No matter how we restrict ourselves, some germ may find us and do us in. Tough!–but only God or some other superhuman entity, if there actually is one, controls our fate and destiny. Not our fallible human self!

Once your clients accept this uncontrollability of the universe, once they accept the uselessness of desperately trying to control it, and once they see what enormous restrictions they would have to place on themselves if they frantically keep trying to stop what inevitably may happen, many of their anxieties will diminish or disappear. They will tend to see that even the most profound worrying doesn't change things and make them safer. Life, to some extent, *is* dangerous; eventually, we all die, anyway. To fully accept this is to worry a lot less about it.

To accept possible and actual dangers also gives people the likelihood of enjoying whatever life they still have. As Michael Abrams and I have shown in *How to Cope with a Fatal Disease,* once they know they are going to die, people have the option of enjoying themselves and living fully while they are still alive. Lewis Thomas, the famous physician and writer, did this for several years after he knew that he was suffering from a rare fatal disease. So did Arthur Ashe, who contracted AIDS from a blood transfusion and who lived heroically with it. Magic Johnson and Anatole Broyard have lived very well with fatal diseases. So did many other less famous individuals, including Warren Johnson, a REBT professor and psychotherapist, who wrote a fine book *So Desperate the Fight.* The knowledge that great danger *has* struck and that you *can* cope with it may lead to a philosophy of acceptance that can make life distinctly uncomfortable but still enjoyable.[6]

The disadvantage of accepting the worst possibilities and not upsetting oneself about them may be that some clients may resort to pollyannaism and conclude that even if the worst thing happens–such as their car sliding on ice and crashing–they will surely be saved. They then may take too few precautions to ward off potential harm and, for example, may drive fast on icy roads.

On the whole, however, if you can help your clients to stop awfulizing about even the worst things that may occur to them, they will tend to accept the low degree of probability that dire catastrophes will occur, will still take proper precautions against them occurring, and will be able to have more fulfilling and enjoyable lives.

People sometimes ask me, "What is the REBT method that you frequently use in your own life, to make sure that you practically never are seriously anxious or depressed about anything that may or actually does happen to you?" A good question!

Answer: I sometimes use an effective variation of the Accepting The Worst Possibilities Technique. I am now 81 years old—and have had insulin dependent diabetes for over 40 years. So some of the worst possible things—such as gangrene of the feet or total blindness—could fairly easily happen to me. What *then*?

Too bad! That would still not be the end of the world. No, it *wouldn't* be awful or terrible.

Do I really believe this?

Definitely! I always have, ever since I originated and started using REBT in 1955. In fact, even before that. In fact, that very rational Belief—and a few others—probably led me to create REBT.

I think I began thinking about human happiness and how to preserve it when one is under real stress when I was seven years old and spent ten months in the Presbyterian Hospital in New York with acute nephritis. I was determined not to be miserable with my restrictions and figured out pretty good ways of being reasonably happy in spite of them. I read a lot, talked to the other children in my ward, made friends with some of the nurses, enjoyed the once-a-week visits from my busy mother (who had my younger brother and sister to take care of), and managed to lead a pretty good existence.

When I adopted the hobby of reading and writing about philosophy, at the age of 16, I concentrated on the philosophy of happiness and soon figured out that as long as I—or anyone else—was alive and not in too much physical pain, I could always find *something* enjoyable to do even if I were sick, alone, despised by significant others, or otherwise deprived of my usual pleasures.

I even figured out, when I was in my late teens, that if I were marooned on a desert island, with nothing to read, nobody to talk to, no radio or phonograph for listening to music, and no writing materials whatsoever, I could still occupy myself by writing an epic poem in my head, remember most of it if I were ever rescued, and thereby give myself something enjoyable and interesting to do. No matter what, I would still stubbornly refuse to be miserable—as long as I was alive and not in too much physical pain. If sickness or accidents did cause me unusual pain, I could then rationally decide to kill myself.

REBT gives everyone a similar ultimate solution to the problem of human Adversity. It teaches them, if they are willing to listen, that only great and constant physical pain is rationally "unbearable" and may possibly—not always—make their lives not worth living. Otherwise, they can find *something*, and usually *several* things, enjoyable and worth living for.

What about your clients being blind and/or cripples? What about their being confined to bed or a wheelchair? What about their being alone and friendless? What about their being without music, reading material, radio and TV, and other regular pleasures that they normally enjoy?

No matter! Or, at least, it doesn't matter *that much*. For it certainly *does* matter if you or your clients are sorely deprived of many or most of your usual interests and enjoyments. It really does.

But as long as your restrictions are not total, as long as your food and shelter are reasonably taken care of, and as long as you are not continually suffering from severe physical pain, you can still—if you undesperately look for it—almost always find *something* to enjoyably live for. Music, art, reading, writing, collecting stamps, knitting, gardening, talking on the phone, helping other people? Yes, *something* that *you* pick, that *you* like, that *you* really enjoy. Yes, in spite of the things you now can't do and relish. Yes, in spite of your damned limitations!

This is one—and, of course, not the only one—solution to life's problems, and to their own personal problems, that you can help your sorely deprived clients to achieve. First, teach yourself, and then strongly teach them that while there's life there's hope. In spite of great restrictions and limitations—which a few of them are *really* afflicted with—they can most probably look for and fairly soon discover *some* real enjoyments in life. *If* they stop needlessly upsetting themselves—otherwise known as *whining*—*about* their deprivations. *If* they keep steadily—and eagerly—*looking for* interests and pleasures that they *still* can find and absorb themselves in. *If*!

So don't, as a therapist, give up. Don't think that it is *hopeless* for some of your severely restricted and physically or socially abused clients to accept the grim social reality (and often injustice) of their lives and still make themselves only *healthily* disappointed and frustrated instead of *un*healthily depressed, terrified, and horrified. Very difficult, yes. But still not *hopeless*. They almost always, if they choose sensible attitudes and actions, *can* live at peace with themselves and the world and *can* find some degree of real, personal enjoyment. If you and they strongly *believe* that they can, they then most probably can.

Once again: Work on getting yourself to believe that if some of the very worst things happen to you and your clients, abject misery and neurotic horror are *not* inevitable. Great trouble and difficulty, yes. Awfulness, terror, and horror, no. That is the REBT message that you had preferably strongly believe—and persistently and powerfully keep trying to teach to your clients.

Are there disadvantages to helping your clients acquire a solid philosophy of almost always being able to find enjoyable pursuits in spite of their being subject to real limitations? There probably are—but I have a hard time thinking of any of them. If you figure any out, by all means let me know!

ANTI-WHINING PHILOSOPHIES

In 1955, shortly after I had created REBT and vigorously used it with a number of my clients, I was surprised, almost shocked, to see that their neurotic attitudes and behaviors really, if they and I honestly faced it, consisted of whining. Just that? Well, maybe not *just* that, but *largely* that.

This became even clearer to me a few years later, when I saw that the dozen or so neurosis-inciting irrational Beliefs (iB's) that I included in my early 1956 paper, "Rational Psychotherapy," could be summarized under three major irrationalities that virtually all humans seem often to strongly hold: (1) "*I* must perform well and win significant others' approval, or else *I* am an inadequate person!" (2) "*You* must treat me kindly and fairly, or else *you* are a *rotten individual!*" (3) "*Conditions* must be the way I want them to be, or the *world* is an impossibly *bad place!*"

Obviously, these three absolutistic musts are grandiose, godlike, and full of hubris. But they are also, all three of them, forms of arrant *whining.* (1) "If I don't do as well as I *absolutely must* do, I'm a worthless, pitiful shit!–whine, whine!" (2) "If you don't treat me as well as you *absolutely should,* you're a contemptible person for being so rotten to poor pitiful me!–whine, whine!" (3) "If the conditions of my life are not totally good, as they *completely must* be, the world's a totally awful place for poor pitiful me!–whine, whine, whine!"

As a therapist, then, you'd better open-eyedly face it: Just about all of your clients are abysmal whiners. Otherwise, why would they be neurotic? Why would they see you for therapy?

So fully acknowledge this—certainly to yourself. You are dealing with a caseload of whiners! Don't, now, upset yourself about this. Don't whine yourself about your clients resisting your noble efforts to help them, coming late to their sessions with you, not paying their bills, and otherwise copping out on their therapeutic responsibilities. Isn't that what whiners often do? Of course!

So don't put them down for their whining. Accept *them* with their crummy, foolish *behavior.* Give them UTA—unconditional therapist acceptance. Then tackle their whining and do your best to help them give it up and acquire an anti-whining philosophy. How? In several important ways:

1. Again: Unconditionally accept *them* with their childish *whining.* (Make yourself *displeased* but not *angry* (demanding) about it.
2. Show them—*un*angrily and *un*demandingly—that they are *choosing,* are *responsible* for their whining. Nobody *made* them (in the past) or *makes* them (in the present) bitch and whine. No one but themselves.
3. Show them how deadly their needlessly bitching and complaining is: Self-defeating. Two-year-oldish. Unattractive. Creating ulcers and high blood pressure. Leading to life-restricting cop-outs. Et cetera!
4. Teach your clients that just about anything they *can* do—like objectionable indulgences in smoking or overspending—they also definitely can *not* do, can *refuse* to do. Including whining.
5. Convince them that it's usually *hard* for them to stop wailing—but much hard*er* if they don't stop.
6. Help them to see that whimpering won't help to change uncomfortable things—and will almost always help make them worse.
7. Show them that the pleasure of moaning and groaning (self-patting and self-pity) is not worth the pain (hopelessness and inactivity).
8. Demonstrate to your clients that their internal and/or external bellowing about life's frustrations will greatly increase rather then decrease their feelings of frustration.

In all these ways, and more if you can think of them, convince your clients that they'd better acquire a strong anti-whining philosophy. No matter *what* happens to them and *what* they make happen badly, they can always resolve, and actively work to *non*-complainingly accept *themselves* whatever they *do* poorly, to non-wailingly accept *other people* however they *act* badly, and to non-whiningly accept *life* whenever its conditions unfortunately erupt.

Strongly encourage your clients, again, to acquire and to keep reaffirming an encompassing anti-whining outlook, which includes the powerful Beliefs that:

- They and others will always be *fallible, nondamnable humans.*
- They and others will often act unkindly and unfairly, for that is their imperfect nature.
- They *can* stand things they never will *like* and still remain alive and reasonably happy.
- Nothing is *terrible, awful,* and *horrible,* although thousands of things and events are highly *inconvenient* and a needless *pain in the ass.*
- Anti-whining leads to much less pining and, usually, much more winning.

UPROOTING THE CANT OF I-CAN'T-ISM

People, let me say once again, are fortunately born constructivists, but are, alas, also innately predisposed destructivists. One of their most natural self-defeating tendencies is to fail to reach some desired goal several times—like passing a test, playing the piano well, or overcoming one of their emotional problems—and then irrationally concluding, "I'll never be able to succeed. *I can't.*" I-can't-ism of this sort is particularly pernicious in therapy. For, as I often tell my difficult clients, "As soon as you say and really firmly Believe, 'I can't change. I've tried many times and failed—so I obviously *can't!*'—as long as you Believe this, you'll make it almost impossible to change. If you strongly Believe you can't, then you really *won't* be able to change. Not because you *really* can't. But because you *Believe* you can't. That's the unkindest cut—*self*-cut—of all!"

I-can't-ism truly sucks. It may not be the worst thing in the world for neurotics. But it also may be! Although I-can't-ism won't *make* you or your clients succeed, it certainly helps. I-can't-ism enormously hinders, often irretrievably and forever. Haven't you found that with your own clients? Look and see.

How can you help your clients kill the cant of I-can't-ism? Not very easily! Still you often can. In these ways:

1. Show them that they are often afflicted—or afflict themselves—with this emotional disease: Whenever they only *lightly* and *mildly* try to make themselves less neurotic. Whenever they work hard at changing for awhile and then fall back to reducing their efforts. Whenever they give up completely and no longer try to change. In all these instances, they are often consciously or unconsciously believing—and probably strongly believing—"I can't. I can't. I can't!"

2. Show your clients that their I-can't-ism is almost always wrong, false, and mistaken. No, they *can't* flap their hands and fly. No, they *can't* always be perfect. No, there are many things they really *can't* do. But changing themselves cognitively-emotively they, at least to some extent, practically always *can* do. If they *think* they can. And if they push themselves to try to do so.

3. Show your clients evidence that they *have* changed in the past—for they invariably have done so. Demonstrate to them—

- That all things change, including mountains and other inanimate objects.
- That humans (and other animals) constantly change.
- That people who swear "I can't change!" actually do.
- That many individuals have made remarkable, almost 180-degree changes—for example, from businessperson to priest or from priest to businessperson.
- That willful and energetically pushed change is certainly likely to work better than hoping for and waiting for spontaneous change.

4. Especially show your clients that I-can't-ism obviously won't "work," because almost anyone who says "I can't do this" or "It's impossible for me to change" will *stop* herself or himself from trying and will thereby "prove" that their "can't" is "true." The view, "I *can* change," is a prime requisite for changing and puts one partly there from the start.

Helping your clients to uproot the cant of their I-can't-ism has obvious advantages. Does it have disadvantages too? Yes, it may have these:

1. If clients strongly believe "I *can* change," they may forget, "but only with much work and practice!" They may try

mildly, or not try at all, and then falsely conclude, "See, I really can't!"

2. Clients easily *say* and *parrot,* "I can change," without really *believing* it. They'd better see the *degree* of their belief in this self-statement and often intensify it.

3. Clients will often say, "I'm sure I can change," to please and pacify *you.* Help them say it and believe it *for themselves.*

4. Clients may tell themselves—and you—"I can change" in order to *avoid* backing this up with hard work and practice. Closely monitor their *determination* to change and their *action* to support this determination.

5. Clients may feel ashamed of not changing and defensively keep saying, "I *can* change" to stave off self-condemnation. If so, show them how to unconditionally accept themselves with their non-changing while continuing to see its undesirableness rather than its "horror."

While monitoring your clients' resistances to believing they can change and to actually pushing themselves to overcome these resistances, consider your own possible irrational Beliefs about helping them. Watch out for: "I *must* help my clients see that they can change and push themselves to do so!" "I *can't stand* working so hard to help my clients and their stubbornly sabotaging my great help!" "Because I'm failing so badly to help George change, I'll *never* be able to do so. How *awful*! What a rotten therapist I am!"

Your own irrationalities in this respect may mirror those of your difficult clients. Try to clearly see and work against *both* these sets of irrational Beliefs!

COMMITMENT TO WORKING FOR CHANGE

According to REBT theory, the great majority of clients can significantly change their thoughts, feelings, and actions because that is their innate constructivist tendency. They easily disturb themselves, but they also are innately changeable.[7] The problem is that they often have a difficult time changing, and they find it even harder to make the kind of profound cognitive-emotive-behavioral change that I refer to as "elegant."

Obviously, therefore, you may have quite a job encouraging your clients to make "normal" changes—and especially to make "elegant" ones.

Some of the things you can push them to do in this regard are the following:

1. They had better have, as I noted above, the knowledge that they partly or largely made themselves disturbed and that they can therefore make themselves less disturbed. Yes, have this knowledge and use it.

2. They had better realize that changing is often very hard and requires a great deal of effort to effect and maintain.

3. Profound or elegant change is even harder and usually means that your clients preferably should commit themselves to a fairly long-range process of working and practicing cognitively, emotively, and behaviorally to break their unhelpful habits and to build healthier ones. To maintain the changes they achieve also requires much work and practice. Yes, much!

4. Forcefully, not namby-pambily, your clients had better change their ideas, modify their feelings, and redo their behaviors, no matter how much difficulty they have in doing so. For they frequently have to do what they are afraid to do and deliberately make themselves *un*comfortable before they become comfortable with their new habits. As Benjamin Franklin said in *Poor Richard's Almanac,* "There are no gains without pains!"

5. To make almost any kind of significant change, and particularly what I keep calling a "deep" or "elegant" one, most clients have to use what is colloquially termed a good deal of "will power." It can endlessly be argued whether or not humans have "free will," because even when they seem to make "free" choices, there are environmental, genetic, and other influences that impel them to make their decisions. Thus, when they order, say, fish instead of beef, they are influenced by their family and cultural rearing, by the cost of both dishes and several factors that make people cost-conscious, by their education regarding "healthy" and "unhealthy" foods, by the genetic endowment of their taste buds, and by several other conscious and unconscious factors. So their "free" choice is really somewhat restricted.

So with therapy. Almost anyone is entitled to go or not go for therapy and to work or not work at it when they decide to go. But their inclination to work and their following up on that inclination are influenced by a number of factors, such as their upbringing, their cultural teachings, their previous life experiences, their past encounters with therapy, their energy level, their tolerance (or lack of tolerance!) for frustration, et cetera.

Nevertheless, practically all clients have something of a will to work and a will not to work at therapy. So how can you help them weaken their will to avoid working?

Well, first let us try to define "will" and "will power." Will seems to mainly mean choice or decision. You choose to do (or not to do) this and you decide to do (or not to do) that. Obviously, as a human, you have some degree of will, choice, or decision-making. Once you will to do something—say, buy and drive a car—you may not have the money to buy it or the ability to drive it. But you can at least try to get the money and try to learn to drive. Will, then, seems fairly simple; the will to change merely means that you decide to change—and then (perhaps!) try to do so.

"Will power," however, is much more complicated. When your clients have "strong will power" to change, it means several things:

First, they decide or will to change. ("Damn it, I think I'll try to change!").

Second, they are *determined* to act on that decision. ("No matter what it takes or how hard it is, I'm going to make some changes!").

Third, they have some knowledge of what to do—or what not to do—to change. ("Change means I have to do some rethinking and to stop my whining!").

Fourth, they *start acting* on their determination and their knowledge. ("Instead of telling myself, 'I'm no good for failing,' I'll force myself to say, '*It's* not good when I fail but *I'm* still a good, worthy person, even if I fail several times!'").

Fifth, clients who have strong "will power" keep steadily creating the decision and determination to change, keep finding out what they have to do or not do to modify their behavior, and keep acting on their determination and their knowledge. ("Now that I am trying to improve my thinking, my feelings, and my behaviors, I am determined to keep striving along these lines, to maintain my progress, and to keep looking for and working on better ways to help myself and to stop blocking myself from changing.").

Sixth, when clients fall back to their old dysfunctional ways, they decide to revert to their more functional ones. They find out, again, how to change their ways, they are determined to act on their decision and their knowledge, and they then force themselves to actually implement their determination, no matter how difficult they discover this action to be.

Will power, then, is not simply will, choice, or decision-making. Its "power" includes (1) *determination* to change, (2) *knowledge* of how to change, (3) taking *action* to change, (4) *persisting* with that action even when it is difficult to carry out, and (5) going through this process again if and when a person falls back to previous or creates new dysfunctioning.

Can you help your clients to achieve this kind of will power? Indeed, you may be able to do so—if you yourself have the will power to work at it! For you can explain to them, again, that they *can* change if they decide to do so and *work* at changing. You can also show them what will power consists of, as described above, and how it is something of a requisite to their changing. You can then persuade and encourage them to make themselves determined to become more functional and less disturbed. How? Once more, you can help them to decide to change, to gain the knowledge of how to do so, to take action to implement their determination and their knowledge, to persist at that action no matter how hard it is to do so, and to go through this process again if and when they fall back to their past dysfunctioning or create new emotional problems for themselves.

You can, in other words, keep showing your clients who have "weak will power" that they will suffer and suffer if they don't increase this power and that they will miss out on many of the best things in life. Don't blame them for their "lack of will power," but show them the real rewards of strengthening it. They *can* direct their own emotional destiny—if they choose to do so and work at implementing their choices!

Disadvantages and hazards of helping your clients get committed to therapy and to changing themselves do exist, so you'd better heed them. Here are some of them.

1. Clients may commit themselves devoutly to some narrow form of therapy—such as psychoanalytic or New Age therapy. They may work hard at this method, but stick to it rigidly and ignore other possible techniques.
2. They may wrongly conclude that hard work guarantees therapeutic success. No, it makes it more likely, but there are no guarantees!
3. They may think therapy is *too* hard and try for magical answers or resort only to easily taken medication.

4. They may view you as a nasty taskmaster, be hostile to you, and even quit therapy.

These disadvantages may be alleviated by your forming a good alliance with your clients, using a number of methods with them, showing them that there is no magical answer to their problems, stressing the advantages that changing will bring, and treating them as individuals in their own right who may sometimes require special methods in order to change themselves.

BALANCED THINKING, FEELING, AND BEHAVING

The well-balanced life has been advocated for humans since at least Aristotle's time, and usually it has much to offer. But not necessarily to all of the people all of the time. Some "screwballs" seem to take an extreme view of themselves, of others, and of the world, and—believe it or not!—lead quite happy lives. People, for example, who have led depressed, dull, or ordinary lives for a number of years suddenly see the Light, join some one-sided political, economic, or religious group, and from there on in seem to be "enlightened" and almost ecstatic. The rest of us tend to think that they are "crazy," and to point out all kinds of limitations to their devout belief systems—such as their certainty that they know the "Secret of It All," their adherence to "nutty" rules (like complete abstinence from sex), and their alienation from and sometimes hostility toward other people who refuse to devoutly follow their rules. But we cannot very well deny that some of them seem to be happier than they ever were before and some of them function well when previously they were dysfunctional.

Shall we, then, advocate this kind of extreme "solution" to some people's problems? Not very quickly! Few would follow our advice; those who did would want us to suggest a particular kind of dogma, religion, or cult that most of us, being therapists, would hardly subscribe to and would hardly promulgate. If, moreover, we generally tried to help people reach such a "therapeutic" position, it is difficult to predict what harm would come to them and the rest of us who would be somewhat forced to live with them.

Back, then, to some kind of balance in the thoughts, feelings, and behaviors for those we would try to help become less disturbed. To an extent, most therapists try to work for such a balance. First, they try to help their clients achieve some degree of balanced thinking. Thus, you probably discourage your clients when they are too rigid, dogmatic, and absolutistic in their thinking; at the same time, you may discourage them when they are too loose and have no regular rules of living or of tending to their problems. You would like them to be focused, but not too narrowly focused, on trying to live successfully with themselves and others.

Second, you would probably want your clients to have somewhat balanced feelings. If they are extremely ecstatic or exceptionally miserable, you would question the advisability of both these states of emotions; when things go wrong in their lives, you would probably want them to feel distinctly sorry, sad, disappointed, and regretful—what REBT calls healthy negative feelings—rather than feel quite panicked, depressed, enraged, and self-hating.

Third, you would usually prefer that your clients not go to one extreme or the other in their actions. On the one hand, you would not think it good if they were continually compulsive and driven, and therefore had to follow certain behaviors rigidly at all times. Nor would you want them to be too lax, inert, or lackadaisical about the things they do, especially when they are at school, at work, or in the throes of raising a family.

A fairly well-balanced life, therefore, seems to be better than a one-sided, rigid one for many people much of the time. Extreme thoughts, feelings, and actions tend to get them into trouble with themselves, especially in their interpersonal relationships. So, in all types of therapy—except a few extreme, religious, and cultish ones—balance seems to be favored. In brief therapy, too, you would often attempt to help your clients in a reasonably short period of time be more well balanced than when they first came to see you, usually in a dysfunctional, less balanced state.[8]

Assuming that balance is desirable, what are its main elements to look for in "deep," "intensive," or "elegant" therapy, and what are some of the ways to help your clients achieve these elements in relatively few sessions?

First, let us consider cognitive balance. I have been showing in this book that cognitive disbalance tends to result in people's thinking rigidly, dogmatically, absolutistically, and musturbatorily. Thus, when they try to solve one of their important life problems—such as how to get more of what they want and less of what they don't want in their love and work endeavors—they had better not pick a single possible solution, insist that it's the only one that is viable, and devoutly hold that they absolutely must achieve it quickly and completely. This kind of inflexible thinking may occasionally produce good results, but it also has its great hazards, especially the production of panic and despair when your clients do not get what they think they absolutely must get and when they do suffer what they think they absolutely must not suffer.

On the other hand, when people are exceptionally labile, changeable, and inconsistent in their thinking, they again will tend to lose out on the things that they want and end up with many conditions they do not desire. Thus, if one of your clients thinks haphazardly about going to school, changes his mind every other day, and focuses only occasionally on the advantages of getting more schooling, he will very likely never finish college and will end up with less education than he would like to have in his later life.

For most people most of the time, therefore, a balance between overly rigid and overly inconsistent thinking will probably give them the best results. This means that if you are to help them make themselves elegantly less disturbable and more functional, you had better show them what degree of rigid and dogmatic thinking they hold and how it is handicapping them. Particularly, as I keep emphasizing, show them their absolutistic musts, shoulds, and oughts, and how to change them back into more flexible preferences.

At the same time, letting your clients be the sloppy, inconsistent thinkers that they often are will also interfere with your serving them adequately. It is usually better if they do some tall thinking for themselves, in regard to picking their goals and values as well as trying to fulfill them. Being dependent on other people's views, including yours as their therapist, is not likely to direct them toward the kinds of satisfactions that they would really like to achieve. Nor will their failing to acquire sufficient data for their decision making, jumping impulsively to thoughtlessly chosen targets, nor deciding and then continually changing their minds and coming up with new goals. The Aristotelian mean between over-compulsiveness and over-impulsiveness in this respect would seem to bring better results. Watch, as you work with your clients, for evidence of both these extremes, and try to help them come back to a more middle ground.

When I first saw her for her severe states of anxiety, Margaret was a real perfectionist who absolutely *had to* do well at virtually everything she did or else felt panicked and self-downing. We worked for three months on her perfectionistic demands and she began to see that even if she failed to do completely well at her marketing job she could still accept herself as a good person and wouldn't have to keep compulsively striving to always do better, always improve. Unfortunately, however, she then went to the other extreme and began to do as little as possible and still get passable results. She began cutting corners at her job and, instead of exercising compulsively, she did much less swimming and jogging and lost the excellent physique that she had previously achieved. She also fell back in her use of REBT to overcome her self-downing.

It took me almost 10 weeks to convince Margaret that although her compulsively insisting on doing well had not done her much good, reverting to a state of practically no discipline was equally or more self-defeating. Whereas she once used to convince herself, "I've *got to* do perfectly well or I'm a crummy person!" she now was convincing herself, "So what if I don't do well. It doesn't matter at all!" Both these extremes were neurotic. She finally adopted the philosophy, "I don't *have to* do well all the time and I can fully accept myself as a person when I don't do well, but having a good degree of discipline will get me far better results than being careless about my personal and work habits. So back to the drawing board I go!" She thereby made her work and her life more effective.

REBT also usually tries to promote a balance in people's states of feelings. If they try to be ecstatic all the time, they are rarely able to achieve this goal and they tend to wear themselves out. Often, they have to resort to drugs or alcohol to keep themselves in a high state; when they are without these boosters, they tend to feel bored and purposeless. On the other hand, when they put themselves in a state of depression, rage, or self-hatred, they experience extreme negative feelings that certainly don't do them much good. Even when they distract themselves from their disturbances in non-thinking ways, such as with meditation, they may temporarily achieve surcease from pain, but they also may become lackadaisical and non-doing, and sometimes they become bored.

A state in between these extremes is that of absorbed activity, or what is sometimes called flow.[9] David, for example, was a frantically busy counselor who *had to* be most helpful to all his clients, as well as to his many friends and relatives, and who became burned out in the process. I tried to help him give up the idea that he had to always be very productive, and particularly in a way that was helpful to other people. I had little success with my argument that if he gave up his *demands* that he must help others he could still *want* very much to do so and allow himself to accomplish this at a less than breakneck pace. He insisted that all humans, but especially himself, had to be devoted to social causes; if they weren't they were leading utterly useless lives. And he saw devotion to others as such an obvious need, and such a "fine" one to fulfill, that nothing but sacrificing himself for others was acceptable.

We got nowhere with this kind of discussion, so I advised him to continue what he was doing, if that was the only plan he could conscientiously follow, and use various kinds of relaxation techniques when he got too uptight about his frantic pursuits. He thought that was a good idea and joined a sect that was into heavy meditation. Meditating for two hours a day did calm David down; he even got a real high from patting himself on the back for achieving a "thoughtless" state and for following some of the other ascetic rules that his group favored. He later found, however, that he spent so much time with his meditation and his rituals that he was doing much less counseling and fewer other activities than he wanted to do.

Impasse again. When, at my suggestion, David finally cut his meditation and his rituals to a minimum and went back mainly to helping people and doing so in an unfrantic and non-ego-bolstering manner, he was able, as he put it, to "go with the flow" and to unanxiously accomplish quite a bit of what he wanted to do. As before, he focused mostly on helping people, but did so for the challenge of doing as good a job as he could in the process, and not for convincing himself that he was therefore a good person. At the same time, he realized that following his cult's rituals perfectionistically also did not make him a worthy individual, so he quit the sect and continued to do some moderate meditation on his own.

Compulsive behavior, such as addiction to alcohol, food, or gambling, may largely be a distraction from feelings of anxiety and/or depression; or it may stem from low frustration tolerance—from the belief that one absolutely must have some substance or activity because it is quite pleasurable and that one cannot forego indulging in this pleasure even though it brings very bad results. Doing nothing, however, about one's severely neurotic feelings and indulging in self-pity, rage, and depression are equally as pernicious as escaping into addictions.[10]

The middle ground, again, is usually the best answer. If you can help your clients to look for what they are doing and thinking to neuroticize themselves, and to unfrenetically work at coping with and changing their dysfunctional thoughts and behaviors, they can much more easily surrender their addictions.

If you help your clients fairly consistently think, feel, and act in a balanced, moderate manner, you will probably serve them well. A few humans seem to naturally achieve this kind of balanced state of living; others remain often at one extreme or another—or actually fluctuate from one extreme to another—and somehow later teach themselves to reach more of an Aristotelian mean between the extremes.[11] A few! Many of your clients can achieve this position with your assistance. But, as usual, your helping them reach it has several possible disadvantages:

1. Some individuals, for a variety of reasons, are natural extremists and are bored with middle-of-the-ground living. They had probably better live somewhat with one-sided thoughts, feelings, and behaviors, as long as they do not seriously sabotage themselves and others by doing so.
2. Some people can get by well enough with a balanced state of living, but their potential for self-actualization will be fulfilled only if they pick some extreme path and "dangerously" follow it. Some of us, as Thoreau said, simply march to a different drummer. If we can do so successfully, without harming ourselves and others, that could be, for us, the best state to be in.
3. The desire to achieve balance can itself be made into a perfectionistic demand, such as, "I *must* achieve proper—or perfect!—balance." Almost any "good" behavior can be driven for absolutely. Then, even balance becomes unbalanced!

ACHIEVING SELF-ACTUALIZATION

Most methods of psychotherapy, whether their proponents are fully aware of it or not, have two main goals: Helping clients, first, to minimize their cognitive, emotional, and behavioral disturbances; and second, while they are doing this, to also achieve more of their potential for human happiness and self-fulfillment. Rational Emotive Behavior Therapy has always specifically sought to help people in these two major ways. Thus, in our original edition of *A New Guide to Rational Living,* which was published in 1961, Robert A. Harper and I came out solidly for our readers not only trying to minimize their disturbances but also to acquire what we called a vital absorbing interest and to work for other means of achieving fuller self-actualization.[12] Some of the points that we advocated that our readers work for in this connection were these:

- Attempt to get vitally absorbed in some persons or things outside of yourself. Loving persons rather than things or ideas has distinct advantages: Other people, in their turn, often love you back and beautifully interact with you. But loving some long-range activity or idea—such as getting yourself vitally attached to an art or profession, or even to building a business or raising a family—also may have its great rewards, and in some respects may turn out to be more durable, varied, and involving than loving another person or several people. Ideally, you can love both persons and things. But if you get, especially for a long period of time, thoroughly absorbed in one or the other, you may still achieve flow and steadily enjoy yourself.

- Try to find some persons or things in which you can honestly absorb yourself for their *own* sake and not for ego-raising reasons. It may seem fine and noble if you devote yourself to your family members or to one of the helping professions—such as teaching, psychotherapy, or medicine. But you have a right, as a human, to devote yourself "selfishly" to an avocation, such as coin collecting or restoring antique cars, that has relatively little social value.

- In devoting yourself to any field that you personally choose to dote upon, try to choose a challenging, long-range project rather than something simple and short-ranged. You may not for very long remain absorbed in simple endeavors, such as stamp collecting, playing checkers, or weight lifting, for you can often quickly master these pursuits and then find them unchallenging and boring. If you want to write a comprehensive history of any of these activities, that will probably take you a lot longer! So try to select a long-range goal like writing novels, making significant discoveries in some science, or becoming an outstanding entrepreneur. You may well find this kind of endeavor intriguing for years or for decades.

- Don't think that your vital absorptions have to be quickly successful. You may, at first, have to push yourself experimentally and forcibly into a chosen field, and may have to persist at it for a reasonable length of time before you get really absorbed in and fascinated by it. Before you abandon a selected project, give it an honest, fairly prolonged try. Then, if you still don't feel enamored, you can look around, experiment again, and choose a different kind of commitment.

• Give some thought to varying your interests and to having some side projects, even while you are absorbed in a major endeavor. If your main involvement may not last forever, have some alternate projects available. If you provide some variety to your hobbies, your circle of friends, and your other involvements, you may remain more vitally alive than if you routinely keep doing the same thing over and over.

Although your clients' acquiring a vital absorbing interest along the foregoing line is desirable, it is, of course, not absolutely necessary that they do so in order to lead a "good" life. Individuals, as usual, are so different and varied that some of them can even be healthy and happy living as beachcombers. Not too many, perhaps. But some!

Over and above urging clients to be vitally absorbed in some project or goal, as well as to be less disturbable, most therapists strongly advocate that they achieve self-actualization, which may be defined as ongoing enjoyment, growth, and development. This concept has been enthusiastically endorsed by Abraham Maslow and many other social thinkers, including Rudolf Dreikurs, S. I. Hayakawa, Carl Jung, Rollo May, Alfred Korzybski, Carl Rogers, and Ted Crawford. It is a part of the humanistic and existential position; and hundreds of books and papers have advocated it.

However, it has its real critics, such as M. Daniels, M. Friedman, Christopher Lasch, and Brewster Smith, who point out that Maslow's version of self-actualization is much too individualistic and nonsocial, that it largely ignores the fact that humans almost always are social creatures, and that if they mainly seek self-actualization they may sabotage some of the best interest of their own group. Adlerians, with their emphasis on social interest, certainly don't push narcissism. However, at times, even they may seem to focus too much on individual rather than on social issues. It has also been noted by Kenneth Gergen, James Hillman, Edward Sampson, and others that self-actualization is largely a Western concept, and that many Asian and other cultures instead stress sociality and put the members of the social group somewhat above the individuals in the group.[13]

Other critics of the concept of self-actualization, such as M. Daniels and A. McIntyre, have also pointed out that self-actualization involves a goal; as we search for progress and choose our goal, we discover more about it and change it. Therefore, a theory of self-actualization is always vague and incomplete. This goes along with the REBT idea that both the theory and the practice of self-fulfillment are almost by necessity experimental, changing, and incomplete.[14]

I think you will find, as a therapist, that the great majority of your clients are definitely interested in actualizing themselves and in thereby increasing their own happiness, as well as in abetting their interpersonal relationships and often helping others. When your clients clearly have these goals, how can they actualize themselves more fully? Some of the things that many therapists have endorsed in this connection and that REBT largely goes along with include the following goals. You can give these some serious thought—but, hopefully, not get yourself dogmatically or one-sidedly stuck on any of them.

Nonconformity and individuality. You can try to help your clients be individuals in their own right—to be "their own person"—while not being overly rebellious against their social group. They can strive for sensible individuality in sex, love, marital, vocational, recreational, and other important areas, while not insisting that that way is the only "right" way and by refraining from antisocial pursuits.

Social interest and ethical trust. Self-actualized individuals had better be importantly devoted to their own goals and values. At the same time, however, as Adler advocated, they should see that we are all members of the social system; if we ignore this and are only self-interested, we tend to be narcissistic and we restrict our interpersonal and love enjoyments. We also may, politically, economically, and ecologically, sabotage the whole human race! So if you can help your clients to be interested both in themselves and in others, they will probably maximize their growth and development and benefit humanity.

Self-awareness. Well-functioning individuals tend to be aware of their own feelings and unashamed of having them. In REBT terms, they acknowledge their negative feelings—as when they feel panicked or enraged—but do not necessarily act on them. They make efforts to change them when they are unhealthy and self-defeating. As S. I. Hayakawa pointed out, they "know themselves" but they also realize how little they know about themselves and keep trying to discover what they "really" want and do not want.[15]

Acceptance of ambiguity and uncertainty. Self-actualizing and "healthy" people tend to accept ambiguity, uncertainty, and some amount of disorder. As I noted in 1983, "Emotionally mature individuals accept the fact that, as far as has yet been discovered, we live in a world of probability and chance, where there are not, nor probably ever will be, absolute necessities nor complete certainties. Living in such a world is not only tolerable, but in terms of adventure, learning, and striving, can even be exciting and pleasurable."[16] Individuals who are more fully functioning are able to take risks just because they do not need to know, in advance, the full outcome of the chances that they take. If they fail, tough! But the earth doesn't stop spinning!

Tolerance. Self-actualizing individuals are, in General Semantics terminology, extensional—that is, responding to similarities and differences—rather than intensional—that is, tending to ignore differences among things that have the same name. They do not see *all* trees as green, *all* education as good, nor *all* modern art as silly. As I have noted, "Emotionally sound people are intellectually flexible, tend to be open to change, and are prone to take an unbigoted (or at least less bigoted) view of the infinitely varied people, ideas, and things in the world around them."[16]

Commitment and intrinsic enjoyment. Self-actualizing people tend to enjoy pursuits (e.g., work) and recreations (e.g., golf) as ends or pleasures in themselves and not mainly as means towards ends (e.g., working for money or playing golf to achieve good health). And as noted above, they tend to commit themselves to vital absorbing interests, rather than only to ephemeral ones.

Creativity and originality. Abraham Maslow, Carl Rogers, S. I. Hayakawa, and many other authorities show that more fully functioning individuals are often, though not necessarily, creative, innovative, and original about their pursuits. Not direly needing others' approval nor cravenly accepting conformism, they tend to be more self-directed than other-directed, more flexible than rigid, and to look more for original solutions to issues and problems that they personally favor rather than for what they "should" go along with.[17]

Self-direction. Healthy and enjoying people tend to be true to themselves as well as to others, and while interdependent with others and at times asking support from them, largely plan and plot their own destiny (albeit within a social context). They do not overwhelmingly need outside support to "make sure" that they do the right thing.[18]

Flexibility and scientific outlook. Science not only uses empiricism and logic to falsify and partially validate its hypothesis, but it also is intrinsically open-minded, undogmatic, and flexible—as Ludwig Wittgenstein, Bertrand Russell, Karl Popper, W. W. Bartley, Gregory Bateson, and other philosophers of science have shown.[19] As REBT emphasizes, people largely neuroticize themselves with rigid, imperative shoulds and musts. They tend to be less neurotic and more self-actualizing when they question and challenge their absolutistic necessitizing and keep their alternative-seeking preferences and desires.

Unconditional acceptance of oneself and others. Paul Tillich, Carl Rogers, and other social thinkers have emphasized the value of people's unconditionally accepting themselves and others.[20] From its start, REBT has held that people will undo much of their self-disturbance and un-block their self-actualizing if they rate and evaluate their thoughts, feelings, and actions only in regard to their goals and purposes and if they refuse to measure their global "selves" or "being." It also encourages them to unconditionally and unbigotedly accept others, and not rate them in an overgeneralized manner on the basis of a few of their acts and deeds. This kind of rating—and non-rating—of people will tend to enhance mental health and self-fulfillment.

Risk-taking and experimenting. Self-actualizing seems to go along with a good degree of risk-taking and experimenting. People had better experiment with many tasks, preferences, and projects in order to discover what they personally really want and don't want. They had better keep risking possible defeats and failures in order to achieve better enjoyments and to live maximally.

Long-range hedonism. Hedonism, or the philosophy of seeking pleasure and avoiding needless frustration and pain, seems almost necessary to human survival and fulfillment. Short-range hedonism—"Eat, drink, and be merry for tomorrow you may die"—has its good points and its distinct limitations. For tomorrow you may well be alive with a hangover! People may often achieve maximum self-actualization by striving for intensive and extensive pleasure today *and* tomorrow.[21]

All of the above-noted goals of therapy have their advantages, but they may also have real limitations. They may all be taken to one-sided extremes. And if your clients frantically run after "becoming the most self-actualized individuals who ever existed!"—that can likely get them into trouble.

Also, as noted above, some of your clients may choose to actualize themselves too damned much. Being overly heedful of what they really want in life, they may psychopathically neglect the other people with whom they choose to live and work and may harm the social group that is largely their habitat. This kind of behavior, as Alfred Adler showed, is hardly the height of mental health. In the long run, it also tends to be self-defeating. For other people usually reinforce one's "good" behavior and penalize one's "bad" deeds. Those, therefore, who gain largely at others' expense can easily wind up jobless, friendless, and without social support. Hardly the best way to actualize one's life!

Another danger is that if you push self-actualization too hard, your clients may wind up devoting themselves to what *you* would like them to do rather than to what *they* really would prefer for themselves. This is what often happens when people join cults. Whatever their leader's or guru's goal, they unassertively and undemocratically follow. Even assuming that these followers get some amount of fulfillment or enjoyment from their adherence to such cults, the amount of *self*-actualizing that they achieve seems to be exceptionally meager!

Therefore, take care about pushing your clients too much or too little with their self-actualization. Your helping them to become both less neurotic and more fully functional sounds great and may well encourage them to achieve a distinctly "better" life. But what is truly self-fulfilling for any individual is not easily ascertainable. From your clients' standpoint, the watchword, once again, is open-minded experimentation. But from your own vantage point, as a therapist, equally open experimenting, especially in pushing the goals that you honestly think are most actualizing for most people, is especially called for in each individual case. Try, if you will, to help each client become both less neurotic and more self-fulfilled. But be ready to retreat and question your (and their) chosen goals when the obtained results appear to be doubtful.

A final word: Musturbation about self-actualization is not very self-actualizing. The need to be *fully* or *perfectly* self-actualized can be very much self-destroying!

USING SELF-HELP MATERIALS

Try to teach your clients several of the points that I describe in this chapter. To help you do this, I strongly recommend that you also use suitable self-help materials. I have found that Rational Emotive Behavior Therapy (REBT), as well as Cognitive Behavior Therapy (CBT), work better when used with these kinds of materials. In fact, there is evidence that self-help resources aid clients in many different types of therapy. Studies showing the effectiveness of these materials have been published by a number of therapists and researchers, including David Barlow and

Michelle Craske, T. Carr, Edna Foa and Reid Wilson, J. T. Pardeck, and S. Starker.[22]

As I have shown in a recent article, self-help materials have their definite disadvantages. Thus, they include some highly dogmatic, antiscientific advice. They are subject to idiosyncratic interpretations by their readers, not all of which by any means are therapeutic. They often give the false impression that personality change is simple and easy.

Many self-help products have obviously been designed mainly to make money and to enhance reputations of their often nonprofessional authors. Some of them discourage people from going for psychotherapy, which they definitely could use. They often lead their users to falsely assess themselves and to treat themselves for disturbances—such as attention deficit disorder—that they may not actually have. They sometimes are rigid and inflexible and offer few benefits, and even some harm, for people with serious personality disorders. They are frequently resorted to by inhibited, passive, depressed, and withdrawn individuals who especially could use help from an active-directive therapist to encourage and push them to take self-changing actions.[23]

In spite of these and other limitations, self-help materials also have a good many advantages. Many disturbed people learn more by reading or by listening to recorded materials than by interacting with a therapist or group. Many who are "allergic" to bibliotherapy do exceptionally well with audio and video materials. A large percentage of therapy clients can deepen their improvement by simultaneously using self-help materials. Unfortunately, many individuals object to the time and expense required for individual or group therapy and prefer to resort to self-help when they might well be better off with regular therapy.

Although being in psychotherapy is no longer considered to be as disgraceful as it used to be, millions of individuals stay away from it because of their feelings of shame about participating and about being known to be in therapy. Many of these avoiders benefit considerably from self-help materials. Millions of people live in communities where few or no therapists are available and where they would have to travel long distances to engage in face-to-face sessions; self-help materials are easily available to them. People who participate in self-help groups, such as Alcoholics Anonymous, Recovery, Inc., Self-Management and Recovery Training, and Rational Recovery, often do a great deal of reading and tape listening to supplement the help they get from these groups.

Readers of and listeners to these materials are also encouraged to join such groups and to get regular psychotherapy.

I first realized that REBT clients benefit from self-help materials when I began providing many of them with reprints of some of my articles early in 1955 and noted that they often got my messages clearer and better through this reading than they did during therapy sessions. Encouraged by this, I wrote my first popular book on REBT, *How to Live with a Neurotic,* in 1956 and soon found that it was helpful to most of my clients who read it as well as to large numbers of readers who were not in therapy or who came to therapy largely because they had read this book. Noting this, I later wrote a number of other self-help books, such as *A New Guide to Rational Living.*

Starting in the 1970's, when Americans began to acquire cassette recorders and other kinds of electronic equipment, our psychological clinic at the Institute for Rational-Emotive Therapy in New York began to make recordings of my and other therapists' talks to the public and to include them in our self-help materials. We also publish a series of pamphlets on REBT and related topics that are given to our clients when they first come to therapy or that they can later purchase. We have always found that these materials, along with posters, sweatshirts, rational emotive behavior training games, and other items help many of our clients to work better at their therapy and often to cut down the number of sessions that they would otherwise require.

For help with REBT, we particularly recommend some of the books in our regular catalogue, such as my own books and books by Paul Hauck, Windy Dryden, Aaron Beck, David Burns, Janet Wolfe, and other cognitive-behavior therapists. A number of these are starred in the bibliography at the end of this book.[24]

To help you provide suitable self-help material for your clients who are willing to work at overcoming their emotional problems and at achieving a greater degree of self-fulfillment, I have written a companion book to this volume entitled *How to Make Yourself Healthy, Happy, and Distinctly Less Disturbable.* Read it and see for yourself whether it is suitable for any of your clients.

I have already tried out these materials with a number of my own clients and find that they usually bring good results. But don't take my word for it. Try them with some of your clients to see how beneficial they are with certain individuals.

NOTES TO CHAPTER 14

1. Barlow, 1989; Beck & Emery, 1985; Bernard, 1991, 1993; Dryden, 1994a, 1994b; Ellis, 1962, 1979b, 1985b, 1986a, 1988a, 1994b; Ellis & Dryden, 1987, 1990, 1991; Wachtel, 1994; Walen, DiGiuseppe, & Dryden, 1992.
2. Pietsch, 1993.
3. Bernard & Wolfe, 1993; Crawford & Ellis, 1989; DiGiuseppe & Muran, 1992, Ellis, 1962, 1969, 1971, 1973a, 1974a, 1979c, 1980b, 1987b, 1989a, 1991b, 1991m, 1993d, 1993j, 1993m, 1994e; Ellis, Young, & Lockwood, 1987.
4. Assaglioli, 1973; Budman, Hoyt, & Friedman, 1992; Ellis, 1994f; Grieger, 1988; Grieger & Woods, 1993; Koss & Shiang, 1994; Kurtz, 1986; Maslow, 1973; May, 1986; Moore, 1992; Stace, 1960; Tart, 1992; Underhill, 1974; Walsh & Vaughan, 1994; Wilber, 1990.
5. Bellak & Small, 1977; Budman, Hoyt, & Friedman, 1992; Ellis, 1962, 1992a, 1995a; Ellis & Velten, 1992; O'Hanlon & Beadle, 1994; Small, 1979.
6. Ellis & Abrams, 1994; Johnson, 1981.
7. Bernard, 1991, 1993; Dryden, 1994a, 1994b; Ellis, 1985b, 1990a, 1990b, 1991a, 1991m, 1992a, 1993d, 1994e, 1995a; Ellis & Dryden, 1987, 1991; Ellis & Velten, 1992.
8. Ellis, 1962, 1993g, 1994e; Ellis & Becker, 1982; Ellis & Harper, 1961, 1975; Epictetus, 1890; Epicurus, 1994; Schwartz, 1993.
9. Csikszentmihalyi, 1990; Ellis, 1994e; Ellis & Harper, 1975.
10. Ellis, McInerney, et al., 1988; Ellis & Velten, 1992.
11. Becker, 1973.
12. Ellis & Harper, 1975.
13. Crawford, 1988, 1993; Crawford & Ellis, 1989; Daniels, 1988; DiGiuseppe, 1991b; Ellis, 1973b, 1988a, 1991a; Ellis & Harper, 1975; Gergen, 1991; Guisinger & Blatt, 1994; Hayakawa, 1968; Hillman, 1992; Jung, 1954; Korzybski, 1933; Lasch, 1978; May, 1969; Rogers, 1961; Sampson, 1989; M. B. Smith, 1973; Snyder, 1994.
14. Daniels, 1988; Ellis, 1991a, 1994e; McIntyre, 1988.
15. Hayakawa, 1968.
16. Ellis, 1983a, 1991g, 1994c.
17. Hayakawa, 1968; Maslow, 1956, 1973; Rogers, 1961.
18. Ellis, 1983a.
19. Bartley, 1984; Bateson, 1979; Mahoney, 1995; Popper, 1962, 1985; Russell, 1965; Wittgenstein, 1922.
20. Ellis, 1985a, 1985c; Hartman, 1967; Hauck, 1991; Miller, 1986; Rogers, 1957, 1961; Satir, 1978; Tillich, 1953; Walker & others, 1992; Woods, 1993; Yalom, 1990.

21. Ellis, 1962, 1994e; Ellis & Knaus, 1977; Epicurus, 1994.
22. Alcoholics Anonymous, 1976; Barlow & Craske, 1989; Coté, Gautier, et al., 1994; Curry, 1993; Ellis, 1959; Foa & Wilson, 1991; Forest, 1987; Gould, Clum, & Shapiro, 1993; Lewinsohn, Antonuccio, et al., 1984; Santrock, Minnett, & Campbell, 1994; Scoggin, Bynum, et al., 1990; Scoggin & McElreath, 1994; Starker, 1988a, 1988b.
23. Ellis, 1993a.
24. Alberti & Emmons, 1990; Beck, 1988; Burns, 1980, 1984, 1989, 1993; Danysh, 1974; DiMattia, et al., 1987; Dryden, 1994c; Dryden & Gordon, 1991, 1993; Ellis, 1957a, 1972a, 1972c, 1972e, 1973c, 1977a, 1979b, 1982, 1986b, 1991k, 1991l, 1992c, 1993f; Ellis and Abrams, 1994; Ellis, Abrams, & Dengelegi, 1992; Ellis & Becker, 1982; Ellis & DiMattia, 1991; Ellis & Harper, 1961, 1975; Ellis & Hunter, 1991; Ellis & Knaus, 1977; Ellis & Lange, 1994; Ellis & Velten, 1992; Freeman & DeWolfe, 1993; Hauck, 1973, 1974, 1991; Nye, 1993; Simon, 1993; Spillane, 1985; Velten, 1987; Watson & Tharp, 1993; Wolfe, 1980, 1993. Many other REBT and CBT materials are included and starred in the References.

15

Verbatim Transcript of a First Session of REBT Brief Therapy*

I originated Rational Emotive Behavior Therapy (REBT) as a pioneering cognitive-behavior therapy (CBT) in 1955 because I had discovered, in working as a psychoanalyst from 1947 to 1953, that just about all forms of psychoanalysis are long-winded and inefficient. REBT was specifically designed, from the start, to be brief but effective for a sizable number of (but not *all*) clients. It assumes that individuals with personality disorders and psychosis are severely disturbed, for biological as well as environmental reasons, and usually require somewhat prolonged therapy, but that a large number of neurotic individuals can be significantly helped in five to 12 sessions and can therefore appreciably help themselves by continuing to practice the main REBT principles they learned during these sessions.

---

*Adapted from "Brief Therapy: The Rational Emotive Method" by Albert Ellis. In S. H. Budman, M. F. Hoyt, and S. Friedman, *The First Session in Brief Therapy* (pp. 36–58). New York: Guilford, 1992. Used with permission.

Although REBT brief therapy uses a number of relationship and experiential methods, it stresses self-help and homework. It actively *teaches* clients how to understand and help themselves in between sessions and after formal therapy has ended or has been temporarily suspended.[1] Here is a verbatim transcript of an actual first session of REBT, with some follow-up material and comments.

CASE ILLUSTRATION

The client was a 38-year-old black male, Ted, a high school graduate, manager of a retail store, married 20 years, with two children. He was referred by his physician, an ex-client, because of his pseudo heart attacks, which were really panic attacks, for which he had been given nitroglycerin for reassurance. Two years before coming to therapy, after worrying about the death of a boyhood friend from a heart attack, he was on a train returning from Manhattan to Jersey City when he started having chest pains and immediately hospitalized himself for two days, only to find that he was in perfect physical condition with no heart problems. Despite medical reassurance, he then became panicked whenever he took the train to work or back to his office, and whenever he even thought about taking a train. In addition, whenever he thought about having intercourse with his wife, he became panicked and lost his erection. He borrowed some Xanax from his mother, but used it only infrequently.

With clients like this, whom I quickly diagnose as severely neurotic, in the first session I get a brief family and personal history (partly from the four-page questionnaire we have all clients at our Institute for Rational-Emotive Therapy fill out just before the session). I especially want to know when the presenting symptom (panic) started, how intense it is, if other close members of the family have it or other symptoms, how anxious and self-downing the client is about having it, and what he or she is doing to cope with and change it. I usually focus the first session on explaining some of the ABC's of disturbance creation to the client, showing him how he mainly constructs and maintains his symptoms and what he can quickly start doing to ameliorate them. I assume that most of the treatment, if the client is not personality disordered or psychotic, can be done in 10 or 20 sessions, and that significant improvement may be effected in perhaps a few weeks.

I feel that the most important things to accomplish in the first session include:

1. Finding the core dysfunctional philosophies the clients are strongly believing that create and maintain their symptoms.
2. Showing the clients what these self-defeating B's are.
3. Showing the clients that, in all probability, they constructed their own irrational shoulds, oughts, and musts and did not merely learn them from their parents and culture.
4. Showing the clients that they can find these core irrationalities and work cognitively, emotively, and behaviorally to change them and ameliorate their influence.
5. Working out with the clients suitable, practical thinking, feeling, and action-oriented homework assignments to perform before the next session.
6. Giving the clients some reading material on REBT to start perusing at home.
7. Summarizing the first session by emphasizing that the clients are to make a note of any dysfunctional C's during the week, observe what A's preceded these C's, and look for their rB's and iB's with which they largely created these disturbed feelings and behaviors.

The First Session

After I had spent less than 10 minutes determining the client's symptoms, when and how they started and were being perpetuated, and a little background about his family (especially his mother's proneness to anxiety), he said that he had borrowed some of his mother's Xanax pills and had taken three or four of them.

Therapist: And does it help you when you take it?

Client: Yes. But the one thing I don't like is to take pills. I know that sometimes you need medication, but I hate it.

T: Well, if we can help you to change your ideas and attitudes about taking trains and about having a heart attack, that will really help you and you won't need medication. You see, you said you were a perfectionist. So you're first making yourself anxious about doing things perfectly well. "I *must* do well! I *must* do well!" Instead of telling yourself, "I'd *like* to do well, but if I don't, I don't. Fuck it! It's not the end of the world." You see, you're rarely saying that. You're saying, "I've *got* to! I've *got* to!" And that will *make* you anxious—about your work, about sex, about having a heart attack, or about almost anything else. Then, once you make yourself anxious, you often tell yourself, "I *must* not be anxious! I *must* not be anxious!" That will make you *more* anxious—anxious about your anxiety. Now, if I can help you to accept *yourself* with your anxiety, first, and stop horrifying yourself about it, and if I can help you, second, to give up your perfectionism—your demandingness—then you would not keep making yourself anxious. But you're in the habit of demanding that things *have* to go well and that, when they don't, you *must* not be anxious about them. "I must not be anxious! I must be sensible and sane!" That's exactly how people make themselves anxious—with rigid, forceful, shoulds, oughts, and musts.

C: Like yesterday. Yesterday was my worst day in a long time.

T: Yes, because?

C: What I did is when I was going to the train, I said: "I need to put something in my mind."

T: To distract yourself from your anxiety that you expected to have when you got to the train?

C: Yes. I said, "I am going to buy some sports things for the children." So I went to one of the stores and I bought some things, and as soon as I got on the train I started deliberately reading. Ten minutes after I was on the train, I still didn't have any anxiety. I was okay. But then I remembered and I said, "Jesus, I feel okay." At that moment, I started feeling panicked again.

T: That's right. What you probably said to yourself was, "Jesus, I feel okay. But maybe I'll have another attack! Maybe I'll get an attack!" You will if you think that way! For you're really thinking, again, "I *must* not get another attack! What an idiot I am if I get another attack!" Right?

C: Yes.

After briefly showing the client that whenever he has a panic attack he really upsets himself and does not actually get upset by the train or anything else, I jump right in and try to teach him that it is not his preferences or wishes for good behavior and good health that upset him but his powerful conscious and unconscious demands, and that if he gives them up, changes them back to preferences, he will lose his anxiety about having a heart attack—and also his anxiety about his anxiety. In REBT, whenever a client like this one has anxiety, and especially panic, I assume that there is a good chance that he also has panic about his panic and that that exacerbates the original panic mightily. So I try to make him aware of this immediately, and I find that very often, as soon as he or she sees that this is so, the panic about the panic subsides—and, often, so does the original panic.

T: Well let me explain to you in a little more detail how humans disturb themselves—what they think and do to make themselves anxious and panicked. They don't *get* disturbed because of the happenings in their early childhood. That's largely psychoanalytic hogwash. They almost always needlessly disturb *themselves—* by first listening to their nutty parents and, more important, taking the goals and standards they are taught and insisting that they absolutely have to live up to them, and that they completely must do well. They are born with the tendency to "*mustr*urbate"; that's their nature. But they can teach themselves not to do so and mainly remain with their preferences. Let me give you a model of most neurotic disturbance, and I know you'll understand it. Suppose you go out of this building at the end of this session into the streets of New York, and you don't know how much money you have in your pocket. It could be a dollar or it could be fifty thousand. You're ignorant of how much you have. And the one and *only* thing you think to yourself is, "I *wish,* I'd *like,* I'd *prefer* to have in my pocket a minimum of 10 dollars. Not a hundred, not 200, just 10. I'd like to have 10 dollars in my pocket because I might eat, take a cab, or go to a movie." Then, you actually look in your pocket and you find nine dollars, one less than 10. Now, how would you feel if you preferred 10 and had nine, one less? What would your feeling be?

C: That I don't have enough of what I want.

T: Yes, but how would you *feel* about not having enough of what you want? You'd like to have 10 dollars, but then you have nine, one less than 10.

C: Slightly disappointed.

T: Fine. That's a very appropriate and healthy feeling, because we wouldn't want you to feel good about not having what you want.

C: Yeah.

T: Okay. Now the second time you're going out, this time you're saying foolishly to yourself—you know it's foolish but you still say and believe it—"*I must, I must, I must,* at all times have a minimum guarantee of 10 dollars. *I have to! I've got to! I must!*" That's what you believe in your head. Then, again, you look in your pocket and you find only nine dollars and you can't get the tenth. Now how would you feel?

C: I would feel very upset.

T: Yes, because of your *must*. It's nine dollars, but this time you're insisting that you absolutely *must* have 10–and, of course, you don't. You see, we humans don't get upset by a bad condition that occurs in our lives. We get upset–or upset ourselves–mainly because of our *musts*. We take our preferences, our wishes, our desires and we often make them into absolute demands, musts, shoulds, oughts. That–your *must*–would be what's upsetting you.

C: I see. My musts.

T: Now, finally, the third time, you go out again and you're still saying to yourself the same thing as the second time: "I *must*, at all times, have a minimum guarantee of 10 dollars in my pocket!" And you look in your pocket and this time you find 15 dollars–more than enough. Now how would you feel?

C: I'd feel okay.

T: That's right. But a minute later, something would occur to you to make you anxious. Now, why would you be anxious a minute later? First, you say to yourself, "Great! I've got 15 dollars–more than enough!" Then, something would occur to make you anxious. Now, why would you become anxious a little later? You've still got the 15 dollars. You haven't lost it and you haven't said, "I must have 20 or I must have 30 dollars." You're still saying, "I must have a minimum of 10. Great, I've got 15!" Now what would make you anxious?

C: Well, I–. I don't really know.

T: Well, don't forget: You're saying to yourself: "I must have a minimum of 10 dollars *at all times*. I *now* have 15. But suppose I spend six. Suppose I lose six. Suppose I get robbed!" All of which could happen, you see, because there *are* no guarantees in the goddamned universe! They don't exist, and you're demanding one.

C: Yes, I see. So I'm still anxious.

T: Right! Now this model shows that anybody in the whole universe–and it doesn't matter what their status is, black or white, young or old, male or female, rich or poor–anybody who takes any desire, any goal, and preference for *anything* and makes it into a *must*, a *got to*, is miserable, first, when he doesn't have what he thinks he must and, second, he's anxious when he does have it—because he could always lose it. Now do you see how that applies to you?

C: Yes, I do. Any must, any real demands.

T: Yes, and you've got two main musts that make and keep making you anxious: (1) "I *must* do well, I *must* be perfect, I *must* do the right thing and not bring on a heart attack!" And (2) "I *must* not be anxious! I *must* not be panicked! I *must* not be panicked!" With these two musts, you're really going to be off the wall. You see?

C: I never thought of that before.

T: But can you see it now?

C: Yes, I think I can.

T: Fine. Now if we can help you to think, "I don't *like* being anxious, but if I am, too damned bad, it won't kill me," you'll get rid of your anxiety about your anxiety, your panic about your panic. If you can convince yourself, "Anxiety is uncomfortable but it won't kill me. It won't lead to a heart attack. And it won't make me an idiot for bringing on my anxiety. It's just uncomfortable. It's not *awful.*" Then you'll get rid of most of your problem. Then, as you rid yourself of your anxiety about your anxiety, you can much more easily go back to your original perfectionism—your demand that you must always do well and not make serious errors. Then, you'll work on being less perfectionistic. You'll still very much *want* to do well, *prefer* to do well, but you'll give up the idea that you *have to.* There's no necessity, you see, in doing well; no necessity for you to be unanxious.

During the first session, I often use this model of someone wanting something and not being anxious about its loss and needing the same thing and being very anxious, and often self-hating, first, when they do not have what they think they need and, second, even when they do have it—for then they could always lose it. Most of my clients understand this model of neurosis and many of them begin right away to use it in their own lives and keep mentioning to me how useful it is to them.

C: What is the best way to react—when you feel that stress is too strong? How can you overcome it?

T: When you're anxious?

C: Yes.

T: You say to yourself very strongly, until you really mean it: "Fuck it! So I'm anxious! It'll pass; it'll pass in a few minutes. It won't kill me. It won't turn my hair gray. It won't send me to the loony bin. Nothing will happen if I just go with the anxiety and relax." So you relax. You sit down and you relax. And you strongly tell yourself, "Too damned bad–so I'm anxious. But it's not the end of the world." Anxiety won't kill you.

C: Well, I know that. But–

T: Well, you don't know that well enough. You're probably saying to yourself, "Yeah, it won't kill me. But maybe it will! Maybe it will! Maybe it will!" Then you'll be *more* anxious!

C: Yeah, I think that I need to be anxious to keep living, to stay alive.

T: Well, you don't! Concerned, yes, about your welfare. But not *over*concerned–anxious. You'd better accept the fact that at times we're all anxious, depressed, or upset. Too bad; tough; that's the way it is. That's the human condition–humans often make themselves very anxious instead of healthily concerned. But all you have to do is relax–do some deep breathing or other relaxation exercises. Do you know any relaxation exercises?

C: Yes, I bought a tape the other day. I think I have it here. It shows you how to breathe freely.

T: What's it called? *How to Turn Stress Into Energy.* That may be all right. If you really follow this tape, or one of our own relaxation tapes that you can get downstairs, then you'll learn to immediately relax and your anxiety will temporarily go away. But if you go back to being a perfectionist and insist that you *must* do well, you *must* not be anxious, your anxiety will come back.

C: Someone told me that when you have great stress, if you do a lot of exercise, you can drain it out.

T: You can distract yourself and feel better. That will temporarily work. But you'd better also change your philosophy–that will work much better. You'd better do two things: (1) Distract yourself with some exercise, then your anxiety will go away temporarily. But it will come back because you're still telling yourself, "I *must* do perfectly well. I *must* not be anxious! I *must* not be upset!" (2) You therefore had better change your attitude, as well as relax. Show yourself that you don't *have to* do that well and that your anxiety won't kill you. Relaxation alone will help, but it will not cure you. Changing your musts—what I call your basic musturbatory philosophy—will help you permanently.

C: So you have to do it physically and mentally?

T: Exactly! You have to do it physically and mentally. And you really have to tell yourself—and *believe*—"Fuck it! If I'm anxious, I'm anxious. Too damned bad! This too will pass. And if I work on it and change my philosophy, I can make it rarely come back."

C: You see, that's what I'm trying to do in regard to the train. I think that my problem is that I think that if I have an attack on the train it will be awful.

T: So suppose you do have an attack on the train? What's going to happen to you then?

C: Something will happen to me.

T: What?

C: Most of the time I've said to myself, "Okay, nothing will happen. Because I know that whatever I have is not a heart problem—it's a mental problem and I create it myself." So I then relax. But what's getting to me is that I have to deal with the same thing every day. Every day I have to deal with it.

T: I know. Because you're saying, "I *must* not be anxious! I *must* not be anxious! Instead of, "I don't *like* being anxious, but if I am, I am!" You see, you're terrified of your own anxiety.

C: That's exactly what it is!

T: Okay. But anxiety is only a pain in the ass. That's all it is. It doesn't kill you. It's only a pain. Everybody gets anxious, including you. And they live with it!

C: It's a *big* pain in the ass!

T: I know. But that's all it is. Just like—well, suppose you lost all the money you had with you. That would be a real pain, but you wouldn't worry about it too much, because you know you'd get some more money. But you're making yourself terrified. "Something awful will happen. Suppose people *see* I'm so anxious! How terrible!" Well, suppose they do.

C: I don't care about that.

T: Well, that's good. Most people are afraid of that and it's good that you're not.

C: When I walk to the train, I know that I am going to start feeling anxious.

T: You know it because you're afraid of it happening. If you said to yourself strongly and really believed, "Fuck it! If it happens, it happens!" then it won't even happen. Every time you say, "I must not be anxious! I must not be anxious!"–then you'll be anxious.

C: I'm getting–not in the train, I mean–yesterday I was like that in the office all day.

T: It doesn't matter where you are. Anytime you say to yourself, "Suppose I'm anxious!" you'll be anxious. Sexually, for example, instead of saying to yourself, "What a great partner my wife is! I'm going to enjoy this!" you say, "Suppose I'm anxious and my goddamned cock goes down!" Then you'll be anxious, not be thinking of sexual enjoyment, and it won't work. Anxiety will take over. But if you didn't give that much of a shit about your anxiety and went back to thinking, "Look, I'd better focus on her body and on sexual enjoyment. That's how I can get and stay erect," then you'll maintain your erection. But, you see, you're not doing that.

C: A couple of months ago, when I was anxious, I did what you're saying. I put a picture in my head, about my wife or about some other sexy woman, and then my anxiety would leave and I'd be all right sexually.

T: Yes, as soon as you focus on anything else, your anxiety will temporarily go. Let me tell you a famous fable. A king didn't want to marry his daughter to a favorite prince, who passed all the tests he was given, so that it looked like he would marry the daughter. But the king was horrified at that, so he said to his wise men, "Look! You find a test this son-of-a-bitch can't pass, or I'll cut your balls off!" The wise men were very horrified about this. So they thought and thought and finally came up with a test that the prince couldn't pass. Do you know what it was?

C: No, I can't think of one.

T: "Don't think of a pink elephant for 20 minutes!" You see, if you say to yourself, as the prince did, "I must not think of a pink elephant! I must not think of a pink elephant!–"

C: Then you're going to think about just that.

T: Right! And that, you see, is exactly what you're doing. You're saying, "I must not be anxious!" Then you'll be anxious. Or, "I must be good sexually." Then you'll make yourself so anxious that you won't be able to concentrate on sexual enjoyment.

Because to do well at sex, you have to focus on sexual thoughts–
on your wife or on some other desirable woman. You have to
have sexy thoughts. But if you say to yourself, "Oh, my God!
Suppose I get anxious! Suppose my cock won't go up and stay
up!" Then it won't! So that's what you're doing. You're *demanding* that you have to do well; and you're also *insisting* that you
must not be anxious. So if we can get you to say to yourself, and
really believe, "I'd *like* to do well, but I never *have* to" and, "I'd
very much *prefer* to be unanxious, but fuck it, if I'm anxious, I'm
anxious!" then you'll get over this nonsense that you're now
telling yourself. Whenever you take a preference, a goal, a desire,
and you say, "I have to achieve it! I must perform well!" you're
making yourself immediately anxious. That's where your anxiety
comes from. And that's what people do: They take their strong
desires and say, "I absolutely must achieve them! I have to; I've
got to!" Instead of, "I'd like to achieve them, but if I don't, tough!
The earth won't stop spinning!"

C: Okay. So the best way is for me to think, if I am anxious?
T: "Too damned bad! It's only uncomfortable! It won't kill me!"
For nothing terrible does happen if you're anxious. You see? Just
like my diabetes. It's a pain in the ass and I have to take care of
it. But it's only uncomfortable and I don't whine and scream
about having it. "I must not have diabetes! I must be perfectly
healthy!" If I did that, I'd be in trouble. So I have diabetes! So?

C: And there's nothing that you can do about it?
T: I take care of it. I stick to my diet and take my insulin regularly.
Too bad! I don't like it, but I don't whine and scream and make
myself miserable by demanding, "I must not have diabetes! I
must not, I must not!"

C: There's nothing you can do. So you just accept it.
T: Yes, we *invent* the horrors. They really don't exist in the world.
Many hassles, many problems do exist. But as a store manager,
you know how to take care of problems. That's your business.

C: Yes, I do that pretty well.
T: So you don't get yourself too excited when there's a problem.
You don't say to yourself, "Oh, my God! I absolutely must solve
it!" Then you'd make yourself anxious and wouldn't be able to
solve it very well.

C: That's right.
T: So if we could get you to take the same attitude toward your

anxiety that you take toward your work, you would do very well and rid yourself of most of your neurotic problems.

C: See, I never thought of that.

T: Yes, but that's what you'd better think of. That's the thing. Life is a series of hassles, and you've had a number of them in your life. So when your children get sick, you don't like it, but you take care of it. Or if you have problems with your wife, you cope with them. Now, we want you to cope with your anxiety, and also give up some of your perfectionism. For when you say, "I have to do well! I have to do well!" you're going to make yourself upset. There are no absolute necessities in the universe—just things we would like, prefer, desire. There are many of those, but we don't *have* to get them. When people like you change these preferences into musts, they upset themselves needlessly. The three main musts are: (1) "I *must* do well and be approved by significant others, or else I'm no good!" This leads people to feel anxious, depressed, and self-hating. (2) "*You* have to treat me well, or you're a shit!" And then people become angry, enraged, homicidal. (3) "Conditions *must* be arranged so that they give me exactly what I want when I want it, and never, no, never give me what I don't want!" Then people have low frustration tolerance and, when conditions are pretty bad, depress themselves. Those three musts really upset people. But, of course, there is no reason why you *have to* do well, or why other people *must* treat you nicely, or that conditions *must* be easy. So whenever you feel upset, or behave foolishly against your interest, about anything, look for your shoulds, look for your musts. You can easily find them, but it takes a good deal of work and effort to give them up. But you can do it!

C: I see what you're saying. It looks like I can do it.

T: Fine, I am sure that you can. Now what I want you to do is take all these forms home with you [*the Millon Clinical Multiaxial Inventory*], fill them all out, and bring them back together and we'll give you some interesting personality scores. Then, for your homework—for we always give homework in REBT—make a note of anything that really bothers you during the week—of any feelings of anxiety, panic, depression, self-hatred, or rage against others. Just a little note to yourself, so that you'll remember these feelings next time you come here. Then note exactly what's happening at point A, your Activating event, just before each of

these feelings happens. Then look for B, your rational and
irrational Beliefs, about A. Rationally, you have preferences and
wishes, that unfortunate A's (or Adversities) preferably should not
occur; and these lead to healthy negative feelings at C, your
emotional and behavioral Consequences, such as sorrow, regret,
frustration, and disappointment. But we are particularly interested in your *un*healthy consequences at C–as I said before, your
really upset feelings. So bring me some of these ABC's–and you
can take one of our self-help report forms, down at the desk
downstairs, to remind you what they are and to help you remember them.

C: Down at the desk?

T: Yes, we always have free forms for you to take and fill out as
homework, during the week, down at the desk. Bring me in a few
filled out, and especially try to find your irrational Beliefs (iB's)–at
point B–your shoulds, oughts, and musts by which you disturb
yourself. But if you don't find them, just bring me in a few A's
and a few C's and I'll show you how to figure out your iB's at
point B.

C: Is that all I have to do during the week?

T: Yes, that's all for this week. Except that we gave you a group of
pamphlets, so start reading these REBT pamphlets. And, preferably, get a copy downstairs of two of my paperback books: *A New
Guide to Rational Living* and *How to Stubbornly Refuse to Make
Yourself Miserable About Anything–Yes, Anything!* And start reading
those books. You don't have to finish all the reading, but let's see
if you can at least start it. The more REBT reading you do and
the more you listen to some of our tape cassettes, the quicker and
better you will see how to help yourself.[2]

C: Oh, I like reading. I find it helpful.

T: Fine. And, as noted in the instructions for therapy, which we
gave you in that envelope, we find it desirable for our clients to
record their sessions and then listen to them later. So next time
you come, if you wish to do so, you can bring a blank cassette, or
get one at the desk downstairs, and record your session and listen
to it a few times in between sessions. I think you'll find that
helpful. Anything else you want to bring up in the last minute or
two of this session?

C: No, I don't think so. I got quite a lot out of the session. I've had
some therapy before, but nothing like this! Thank you for

helping me. I got a lot.

T: Fine. I am glad you enjoyed the session. Just make another appointment downstairs to see me in a week or so, and I'll look forward to continuing to see you.

C: Fine. Thank you.

Notice how I go over some of the essentials of REBT, and particularly the point that the client upsets himself with his musts and then makes himself anxious about his anxiety with more musts, several times. I directly, forcefully, and briefly keep repeating this message, especially during the first session, to achieve several results: (1) explain some of the basic principles of human disturbance and of REBT to the client; (2) try to get quickly to a central problem, so that he or she can see right away how it is largely created by himself or herself and that he or she can immediately start to do something about it; (3) try to get the idea over that the client can quickly start changing himself or herself, but that to do so permanently will require a longer period of time; (4) try to show the client that the REBT sessions themselves can be relatively brief (usually, half-hour sessions) and infrequent (from 5 to 30 sessions for most clients), but only because the client does most of the therapeutic work himself, in between sessions; and (5) give bibliotherapy homework as well as some kind of cognitive, emotive, or behavioral homework.

The second session with this client took place one week after the first session and showed fair progress:

He said, "I feel okay, this week only a couple of times have I had some anxiety."

On a fairly crowded train, he forced himself to read my book *How to Stubbornly Refuse to Make Yourself Miserable About Anything—Yes, Anything* and distracted himself from his feelings of panic.

He kept strongly convincing himself that he was creating his panic and that he was not going to have a heart attack and felt uncomfortable rather than anxious.

In his office, he began to tell himself that he did not have to do everything fast or perfectly well. "And two minutes later, I feel like I can face myself. My anxiety—it is gone..."

"Last week when I got to the train, I started getting anxiety. This week
      I got anxious only one time. I got to the train and I said to
      myself, 'There's nothing to worry about. Nothing will happen.
      So you're creating your anxiety, just like you put wood on a fire.
      So you can go the other way.' So five minutes later I forgot about
      it and I didn't have that problem."

"Before last session, I didn't understand what was going on with me. Now I know my anxiety is a problem that I am creating. I can live with that, and one of these days, I won't have that problem. I think I can really convince myself. I don't feel the way that I felt a week ago. Then I was getting crazy. Now I know that anxiety doesn't matter that much. Any time I can take the train and maybe the first couple of minutes I have to deal with myself, and I say, 'You don't have to feel panicked. You can feel the other way.'"

For the first time, he confessed to some of his friends that he had an anxiety problem and was seeking help. "I no longer care that much what they think. Because I don't think I'm that crazy. I just have a minor problem. You don't have to be crazy to see a psychologist."

He kept repeating that he was creating his anxiety himself and that he didn't have to do so.

Two weeks later, during the third session, the client showed that he had several real breakthroughs as he kept working on his anxiety and kept reading the REBT materials. Here are some excerpts from the session:

"I'm feeling better. Whatever I'm feeling, like anxiety, is not it. I'm creating it. Whatever I'm feeling I can make it go away in a couple of minutes and if I get upset about my anxiety, I can talk to myself about that."

"When I get to the train I'm not that anxious. Like this morning, I completely forgot about it until I was on the train. Then I remembered and started saying to myself, 'It's nice to be feeling the way I'm feeling now.' It doesn't bother me anymore. And last week, a couple of days, I'm going home, I fall asleep on a train, and I wake up at my station and I said to myself, 'Whatever happened a couple of months ago is gone.'"

"And even in my work I don't feel anxious. I am working better than before without feeling that, uh, anxiety to make everything fast and quick. I can pace myself better than before. Another thing I learned to do: not to upset myself about the others in my office who act badly. If I get upset, they're going to act the same way."

"Before, I thought my anxiety meant something was physically wrong. Now I see that I'm creating it. It's not that I am sick....I used to

say, while going to the train, 'I'm sure I'm gonna get sick.' Now I
see that I'm creating that sick feeling. Two or three minutes later,
I am okay. Two weeks ago it would have taken me 15 minutes to
be less anxious. Now it takes me two or three minutes and there
are days when I don't feel panic."

"The other day I got to the train when it was almost full, and I couldn't
sit down and read and distract myself. But it didn't bother me
and I didn't wait for another train as I used to have to do. I can
talk to myself and say, 'Look, whatever anxiety you feel, you
created it. And you can uncreate it.'"

"Your book [*How To Stubbornly Refuse To Make Yourself Miserable About
Anything–Yes, Anything!*] is not only helping me with this anxiety
problem, but it's also helping me to deal with other people. If
they didn't do things the way I wanted it, I just would get upset.
Now if they don't, it's not like before, I don't upset myself. I can
deal with people better and I can deal with myself–not making
myself crazy. I used to get angry with them and feel enraged for a
long time. But now I tell myself, 'If I'm getting angry it's because
I'm creating the anger.' It doesn't pay for me to do that and feel
like that."

"I still try to do things better in the office but when I think that I have
to do it perfectly, I say to myself, 'Please! That is impossible. I
will do the best I can–and that's it.'"

"Sexually, I am better now than before. Less anxious. I was having
problems with erections because I started thinking, 'I won't have
it. Suppose I don't have it!' Now, I'm doing what you say in the
book: 'Maybe I can make it, maybe I cannot. Okay, if I don't,
tomorrow maybe it will be better.' And things like that, I am
enjoying it more. The whole thing is changing because if I start
thinking, 'I can't,' then I won't be able to. But if I don't think like
that, then it will be fine. That's what's helping me a great deal."

"Since I was feeling better this two weeks, I thought that I don't have
to be here every week. I would like every two weeks or every
three weeks, to see how I can do by myself. I know that I am not
100% better, but I feel I am getting there."

"I think the book helped me a lot. The way you described in it how to
overcome your anxiety–to deal with just about any problem you
have. The chapters that I read, I read them intensely, like trying
to absorb a hundred percent of it, you know. It's not that I have
the will to practice everything I read over a month. But I was

feeling so awful that I said that the only way for me to get better is to really confront my problem and then to follow through on it in whatever way I can."

[Therapist asks, "Anything else that's been bothering you at all recently?"] "Not really. What was bothering me was worrying about when I get to the train. And then I was feeling anxious in the office. But now with that and in the home and in the office, I said I couldn't control my anxiety and that I had to do so. But now I think that it's better to see what the problem is and use my thinking to make the problem go. Work it out, no matter how bad it is."

Follow-Up

I expected to have several more sessions with Ted, because I usually see people like him from five to 10 times, but actually this was his last individual therapy session. He and his wife started to attend my regular Friday night workshops at the Institute for Rational-Emotive Therapy in New York, where I interview volunteer clients each week before an audience of 100 or more people. After working with each client for about a half hour, I throw the discussion over to the audience and let them question and advise the volunteer as I supervise. Ted has participated in these workshops quite actively, as well as in several of our four-hour workshops for the public, such as one on low frustration tolerance. He has continued to read REBT books and to listen to Institute cassettes, especially my tapes *Solving Emotional Problems* and *Unconditionally Accepting Yourself and Others.*[3]

I have spoken with him several times and also with his wife, Myra, who agrees that he is continuing the gains that he indicated during his third session and that he is making still further progress. He has almost completely lost his panic about trains and has also begun to take plane trips, which he was previously afraid to do but had never discussed in his sessions with me. He is rarely anxious or angry at the office, and sex with his wife is "by far the best I ever had." His wife corroborates his progress.

At the present time, five years have passed since I saw Ted for therapy, and he continues to hold his ground. I expect that I may see him occasionally again, as new crises arise in his life, but that he will generally hold the gains he has already made. My guesses about why he was able to make such good gains in the course of three half-hour sessions in one month's time include these: (1) He was a classic neurotic, unlike many personality disorders I often see. On the Millon Clinical Multiaxial Inventory II, his only really high score was on the anxiety scale, with his compulsive and somataform scores somewhat above average. (2) He was highly motivated to reduce his anxiety and from the first session worked hard to do so. (3) He was competent and hardworking in his business and social life. (4) He took very well to my highly active-directive REBT approach and kept echoing my insistence that he was responsible for his own anxiety and anger and that he had the ability to work at reducing these disturbances. (5) He read and listened to our REBT self-help materials most intently and frequently used my book, *How to Stubbornly Refuse to Make Yourself Miserable About Anything—Yes, Anything!*. (6) After therapy ended, he continued assiduously to attend REBT workshops and to work with REBT materials.

SOME QUESTIONS ABOUT THE TREATMENT

Q: It appears that the client was a man who liked the therapist from the beginning. His personality seems to fit well with the REBT model. He was enthusiastic and willing to comply with your requests. What if he had been resistant, difficult, and ornery and had a significant personality disorder? How would your method and technique vary?

A: In that situation, I probably would have tried to show him that he was going to have a difficult time changing and that therefore he had better work harder and longer at doing so. I would probably let him know that he very likely had a strong innate tendency to be the way he was, exacerbated by his life experiences and reinforced by his own creating and practicing dysfunctional thoughts, feelings, and behaviors, and that only very hard work and practice—yes, work and practice—to overcome this tendency would probably be effective in his case. I would stress the pain he was in and how disadvantageous it would be for him to prolong it, and I would vigorously show him that, in all probability, he could significantly change if he *chose* to keep working at doing so. I would try to get him to learn REBT and to keep using it to help others, and would encourage him to spend considerable time helping himself be much less miserable than he presently was.

Q: What do you usually tell a client about the course and prognosis of treatment? When and how do you determine and discuss length of treatment? How do you motivate the client?

A: I usually tell clients that the treatment will be relatively brief–a matter of months rather than years–*if* they work very hard in between sessions at using the REBT methods we go over during the sessions. I motivate them in several ways: (1) by emphasizing their present emotional-behavioral misery and showing them that they definitely can reduce or eliminate it; (2) by strongly showing them that they largely create their *own* disturbances and that, therefore, they can almost alleviate or undo them; and (3) by pointing them toward the greater pleasures they can have if they work at reducing their disturbances *and* at enhancing hedonic pursuits and at personal self-actualization.

Q: There was a flexible use of time in this case. You advised having the next appointment in a week or so, but later the client indicated spacing out sessions. What guides about length of sessions, frequency, and spacing do you use?

A: I usually suggest fewer or more-spaced-out sessions after several weeks of therapy, providing that the client is improving. If clients want fewer sessions than I suggest, I say, "Let's try it your way and see how it goes. If you will work hard in between sessions, and keep reading our material and doing your homework, you will probably do a good therapeutic job on yourself and therefore require fewer sessions. If not, we'll soon see a lack of progress and you can arrange for more sessions again."

Q: Did you screen for alcohol abuse? Suppose the client were alcoholic–would you approach the problem in the same way?

A: Yes, I asked the client about alcohol abuse and he indicated that he only did mild social drinking, and I accepted this answer. If there had been alcoholic abuse, I would have worked on his problem drinking from the start, ferreted out the dysfunctional Beliefs leading to it–including his self-denigration, his low frustration tolerance, and his squelching of other emotional problems by his drinking–and I would have helped him to stop denigrating himself for his drinking, to work on his low frustration tolerance, and to use a number of cognitive, emotive, and behavioral techniques that are commonly used in REBT with problem drinkers.[4]

Q: If the client had come to you on medication for panic disorder, how would you proceed?

A: I would proceed in much the same way that I did in this case, but I would talk to his psychopharmacologist to see what medication he was taking, what dosage, how long he was expected to take it, what side effects he might have, etc. Depending on the information received, I might modify some of my treatment methods and the homework assignments worked out with the client.

Q: How would you focus with a client whose problems were more vague or unclear?

A: I would get him to clarify his problems by asking him questions about when and where the problems occurred, why they troubled him, what his goal was in regard to them, what he was thinking when the problems occurred, etc. Usually, after a few sessions, I would wind up with a pretty clear idea of his central problems and I would almost always discover at least one specific issue that was clear to both of us and that he or she wanted to work at.

Q: In the case presented, if the client had not responded well, what are some of the issues you might consider? How might you change your approach?

A: I would consider: (1) how well the client understood the ABC's of REBT and knew what he could do about disputing his dysfunctional B's; (2) how he was actually working to use the ABC's of REBT and how he was doing the homework we had agreed on; (3) what he was specifically telling himself when he did not do his cognitive, emotive, and behavioral homework; (4) whether he was really willing to change and to work at changing himself; (5) what, if anything, were his "neurotic" gains from remaining the way he was and from not changing; (6) what unexpressed problems he had that may have been blocking him from working on the expressed ones; and (7) how he was reacting to me, and if his positive or negative attitudes toward me were interfering with his working at changing himself.

Q: If the client said that he saw what he was telling himself, was doing REBT disputing of his irrational and dysfunctional Beliefs, and was still not changing, what would you then do?

A: I would tell him that it was quite probable that he was seeing his dysfunctional Beliefs and disputing them, but mainly doing this lightly, unvigorously, and not often enough. I would show him, if

I had not already done so, that practically all disturbed people have *two* simultaneous sets of beliefs: one rational and self-helping and the other irrational and self-defeating, and that one is usually held lightly and mildly and the other is held strongly and powerfully. In his case, the irrational beliefs were probably *still* being held much more powerfully than the rational beliefs, and therefore he had better see that this was so and keep vigorously and powerfully disputing the former and replacing them with the latter. At the same time, he had better work very strongly to change his feelings and work powerfully and repetitively to change his behaviors, so that these, also, which have been inter-acting with his crooked thinking, can now significantly help him change that thinking. I would show him that REBT always has highly emotive and behavioral components, not merely impor-tant cognitive elements, and that he had therefore better keep working and practicing—yes, keep working and practicing—the REBT methods and do so very forcefully and committedly until he truly believed, felt, and acted on the rational philosophies that he was now (at times) presumably telling himself.

Q: How did you become a brief therapist?

A: I became a brief therapist in the early 1940's, when I started to do a great deal of sex and marital therapy and found that most clients wanted to come for only a few sessions and had no inten-tion of making basic personality changes. To help some of them who wanted depth therapy, I was analyzed, was trained as an analyst, and practiced psychoanalysis for six years. Doing so, I found that psychoanalysis intensively goes into every irrelevancy under the sun and, alas, misses just about all the philosophic relevancies by which people mainly disturb themselves. Like many therapies that stem from it, psychoanalysis is obsessed with people's past history, which influenced their goals and values but did not really *make them* disturbed. It largely ignores how they mainly *constructed* their dysfunctional thoughts, feelings, and behaviors and what they are now actively doing to keep con-structing them. So, in 1955, I founded and started using Rational Emotive Behavior Therapy and specifically designed it to be an efficient and brief therapy for most neurotic clients, although it is often more prolonged and intensive for individuals with personal-ity disorders, psychosis, and other serious disturbances.[5]

NOTES TO CHAPTER 15

1. Bernard, 1991, 1993; Dryden, 1994a, 1994b, 1995; Dryden & Neenan, 1995; Ellis, 1957a, 1962, 1965b, 1971, 1973c, 1977a, 1979c, 1985b, 1988a, 1994e; Ellis & Grieger, 1977, 1986; Walen, DiGiuseppe, & Dryden, 1992; Woods, 1990.
2. Ellis, 1988a; Ellis & Harper, 1975.
3. Ellis, 1982, 1988a.
4. Ellis, McInerney, et al., 1988; Ellis & Velten, 1992.
5. DiMattia & Lega, 1990; Dryden & Ellis, 1989, 1990; Ellis, 1990d; Palmer, Dryden, et al., 1995; Warga, 1988; Weinrach, 1980; Wiener, 1988; Yankura & Dryden, 1990.

16

Some Conclusions

As you have probably seen from reading this book thus far, you and I are indeed tackling a complicated subject. The question of how you (or anyone) can do better, deeper, and more enduring brief therapy is quite complex, has no final or absolute answers, and includes many controversial issues. The views I present here are somewhat different from those that I have previously held, are far from being written in stone, and may well change as I keep practicing and reading about psychotherapy. So please consider them carefully—but not devoutly!

As I start writing this final chapter, I see that I have omitted some important aspects of therapy that I had better deal with before I finish up. So let me deal with them in this chapter and show how they relate to better and more "elegant" brief therapy.

HELPING CLIENTS CHANGE THEIR THINKING
AND THEIR LANGUAGE HABITS

As I have tried to indicate in the previous section, you, as a therapist, can significantly limit yourself and the help that you give to your clients if you take an either/or rather than an and/also attitude toward using psychotherapy. If you are a devout psychoanalyst or a pious Reichian therapist, you will tend to use only the rigid theory and the limited practices that your school swears by. You will then have a hard time fitting all your clients into the Procrustean bed of your procedures and you will be particularly limited with the unusual clients who somehow won't, or even cannot, follow your prescriptions. Therefore, it is probably best to pick one central theory and practice—because pure eclecticism has its own hazards, and rarely seems to exist—but also leave your door open for other ideas and procedures that are not quite encompassed by your monolithic orientation. As noted in Chapter 12, you can use several of the methods of solution focused therapy—but you had also better use some of the "elegant" methods of REBT as well. By the same token, you can generally use REBT—especially because it includes a large variety of cognitive, emotive, and behavioral methods—but you can also at times include with it some of the specific theories and practices of solution-focused therapy. As Alfred Korzybski and his general semantics followers have shown for over 60 years, either/or thinking (sometimes called Aristotelian thinking) frequently gets you into needless difficulties, while and/also (or nonAristotelian thinking) is more useful.[1]

For this reason, REBT has always followed some of the principles of general semantics and of other forms of lateral (rather than rigid) thinking and has included these in its practice. Thus, as I briefly indicate in the early chapters of this book, you can help your clients to watch their usual forms of language and to change these forms when they encourage emotional disturbance.

If, for example, your clients keep telling themselves, "Now that I have failed several times to achieve a close relationship, I will *never* be able to do so and will *always* fail in this important respect," they are unrealistically overgeneralizing and may create a self-fulfilling prophecy. If, on the other hand, they tell themselves, "Because I have failed several times to achieve a close relationship that I want to achieve, I find this difficult to do and I'd better seriously think about changing my actions in regard to relating," they then may avoid overgeneralizing and see that they are hardly the basket cases that they have wrongly concluded they are.

The important point is that if you want to help your clients to achieve a more permanent, deeper kind of personality change, one way to do this is to show them how to become much more conscious of their thought and language difficulties. Show them, in particular, that probably the whole human race, and particularly people in some cultures like our own, often think crookedly, incorporate their disordered thinking into their language system, and then have this language system contribute to their thinking more destructively.

Why is this so? Because, as Korzybski and other psycholinguistic authorities have indicated, humans easily and naturally do think poorly as well as sensibly, and their language systems both help and limit their thinking. What we think is never perfectly represented in the language we use to describe our thinking; and although our verbalizations (as well as our other forms of communication) greatly help us in our artistic, scientific, and other creativity, they have distinct limitations and can also be hindrances.

It is important, therefore, that you show your clients some of the main limitations of their thoughts and verbalizations and how to overcome these limitations. You had better especially show them (and yourself) that we'd better watch and suspect the ways in which we talk to ourselves and to others. As Korzybski said, "The map is not the territory." The language maps that we commonly use do not exactly describe the full territory of our thinking, feeling, and behaving.

If you say to someone, for example, "I really love you and care for you," you are probably meaningfully revealing some of your feelings for this person. But your using a metaphor, a poem, a novel, a drama, a drawing, a musical composition, or some other form of communication may express what you feel more than the mere verbal statement that you make. Moreover, you often may have such unique feelings of love for this person that there is actually no way in which you can accurately describe them. So you–and the recipient of your love–may have to be satisfied with only a linguistic approximation of your feelings.

My main point here is this: If your clients are to make a profound philosophical-behavioral change and make themselves less disturbable for the rest of their lives, they had better clearly see how they (and the rest of us humans) often create defeating overgeneralizations and incorporate them into our language. They had better become prophylactically cautious in this regard, suspect that they and others are frequently overgeneralizing and suspect that their tendency to do this is part of the English language and of other languages.

David Bourland, Jr., following Alfred Korzybski, has pointed this out by showing that our use of the verb *to be* encourages "unsane" thinking and that we had better, instead, use E-prime, an English-language system that largely eliminates this usage.[2] Thus, if you say, "I *am* doing badly," you imply not only that right now you are acting poorly, but also that in the future you will keep doing so. You can also easily jump from, "I presently am performing badly," to "Therefore I always will do so and consequently I am a bad person." Then, by calling yourself a "bad person," you imply that you can never change and will always have to act badly for the rest of your life. But if you say, "I *do* badly at this moment," you stop overgeneralizing and create less "emotional" trouble for yourself.

As Bourland and other advocates of the use of E-prime have acknowledged, getting rid of *to be* will never completely make you and your clients think clearly, sensibly, and undisturbedly–though it may well help. Also, if you completely get rid of your overgeneralizing you may be in danger of giving up generalizing and abstracting–which are often great assets to human communication and self-communication. So don't go from one extreme to the other and throw out the baby with the bathwater!

Anyway, try to become aware of your own, your clients', and just about everyone's human tendency to overgeneralize and to use imprecise forms of language. Caution your clients to watch out for this tendency and teach them to minimize it. This, perhaps, is one of the best ways of helping them to achieve an "elegant" change in their thinking and behaving.

As I was finishing this book, I read Kevin Everett FitzMaurice's leaflet, "Introducing the 12 Steps of Emotional Disturbance," which he uses to show his clients his form of Ego Uprooting Therapy (EUT). Kevin has for a number of years been one of the leading therapists to apply some of the main theories of Alfred Korzybski's General Semantics to psychotherapy and counseling. His booklet, "Self-Concept: The Enemy Within," and several of his other writings are outstanding in this respect.

Let me summarize, in my own words, the gist of Kevin's important concept of reifying, which he says that you and your clients do to disturb yourselves, and which you can teach your clients to notice and to change. You can say to the clients something like this:

> You *reify* some of your thoughts (perceptions or beliefs) about a "bad" Activating Event (A). You reify your thoughts by *labeling* or *identifying* the event as a *negative thing.* Your reifying or identifying your *thought* as a *thing*–and thereby manufacturing a *thought-thing*–is based on your mistaken Belief (B) that if you strongly *know* something it has an *independent existence*, it exists in its own right as a *real thing.* You take your thought, "I *know* this is so," and you then insist, "Therefore, it *is* so–the *thing* or *event* I am *thinking* about really *is* exactly what I *think* it is." To paraphrase Descartes, "I think it exists, therefore it does."

Your thought, as Alfred Korzybski showed in *Science and Sanity*, is a *representational* system that describes–and partly *creates*–"what is." Because it is only a thought, it is never *equal to*, can never *become* what is. Your *description* can never become what you describe. But you are "sure" that it does become just that!

You tell yourself, for example: "I *think* (or *see*) what happened was bad," and you falsely make it become, "Because I *think* what happened was bad, it *was* bad." And you take your thought, "I *view* what I did as bad," and you "make" it become "I *absolutely know* it was bad, and therefore it *absolutely was* bad." Again, when you note, "I *think* what they did was bad," you cannot legitimately (logically and empirically) prove, "Therefore, I *completely know* it was bad and therefore it *absolutely was* bad." But you *convince* yourself of this "truth"!

Because, however, you are a natural reifier (that is, crooked thinker and user of overgeneralized language), you often (not always) take your thoughts and inaccurately make them into thought-things. Then you devoutly *Believe* (B in the ABC's of REBT) that your thought-things are *real* things or events–and get yourself into more emotional trouble!

If you will use material like this to show your clients how important their conception of themselves is and how their easy and natural creation of what Kevin FitzMaurice calls thought-things, and what I call overgeneralized, crooked thinking, gives them severe ego–and other!–problems, you may help some of them to arrive at the "elegant" solutions to their emotional disturbances that I keep advocating in this book.

RELAPSE PREVENTION

REBT, like Cognitive Behavior Therapy (CBT), includes the concept and the work of relapse prevention–particularly in the area of addiction. As I and my collaborators have shown in our writings on dealing with people who have serious problems with alcohol, substance abuse, overeating, and other compulsive disorders, addicts (and people afflicted with obsessive-compulsive disorder) not only have a very difficult time making themselves nonaddicted but also, once they accomplish this, they frequently fall back to their overindulgence. Even after they have been "cured" for a number of years, a surprisingly large number of them take one drink and then finish the bottle, one piece of candy and polish off the whole box, go on one spending spree and then run up a huge credit card bill.[3]

Why? For various reasons. Some of them overcome their addiction by laboring very hard to do so—but then stop striving that hard, or become bored with this work, and addict themselves again. Some of them have biologically impelled cravings for different substances or behaviors and have to fight their addictive tendencies all their lives. Some of them use their addiction to sedate their emotional disturbances—for example, they resort to too much alcohol in order to overcome their social shyness or their panic about succeeding at their profession.

In any event, because relapses are frequent, and often enormously destructive, REBT and CBT have developed a series of relapse prevention methods, which I have outlined elsewhere, and which other cognitive-behavior therapists such as Alan Marlatt and J. R. Gordon have described in detail. These largely consist of showing clients, when they are about to relapse or have actually done so, how to look at their self-statements and their irrational Beliefs about giving in to their urges, helping them actively and forcefully Dispute these iB's, and encouraging them to arrive at an Effective New Philosophy that will not exactly guarantee their never relapsing again but will greatly diminish the chances of their doing so.[4]

Along with these potent cognitive methods of helping addicts to cut short their tendencies to relapse, practitioners of REBT and CBT also provide them with a number of emotive-evocative and behavioral methods of staving off backslides. Emotively, for example, they can devise a set of rational coping statements and very vigorously and repetitively recite them to help them refrain from indulging. Or they can put some of their irrational Beliefs about weakening again on a cassette tape recorder, powerfully refute these Beliefs, and have their therapist, group members, or friends listen to their Disputation to see how strong it is. Behaviorally, they can use stimulus control, so that they stay away from settings where they may be tempted to indulge again, and they can avoid "friends" who encourage them to make themselves readdicted. Or they can use reinforcements and penalties to combat their tendencies to revert to destructive habits.

Addicts, of course, are hardly the only individuals who return to previously unhealthy behaviors after they have once overcome them. Disturbed people who are not addicted often do so, too. Thus, people give up their phobias about planes, trains, or bridges, and then afflict themselves with them again. Or they stop depressing themselves about the end of one love affair and then debase themselves all over again when another love relationship breaks up. Just about any emotional and behavioral hang-up can be temporarily relieved—and then brought back in full or even greater force.

REBT, consequently, uses relapse prevention both with addicts and with nonaddicts who go back to dysfunctional thoughts, feelings, and behaviors. As noted above, it assumes that when people reinstitute their unhealthy actions they are once again reverting to dysfunctional Beliefs. It assumes, too, that these Beliefs almost always include absolutistic shoulds, oughts, and musts. So, if you use REBT, you can teach your clients that when they relapse, or when they are even seriously thinking about backsliding, they are predisposed to give themselves rationalizations, excuses, and other irrationalities. Such as: "I *must* have the joy I once had by drinking and *can't stand* the horrible pains of abstinence!" "I *deserve* a smoke. If I smoke a few cigarettes, I'll easily go back to giving them up again." "Staying on my diet forever is much *too hard.* I can't be happy *at all* if I keep on a healthy food regimen!" "I'm *no good* for taking a single drink again, so how can a *rotten person* like me keep refraining from drinking?"

You can show your relapsing and relapsed clients that if they devoutly believe these demands, their awfulizing, their I-can't-stand-it-itis, and their needless self-deprecation, they will keep reindulging. But, instead, they *can* find these irrationalities quickly and *can* minimize them. Just because they once surrendered them and know how to do this, they can definitely do so again. In addition, they can use several other REBT emotive and behavioral techniques to interrupt and to change their irrational Beliefs and, once again, to make themselves considerably less anxious, depressed, enraged, self-hating, and self-pitying. So, because you have presumably helped them significantly in these respects before and because they have worked with you in regard to decreasing their disturbances, they can do so again and can stop their reversion in its tracks.[5]

Even better than this, however, is REBT's concept of deep, intensive, and "elegant" personality change. Because if you keep working with your clients along the lines that are described in this book, even when you help them to become less dysfunctional, you will not stop there but will go on to urge them to make more thoroughgoing changes. Suppose, for example, that one of your clients, Deborah, is very angry at her teenage son, Tim, because he takes all the love and the help she gives him—which she is convinced is enormous—and he acts most inconsiderately to her, keeps getting into trouble for which she chooses to bail him out, and demands that she give him more money and other things that he wants, but he refuses to do anything to help get them himself. In these respects, Tim is also radically "worse" than his fraternal twin brother, Tom, who is kind, considerate, and hardworking.

In a case like this, you show Deborah that her son may well be "wrong" and "unfair," but that his behavior is not really *making her* incensed and is not *causing her* to have an ulcer. Instead, her rage largely stems from her grandiose demands that Tim *absolutely must not* act the "horrible" way that he does, from her insistence that therefore he is "a rotten son and a despicable person," and from her viewing herself as "an incompetent mother" for raising such a "bad child." You also show her that she obviously did not raise his twin brother Tom that badly, and there well could be biological aspects of Tim's behaving the way he does, that she is hardly totally responsible for his poor behavior, and that even if she were responsible she would be incompetent at some aspects of mothering but she would hardly be "an incompetent mother" or a "rotten person" for having some incompetence in the mothering area.

If you succeed in these respects with Deborah and you encourage her to do various REBT emotive and behavioral exercises to facilitate and add to her cognitive changes, she will very likely wind up, after perhaps only a few sessions, still sorry and displeased about Tim's "bad" behaviors but not enraged at him or at herself. So you and your therapy will have considerably helped her. However, if you use REBT still further, to encourage her to make a more "elegant" and permanent change in her disturbed thoughts and feelings, you will also tend to show Deborah several more aspects of social reality, such as these:

1. Tim is hardly the only teenager who behaves as badly as he does, in spite of her presumably treating him exceptionally well and trying to train him to be more responsible, considerate, and hardworking. Many other sons, somewhat like him, often act badly, for a variety of biological, environmental, and self-created reasons.

2. Not only does Deborah upset herself about her son's actions—seeing these actions themselves as the "real" or "sole" source of her upsetness—but she also has a biosocial tendency to do the same thing in a number of other ways. She easily can enrage herself, for example, about the "bad" behaviors of her husband, her other children, her relatives, her friends, and just about anyone else. She had better, therefore, acknowledge fully that she, as a "normal" member of the human race, has this strong tendency and that she frequently indulges in it—to her own disadvantage

and also to the disadvantage of her relationships with her son and with other people whom she needlessly enrages herself about.

3. Fortunately, again because of her humanity, she has an innate constructivist proclivity that she can just about always use to minimize her rage and to make herself less like her son (and other inconsiderate individuals). She definitely can control her own emotional destiny and get herself to the point where, first, she unenrages herself whenever she feels furious at her son (and at others); and, second, brings herself to the point where she makes herself less generally enrageable, less prone to fly off the handle when he (and others) act "badly."

4. She can do this by giving up her rage every time she feels it engulf her and by reminding herself over and over again that her son (and other people) will often do what they do, that right now that is their nature, that there is no reason why they *must* be different, that she can *stand* their unfortunate doings, and that they are fallible individuals rather than "utterly rotten people."

You can see, then, that while you first work with Deborah to help her overcome her rage at Tim and her self-downing about this rage, you can also work with her general attitudes, especially her self-defeating attitudes, about herself and others. You can show her how, on the whole and in many different kinds of "bad" conditions, she can stubbornly refuse to upset herself about practically anything. She will then get close to reaching what I call the "elegant" solution to her emotional and mental problems.

The closer your clients get to achieving this solution—and most of them, of course, are not likely to fully achieve it—the fewer relapses they will tend to have and the less disruptive their relapses will be when they do have them. Also, what I call their achieving the "elegant" solution includes, when they fall back again to their former disturbances, or when they construct new neurotic conditions, their remembering what they previously did to make themselves less neurotic and their repeating these same steps to minimize their new disturbances.

Thus, if Deborah gives up her rage at her son, Tim, while seeing you for therapy, and if she subsequently makes herself furious at him again (or at someone else who, in her eyes, acts very "badly"), she can, if you helped her to reach an "elegant" level of minimal disturbance, go back over the procedures that she had used while seeing you and use them once again to give up her rage. If, for example, Tim begins to behave worse than ever and if she makes herself furious at him once more, she can refer to her basic Effective New Philosophy and tell herself something like, "Well, there he goes again. He wasn't so bad for awhile but now he has gone back to his execrable ways. But since I feel so enraged at him once more and since I am foolishly stirring up my own gut and getting nothing from him but returned hostility and additional poor behavior, I'd better fully admit that I am upsetting myself and that *he's* not really making me as furious as I now feel. Now why don't I go back to really accepting that it is his nature to often act in this abominable way, that he has a perfect right to be just as bollixed up as he is, that I can't very well change him, and that that's just too bad. But he doesn't *have to* act differently. I *can* stand it if he continues to behave poorly. It's not *awful*. And I can still lead a happy life in spite of his rotten antics. Tough! But, again, that's the way he behaves right now and I'd better not play God and *demand* that he *absolutely must not be* the way he indubitably, right now, is."

Doing this, your client Deborah, if she really has reached a state of less disturbability, will almost automatically do her own relapse prevention if she falls back to her former level of disturbance. As I noted above, she probably rarely will seriously retrogress to her old state of fury about Tim. But on those occasions when she actually does revert, she will to some extent replay her therapeutic tapes, as it were, and bring herself back to a state of relative healthfulness.

Let me repeat: If you help any of your clients to achieve better, deeper, more enduring, and more "elegant" solutions to their cognitive-emotional-behavioral difficulties, you will provide them with a built-in facility for using relapse prevention. When they fall back to their old disturbances, they may benefit from a few additional sessions with you, so you can then remind them of the best REBT methods they can use to unupset themselves again. But if they reach an "elegant" solution they will require only a few of these reminders and will themselves, without much help from you or anyone else, be able to calm themselves down and deal effectively with their returned neurotic symptoms.

Deborah, actually, was one of my clients who was exceptionally enraged at her son, Tim, for his "stupid," "irresponsible," "utterly goofing" behaviors and who came within a hair of throwing him out in the snow during a winter storm, of having a fist fight with her husband about his not supporting her against Tim, and of never speaking to Tim again in her whole life. Once I helped her make herself much less angry with her son, though highly displeased with much of what he did, she kept something of a distance between them, but practically never lost her temper with him.

When, a year after Deborah's 10 weeks of therapy with me ended, Tim irresponsibly smoked marijuana in his bedroom, started a fire in his bed, and almost burned down the family house, Deborah again made herself quite enraged at him. But, going back to the anti-anger methods she had effectively used when seeing me, she overcame her rage within a few days and wrote me a long letter saying how pleased she was that she did not have to return to therapy to deal with her feelings but had handled them successfully on her own. She and her husband then decided that Tim was not to live in their house anymore, because they couldn't trust him to refrain from being destructive there. So they sent him to boarding school. But Deborah maintained good intermittent relations with Tim, and even enjoyed being with him when they got together several times a year.

THE PREVENTIVE USE OF
RATIONAL EMOTIVE BEHAVIOR THERAPY AND
COGNITIVE BEHAVIOR THERAPY

As I have noted several times in this book, practically all humans are born and reared with strong tendencies to think, feel, and act neurotically and self-defeatingly. Many of them, also, have innate and acquired predispositions to be even more seriously disturbed and therefore to be steadily handicapped in their educational, vocational, social, and intimate relationships. Quite a few of them, at least in the United States, come for therapy; and even more of them join self-help, support, religious, and other groups, and use self-help materials to make it easier for them to cope with their disturbances.

All this kind of mental and emotional help, however, is not exactly the basic answer to the problem of human disturbability. The real answer, as I and others—such as George Albee and Nicholas Cummings—have noted for several decades, is prevention. How can we rear people—in our families, schools, civic organizations, and business and professional enterprises—so that they will not make themselves too disturbed, in the first place, and so that they will be able to deal effectively, in the second place, if they do upset themselves?[6]

The answer, I say, is psychoeducational. Even if I am right about humans being born easily disturbable, this does not mean they cannot largely overcome this tendency. For, once again, humans are innate constructivists. They have the ability and power to change themselves at times remarkably and radically, if not completely. They not only think but also think about their thinking and think about thinking about their thinking. If, therefore, REBT and CBT are correct in seeing that emotional disturbance has a strong cognitive element and that we can teach ourselves how to change our disturbed cognitions, we can be truly hopeful about helping ourselves, our children, and our great great grandchildren to become significantly less disturbable.

Perhaps this had better be the main goal of effective psychotherapy—not only remediation, but prophylaxis against incipient trouble. Preventive therapy, I contend, is particularly the province of REBT and CBT. Because it obviously had better be done on a mass scale, and taught to children, adolescents, and adults, from early childhood to old age. All of us, and not merely those of us who are so neurotic—and so sensible!—that we seek out some form of individual or group therapy, had better learn some of the main principles of REBT, especially its ABC's. We had better learn through our parents, teachers, community, and other organizations that we largely make ourselves panicked, depressed, enraged, self-hating, self-pitying, avoidant, and compulsive, and that we have the capacity not to do so, as well as the ability to undisturb ourselves after we have already made ourselves gratuitously suffer.

I say—and other preventionists say—that we can learn to use our constructive abilities to think, plot, plan, scheme, feel, and act more creatively and productively, and that we can do so by using mass media communication. Thus, in our regular school system we can teach nearly all the children the ABC's of human disturbance, how to Dispute their dysfunctional, irrational Beliefs, how to work on their disordered feelings, and how to change their self-sabotaging and socially destructive behaviors.

How can we set up our school system to do this kind of teaching? Mainly by teaching our teachers how to do it and by devising for them and their pupils abundant self-help materials. These materials, from toddler level up to postgraduate levels at schools, and from infancy to older ages outside of school, can be prepared and tested. They can consist of written materials, audiovisual aids, interactive television, computer programs, and any other feasible method of mass communication.

In the schools, these self-help ingredients would be used along with teachers. Outside of schools, they might be used with counselors, therapists, self-help groups, support groups, and by themselves. They would be constructed so that almost anyone could understand and benefit from them. They could include all kinds of homework exercises, and perhaps self-administered tests, so that their consumers could check on using them properly and see what results they derive from them.

This kind of a prevention program, through which millions or billions of people can discover how to stave off neuroticizing themselves and to work at unupsetting themselves in case they still fall into self-defeat, is perhaps even more important than using REBT and other therapies with already disturbed individuals. Not that the two efforts are mutually exclusive. Even with an excellent preventative program, many people will still behave neurotically. These people, in addition to gaining as much as they can gain from the preventive program, can also use psychologists, therapists, counselors, physicians, psychiatrists, remedial teachers, and other specialists to help them with various forms of psychotherapy.[7]

If the preventive program that I have just briefly outlined were actually established it would still leave room for several therapeutic purposes and goals. First, it would help people—ideally, billions of people—to make themselves less neurotic than practically all of them seem, to some extent, to make themselves today. Second, it would show them what to do to reduce their symptoms when they became neurotic or are afflicted with more serious emotional disorders, such as severe personality disorders, organic and neurological problems, and psychoses. Third, it would encourage disturbed individuals to be psychopharmacologically assessed, to see whether they could benefit from psychotropic medication and other kinds of medical procedures. Fourth, it would not only push people with disturbances to minimize their presenting symptoms (and their secondary symptoms about having this presenting symptoms) but also try to show them how to achieve the kinds of deep, intensive, "elegant" personality changes that are the main subject of this book. Fifth, it would show both disturbed and nondisturbed people how to actualize themselves and thereby to lead happier, more creative, more fulfilling lives than they would otherwise tend to have.

Pretty good—eh? I certainly think so. But let me again bring up a word of nonutopian caution. Unless we significantly change our genes and our basic biological structure—which some day we may actually be able to do—none of us is likely to wind up becoming or making ourselves thoroughly non-neurotic and non-self-defeating. All our lives we will keep having realistic practical problems to contend with—such as economic, educational, political, and social problems—and senselessly disturb ourselves about them. No rest for the weary! Therefore, using all the resources that we can derive from Rational Emotive Behavior Therapy and from other forms of effective therapy, let us do the best we can to minimize, but not as yet totally eradicate, neurosis and other emotional disorders. Yes, minimize, but not completely erase.

As counselors and therapists, you readers of this book can consider the points that I have been making, view them thoughtfully and skeptically, and decide which of them, if any, you will use in your own work. Think carefully about this. Then thoughtfully act!

A SOMEWHAT POSTMODERNIST FINAL WORD

If I were writing the conclusion to this book a number of years ago I would have repeated what I have said in most of my former writings: namely, that I am pretty well convinced that the hypotheses I have expressed about brief therapy, and especially about deep, intensive, and "elegant" brief therapy, are "true" or "valid." Why? Because I have tried them out literally hundreds of times with my own clients, have similarly tested the hypotheses of many other schools of psychotherapy, and fairly consistently find that my REBT ideas, when I carry them into practice, bring better results for most of my clients most of the time. Nonetheless, I always add, this is only my own observation and opinion; to check it out scientifically, a great deal of controlled experimentation had better be done to see if I, for all my strongly held convictions, am really on the right track.

I still essentially make this statement. But when I first originated REBT in January of 1955, I was a logical positivist and believed that somewhere in the universe "real" or "objective" truth existed and that it could fairly accurately, though not for all time under all conditions, be found by scientific observation and experimentation. Alas, I was largely wrong about this.

I now have abandoned logical positivism and am largely in Karl Popper's camp, which he calls critical realism. Both Popper and I are liberal, and not extreme or radical, postmodernists. In my own case, I believe that there is no absolute and incontestable truth and that what we call "reality" is largely social reality.[8] We humans see the world and ourselves through our own limited eyes, nervous system, and intrinsic prejudices. We temporarily "see" and are "sure" that things and human events are one way; then, a year, a decade, or a century later, we "see" them differently and change our strict views about them. This is because things themselves change, our information about them changes, and our perceiving and thinking apparatus (our "selves") change. Moreover, our environment distinctly affects and modifies us, and we, in our turn, distinctly affect and modify our environment. So, if we and the environment are in constant flux, and if we interactionally affect and will continue to affect each other, nothing seems to be absolutely "true" and "final." All things and all humans indeed change!

Our best theories and hypotheses, moreover, about ourselves and the world never seem to be thoroughly validatable—because we can always presumably find new data that may well lead to our modifying them or abandoning them. As Popper has shown, we can fairly easily invalidate or falsify many of our hypotheses, and we learn much by doing so. But we cannot substantiate any of them with certainty and can only support them with a high degree of probability.

This goes for psychological and psychotherapeutic theories as well as for other "scientific" theories. I once thought that rationality and reason were easily definable, especially because in REBT "rational" is taken as meaning (as John Dewey and other pragmatists would put it) "leading to good or beneficial results." I still largely endorse this view and hold that once you set up a goal or purpose—such as your being less panicked and less depressed—it is "rational," "sensible," or "effective" for you to do one thing (such as prefer to reach that goal) rather than to do another thing (such as demand and command that you absolutely must, under all conditions at all times, reach it). I still mainly believe this and have kept it as a fundamental tenet of REBT.

Mainly, but not dogmatically or absolutely! Because we can set up human goals and purposes only somewhat definitionally. We decide that it is "good" for us to stay alive, to be less panicked and depressed, and to live "more happily" than we are now living because—well, because we decide this. Someone else could argue against all our goals and strongly contend that they are "bad," "evil," "useless," and the like. How can we definitively prove this individual to be "wrong"? I doubt whether we can.

In spite of this uncertainty and indeterminacy, all is not in vain in the field of mental health. For once we decide on a goal—such as, again, minimal panic and minimal depression—we can to some extent determine whether that goal is reachable and what are the best (and the worst) ways to achieve it. Perhaps we cannot determine this under all conditions and for all time to come. But for the present, and under certain conditions, we can reasonably determine it.

The main point I am making as I conclude this book is this: If we assume (and not absolutistically aver) that "emotional health" is good and desirable and if we assume that "emotional disturbance" (including panic and depression) are less good and less desirable, we are back in the business of psychotherapy—yes, even if we cannot absolutely prove or validate our assumptions. So I and other therapists do this kind of assuming and set up principles and practices that can presumably "show" that one set of therapeutic methods usually, under most conditions, works "better" for our defined mental health goals than another set works.

This is where what we call "science" or the "scientific method" comes in. I (like practically all other psychotherapists) assume that conditions like "neurosis" or "emotional disturbance" are undesirable and that they accompany certain "dysfunctional" or "irrational" thoughts, feelings, and behaviors. I then adapt and devise methods of helping "disturbed" people to change their "maladjustments." My own observations and conclusions about how well my methods work may be interesting and valuable, but hardly too reliable—because I am a highly prejudiced observer and concluder. Therefore, I try to set up controlled experiments (as well as other methods) of testing my therapeutic hypotheses, to see how well they work out in actual practice.

The experiments that I (and other scientists) set up to falsify these hypotheses have all kinds of flaws and hazards; no special means of doing them has as yet been universally accepted and agreed upon as "good" or "perfect." Nor will it probably ever be. But as a psychologist and a scientist, I do the best I can, and try to help other experimenters do the best they can, to disprove my therapeutic hypotheses and to come up with fairly hard "data" and "facts" that will help me change or abandon them, and that will at times also give me a reasonably strong indication that they probably—but never certainly—are accurate or "true."

I don't take these "falsifying" and "partially confirming" experiments too seriously—for they are always prone to include errors and a good many different kinds of interpretations. But I take them with a moderate degree of seriousness, and I keep experimenting to come up with more definitive data that will again falsify them or at times seem to—yes, only seem to—support them.

So, this book this is what I again "scientifically" advocate. As a therapist, try out the brief methods of therapy that I have described in this book, both the "inelegant" and the "elegant" ones. Try to put aside many of your preconceptions and prejudices and see for yourself which of them "work" or "work better" for you and your clients. Also, if you have the time and energy, do some controlled or "scientific" studies to try to falsify and partially validate your clinical observations. The more such studies that you and other therapists and theorists do, the more substantial and/ or unsubstantial my brief therapy hypotheses will seem. Yes, seem! I, naturally, think that my observations and tentative conclusions about them will often (not always) nicely work out. But don't take my word for it. Be skeptical. Let us see what we shall see!

NOTES TO CHAPTER 16

1. Bourland & Johnston, 1991; DeBono, 1991; Dryden, 1987; Ellis, 1993e, 1994a; FitzMaurice, 1991; Hayakawa, 1965; Johnson, 1946; Johnston, Bourland, & Klein, 1994; Korzybski, 1933; Kwee, 1982; Watzlawick, 1978.
2. Bourland & Johnston, 1991; Johnston, Bourland, & Klein, 1994.
3. Ellis & DiGiuseppe, 1994; Ellis, McInerney, et al., 1988; Ellis & Velten, 1992; Tate, 1993 Trimpey, 1989.
4. Marlatt & Gordon, 1989; Wilson, 1992.
5. Ellis, 1965b, 1972, 1979, 1985b; Ellis & Abrams, 1994; Ellis & Velten, 1992; Ellis, Young, & Lockwood, 1987.
6. Albee, 1994; Cummings, 1994.
7. Ellis, 1994e.
8. Ellis, 1994e; Popper, 1985.

Bibliography

Note: The items preceded by an asterisk (*) in the following list of references are recommended for readers who want to obtain more details of Rational Emotive Behavior Therapy (REBT) and cognitive behavior therapy (CBT). Those preceded by two asterisks (**) are REBT and CBT self-help books and materials. Many of these materials are obtainable from the Institute for Rational-Emotive Therapy, 45 East 65th Street, New York, NY 10021-6593. The Institute's free catalogue and the materials it distributes may be ordered on weekdays by phone (212-535-0822) or by FAX (212-249-3582). The Institute will continue to make available these and other materials, and it will offer talks, workshops, and training sessions, as well as other presentations in the area of human growth and healthy living, and list these in its regular free catalogue. Some of the references listed here are not referred to in the text, especially a number of the self-help materials.

Abelson, R. P. (1963). Computer simulation of "hot" cognitions. In S. S. Tompkins & S. Messick (Eds.), *Computer simulation of personality.* New York: Wiley.

*Abrams, M., & Ellis, A. (1994). Rational emotive behavior therapy in the treatment of stress. *British Journal of Guidance and Counseling, 22,* 39–50.

Abrams, M., & Abrams, L. D. (1994). Depth therapy and cognitive psychology. Unpublished manuscript.

**Adler, A. (1927). *Understanding human nature.* Garden City, NY: Greenberg.

**Adler, A. (1958). *What life should mean to you.* New York: Capricorn.

*Adler, A. (1964a). *Social interest: A challenge to mankind.* New York: Capricorn.

*Adler, A. (1964b). *Superiority and social interest.* Ed. by H. L. Ansbacker & R. R. Ansbacker (Eds.). Evanston, IL: Northwestern University Press.

Ainslie, G. (1974). Specious reward: A behavioral theory of impulsiveness and impulse control. *Psychological Bulletin, 82,* 463–496.

Albee, G. (1994, February). Comments on prevention of disturbance. Assembly of the 21st Century, American Psychological Association, Washington, DC.

**Alberti, R. F., & Emmons, M. L. (1990). *Your perfect right,* 6th rev. ed. San Luis Obispo, CA: Impact.

Alcoholics Anonymous. (1976). *Alcoholics Anonymous: The big book,* 3rd ed. New York: Alcoholics Anonymous World Services.

Alexander, F., & French, T. M. (1946). *Psychoanalytic therapy.* New York: Ronald.

Alford, B. A., Richards, C. A., & Hanych, J. M. (1995). The causal status of private events. *Behavior Therapist, 18*(3), 57–58.

American Psychiatric Association. (1994). *Diagnostic and statistical manual of mental disorders,* 4th ed. Washington, DC: American Psychiatric Association.

*Ansbacher, H. L., & Ansbacher, R. (1956). *The individual psychology of Alfred Adler.* New York: Basic Books.

Arnold, M. (1960). *Emotion and personality,* 2 vols. New York: Columbia University.

Ascher, M. (Ed.) (1989). *Paradoxical procedures in psychotherapy.* New York: Guilford.

*Assaglioli, R. A. (1965). *Psychosynthesis.* New York: Hobbs-Dorman.

Assaglioli, R. (1973). *The act of will.* New York: Viking.

*Baisden, H. E. (1980). *Irrational beliefs: A construct validation study.* Unpublished doctoral dissertation. University of Minnesota, Minneapolis.

**Baldon, A., & Ellis, A. (1993). *RET problem solving workbook.* New York: Institute for Rational-Emotive Therapy.

Balint, M., & others (1972). *Focal psychotherapy.* London: Tavistock.

Bandler, R., & Grinder, J. (1978). *The structure of magic,* 2 vols. Palo Alto, CA: Science and Behavior Books.

*Bandura, A. (1986). *Social foundations of thought and action: A social cognitive theory.* Englewood Cliffs, NJ: Prentice-Hall.

Barber, T. X. (1966). The effects of "hypnosis" and motivational suggestions on strength and endurance. *British Journal of Social and Clinical Psychology, 5,* 42–50.

*Bard, J. (1980). *Rational-emotive therapy in practice.* Champaign, IL: Research Press.

*Barlow, D. H. (1989). *Anxiety and its disorders: The nature and treatment of anxiety and panic.* New York: Guilford.

**Barlow, D. H., & Craske, M. G. (1989). *Mastery of your anxiety and panic.* Albany, NY: Center for Stress and Anxiety Disorders.

Barrish, I. J. (1995). Using what works. *Behavior Therapist, 18*(3), 61.

Bartley, W. W., III. (1984). *The retreat to commitment,* rev. ed. Peru, IL: Open Court.

Bateson, G. (1979). *Mind and nature: A necessary unit.* New York: Dutton.

*Beck, A. T. (1976). *Cognitive therapy and the emotional disorders.* New York: International Universities Press.

**Beck, A. T. (1988). *Love is not enough.* New York: Harper & Row.

*Beck, A. T. (1991). Cognitive therapy: A 30-year retrospective. *American Psychologist, 46,* 382–389.

*Beck, A. T., & Emery, G. (1985). *Anxiety disorders and phobias.* New York: Basic Books.

*Beck, A. T., Freeman, A., & Associates. (1990). *Cognitive therapy of personality disorders.* New York: Guilford.

*Beck, A. T., Rush, A. J., Shaw, B. F., & Emery, G. (1979). *Cognitive therapy of depression.* New York: Guilford.

Becker, E. (1973). The denial of death. New York: Norton.

Bellak, L., & Small, L. (1977). *Emergency psychotherapy and brief psychotherapy.* New York: Grune & Stratton.

Benjamin, L. S. (1993). *Interpersonal diagnosis and treatment of personality disorders.* New York: Guilford.

**Benson, H. (1975). *The relaxation response.* New York: Morrow.

Bereiter, C. (1994). Implications of postmodernism for science, or science as progressive discourse. *Educational Psychologist, 29,* 3–13.

Bergin, A. E., & Garfield, S. L. (1994). Overview, trends, and future issues, In A. E. Bergin & S. L. Garfield (Eds.), *Handbook of psychotherapy and behavior change* (pp. 821–830). New York: Wiley.

*Berkowitz, L. (1990). On the formation and regulation of anger and aggression. *American Psychologist. 45,* 494–503.

*Bernard, M. E. (Ed.). (1991). *Using rational-emotive therapy effectively: A practitioner's guide.* New York: Plenum.

**Bernard, M. E. (1993). *Staying rational in an irrational world.* New York: Carol Publishing.

*Bernard, M. E., & DiGiuseppe, R. (Eds.). (1989). *Inside RET: A critical appraisal of the theory and therapy of Albert Ellis.* San Diego, CA: Academic Press.

*Bernard, M. E., & Joyce, M. R. (1984). *Rational-emotive therapy with children and adolescents.* New York: Wiley.

*Bernard, M. E., & Wolfe, J. L., (Eds.). (1993). *The RET resource book for practitioners.* New York: Institute for Rational-Emotive Therapy.

Berne, E. (1961). *Transactional analysis in psychotherapy.* New York: Grove.

Berne, E. (1972). *What do you say after you say hello?* New York: Grove.

*Bernheim, H. (1947). *Suggestive therapeutics.* New York: London Book Company. (Original publication, 1986).

*Beutler, L. E., Engle, D., Mohr, D., Daldrup, R. J., Bergan, J., Meredith, K., & Merry, W. (1991). Predictors of differential response to cognitive, experiential and self-directed therapeutic procedures. *Journal of Consulting and Clinical Psychology, 59,* 333–340.

Bjork, D. W. (1993). *B. F. Skinner: A life.* New York: Basic Books.

Blakeslee, S. (1994, December 6). Tracing the brain's pathways for linking emotion and reason. *New York Times,* pp. C1, C3.

*Blatt, S. J., & Felsen, I. (1993). Different kinds of folks may need different kinds of strokes. *Psychotherapy Research, 3,* 245–259.

*Blau, S. F. (1993). Cognitive Darwinism: Rational-emotive therapy and the theory of neuronal group selection. *ETC: A Review of General Semantics, 50,* 403–441.

Bloom, B. S. (1991). *Planned short-term psychotherapy: A clinical handbook.* Needham Heights, MA: Allyn & Bacon.

**Bloomfield, H. H., & McWilliams, P. (1994). *How to heal depression.* Los Angeles: Prelude Press.

Bolter, K., Levonson, H., & Alvarez, W. F. (1990). Differences in values between short-term and long-term therapists. *Professional Psychology, 21,* 285–290.

Bordin, E. S. (1979). The generalizability of the psychoanalytic concept of the working alliance. *Psychotherapy, 16,* 252–260.

Bourland, D. D., Jr., & Johnston, P.D. (Eds.). (1991). *To be or not: An E-prime anthology.* San Francisco: International Society for General Semantics.

Bowlby, J. (1969). *Attachment and loss: I: Attachment.* New York: Basic Books.

Bowlby, J. (1973). *Attachment and loss: II: Separation.* New York: Basic Books.

Bowlby, J. (1980). *Attachment and loss: III: Loss: Sadness and depression.* New York: Basic Books.

Brammer, L. M., & Shostrom, E. L. (1968). *Therapeutic psychology.* Englewood Cliffs, NJ: Prentice-Hall.

Branden, N. (1970). *The psychology of self-esteem.* New York: Bantam.

Breuer, J., & Freud, S. (1965). *Studies in hysteria.* Vol. 2 of *The standard edition of the complete psychological works of Sigmund Freud.* New York: Basic Books. (Originally published, 1897).

*Bricault, L. (1992). "Cherchez le 'should'! Cherchez le 'must'! Une entrevue avec Albert Ellis, l'initiateur de la méthode émotivo-rationelle. *Confrontation, 14,* 3–12.

Brislin, R. W. (1993). *Understanding culture's influence on behavior.* Ft. Worth, TX: Harcourt Brace Jovanovich.

**Broder, M. S. (1990). *The art of living.* New York: Avon.

**Broder, M. S. (1994). *The art of staying together.* New York: Avon.

Brown, C. (1985). *Down all these years.* New York: Bantam.

*Brown, G., & Beck, A. T. (1989). The role of imperatives in psychopathology: A reply to Ellis. *Cognitive Therapy and Research, 13,* 315–321.

Buber, M. (1984). *I and thou.* New York: Scribner.

*Budman, S. H., & Gurman, A. S. (1988). *Theory and practice of brief therapy.* New York: Guilford.

*Budman, S. H., Hoyt, M. F., & Friedman, S. (Eds.). (1992). *The first session in brief therapy.* New York: Guilford.

**Burns, D. D. (1980). *Feeling good: The new mood therapy.* New York: Morrow.

**Burns, D. (1984). *Intimate connections.* New York: Morrow.

**Burns, D. D. (1989). *Feeling good handbook.* New York: Morrow.

**Burns, D. D. (1993). *Ten days to self-esteem.* New York: Morrow.

*Cade, B., & O'Hanlon, W. H. (1993). *A brief guide to brief therapy.* New York: Norton.

*Carlson, C. R., & Hoyle, R. H. (1993). Efficacy of abbreviated progressive muscle relaxation training: A quantitative review of behavioral medicine research. *Journal of Consulting and Clinical Psychology, 61,* 1059–1067.

Carey, G., & DiLalla, G. (1994). Personality and psychopathology: Genetic perspectives. *Journal of Abnormal Psychology, 103,* 32–43.

Carnegie, D. (1942). *How to win friends and influence people.* New York: Pocket Books.

*Cloitre, M. (1993, Winter). An interview with Martin Seligman. *Behavior Therapist,* pp. 261–263.

Cloninger, C. R., Svrakic, D. M., & Przybek, T. R. (1993). A psychobiological model of temperament and character. *Archives of General Psychiatry, 50,* 975–990.

*Cocker, K. I., Bell, D. R., & Kidman, A. D. (1994). Cognitive behavior therapy with advanced breast cancer. *Psycho-oncology, 3,* 233–237.

*Cohen, E. D. (1992). Syllogizing RET: Applying formal logic in rational-emotive therapy. *Journal of Rational-Emotive and Cognitive-Behavior Therapy, 10,* 235–252.

*Corey, G. (1995). *Theory and practice of counseling and psychotherapy,* 5th ed. Pacific Grove, CA: Brooks/Cole.

*Corsini, R. J. (1979). The betting technique. *Individual Psychology, 16,* 5–11.

Corsini, R. J. (1989). Introduction. In R. J. Corsini & D. Wedding (Eds.), *Current psychotherapies* (pp. 1–16). Itasca, IL: Peacock.

*Corsini, R. J., & Wedding, D. (1995). *Current psychotherapies.* Itasca, IL: Peacock.

Costa, P. T., & Widiger, T. A. (1994). *Personality disorders and the five factor model of personality.* Washington, DC: American Psychological Association.

*Coté, G., Gautier, J. G., Laberge, B., Cormier, H. J., & Plamondon, J. (1994). Reduced therapist contact in the cognitive behavioral treatment of panic disorder. *Behavior Therapy, 25,* 123–145.

**Coué, E. (1923). *My method.* New York: Doubleday, Page.

*Cramer, D., & Ellis, A. (1988). Irrational beliefs and strength in appropriateness of feelings: A debate. In W. Dryden & P. Trower (Eds.), *Developments in rational-emotive therapy* (pp.56–64). Philadelphia: Open University.

**Crawford, T. (1988). *The five coordinates for a good relationship and better communication.* Santa Barbara, CA: Author.

**Crawford, T. (1993). *Changing a frog into a prince or princess.* Santa Barbara, CA: Author.

*Crawford, T., & Ellis, A. (1982, October). Communication and rational-emotive therapy. Workshop presented in Los Angeles.

*Crawford, T., & Ellis, A. (1989). A dictionary of rational-emotive feelings and behaviors. *Journal of Rational-Emotive and Cognitive-Behavioral Therapy,* 7(1), 3–27.

**Csikszentmihalyi, M. (1990). *Flow: The psychology of optimal experience.* San Francisco: Harper Perennial.

*Cummings, N. (1994, February) Comments on programmed material and psychotherapy. *Assembly of the 21st Century.* American Psychological Association, Washington, DC.

*Cuon, D. W. (1994). Cognitive-behavioral interventions with avoidant personality: A single case study. *Journal of Cognitive Psychotherapy, 8,* 243–257.

*Curry, S. J. (1993). Self-help interventions for smoking cessation. *Journal of Consulting and Clinical Psychology, 61,* 790–803.

Daniels, M. (1988). The myth of self-actualization. *Journal of Humanistic Psychology, 28*(1), 7–38.

**Danysh, J. (1974). *Stop without quitting.* San Francisco: International Society for General Semantics.

Davies, M. F. (1993). Dogmatism and persistence of discredited beliefs. *Personality & Social Psychology Bulletin, 19,* 692–699.

**DeBono, E. (1991). *I am right—You are wrong: From rock logic to water logic.* New York: Viking.

*Dengelegi, L. (1990, April 25). Don't judge yourself. *New York Times.* p.C3.

*de Shazer, S. (1985). *Keys to solution in brief therapy.* New York: Norton.

*de Shazer, S. (1990). Brief therapy. In J. K. Zeig & W. M. Munion (Eds.), *What is psychotherapy?* (pp. 278–282). San Francisco: Jossey-Bass.

Dewey, J. (1929). *Quest for certainty.* New York: Putnam.

*DiGiuseppe, R. (1986). The implication of the philosophy of science for rational-emotive theory and therapy. *Psychotherapy, 23,* 634–639.

**DiGiuseppe, R. (Speaker). (1990). *What do I do with my anger: Hold it in or let it out?* Cassette recording. New York: Institute for Rational-Emotive Therapy.

*DiGiuseppe, R. (1991a). Comprehensive cognitive disputing in RET. In M. E. Bernard (Ed.), *Using rational-emotive therapy effectively,* pp. 173–196. New York: Plenum.

**DiGiuseppe, R. (Speaker). (1991b). *Maximizing the moment: How to have more fun and happiness in life.* Cassette recording. New York: Institute for Rational-Emotive Therapy.

*DiGiuseppe, R., Leaf, R., & Linscott, J. (1993). The therapeutic relationship in rational-emotive therapy: A preliminary analysis. *Journal of Rational-Emotive and Cognitive Behavior Therapy, 11,* 223–233.

*DiGiuseppe, R. A., Miller, N. J., & Trexler, L. D. (1979). A review of rational-emotive psychotherapy outcome studies. In A. Ellis & J. M. Whiteley (Eds). *Theoretical and empirical foundations of rational-emotive therapy* (pp. 218–235). Monterey, CA: Brooks/Cole.

*DiGiuseppe, R. A., & Muran, J. C. (1993). The use of metaphor in rational-emotive therapy. *Psychotherapy in Private Practice, 10,* 151–161.

*DiGiuseppe, R., Tafrate, R., & Eckhardt, C. (1994). Critical issues in the treatment of anger. *Cognitive and Behavioral Practice, 1,* 111–132.

*DiMattia, D., & Lega, L. (Eds.). (1990). *Will the real Albert Ellis please stand up? Anecdotes by his colleagues, students and friends celebrating his 75th birthday.* New York: Institute for Rational-Emotive Therapy.

**DiMattia, D. J., & others (Speakers.). (1987). *Mind over myths: Handling difficult situations in the workplace.* Cassette recording. New York: Institute for Rational-Emotive Therapy.

*Dobson, K. S. (1989). A meta-analysis of cognitive therapy for depression. *Journal of Consulting and Clinical Psychology, 57,* 414–419.

*Dougher, M. J. (1993). On the advantages and implications of a radical behavioral treatment of private events. *The Behavior Therapist, 16,* 204–206.

*Dougher, M. J. (1994). More on the differences between radical behavioral and rational emotive approaches to acceptance: A response to Robb. *The Behavior Therapist, 17,* 103–105.

*Dryden, W. (1987). Language and meaning in rational-emotive therapy. In W. Dryden (Ed.). *Current issues in rational-emotive therapy.* London: Croom Helm.

*Dryden, W. (1990). *Dealing with anger problems: Rational-Emotive therapeutic interventions.* Sarasota, FL: Professional Resource Exchange.

*Dryden, W. (1994a). *Invitation to rational-emotive psychology.* London: Whurr.

*Dryden, W. (1994b). *Progress in rational emotive behavior therapy.* London: Whurr.

**Dryden, W. (1994c). *Overcoming guilt!* London: Sheldon.

Dryden, W. (1995). Brief rational emotive behavior therapy. London: Wiley.

*Dryden, W., Backx, W., & Ellis, A. (1987). Problems in living: The Friday Night Workshop. In W. Dryden (Ed.), *Current issues in rational-emotive therapy.* (pp.154–170). London and New York: Croom Helm.

*Dryden, W., & DiGiuseppe, R. (1990). *A primer on rational-emotive therapy.* Champaign, IL: Research Press.

*Dryden, W., & Ellis, A. (1989). Albert Ellis: An efficient and passionate life. *Journal of Counseling and Development, 67,* 539–546. Reprinted: New York: Institute for Rational-Emotive Therapy.

**Dryden, W. & Gordon, J. (1991). *Think your way to happiness.* London: Sheldon.

**Dryden, W., & Gordon, J. (1993). *Peak performance.* Oxfordshire, England: Mercury.

*Dryden, W., & Hill, L. K. (Eds.). (1993). *Innovations in rational-emotive therapy.* Newbury Park, CA: Sage.

*Dryden, W., & Neenan, M. (1995). *Dictionary of rational emotive behavior therapy.* London: Whurr.

*Dryden, W., & Yankura, J. (1992). *Daring to be myself: A case study in rational-emotive therapy*. Buckingham, England and Philadelphia, PA: Open University Press.

*Dubois, P. (1907). *The psychic treatment of nervous disorders*. New York: Funk & Wagnalls.

*Dunlap, K. (1932). *Habits: Their making and unmaking*. New York: Liveright.

**Dyer, W. (1977). *Your erroneous zones*. New York: Avon.

*D'Zurilla, J. (1986). *Problem-solving therapy*. New York: Springer.

Edelman, G. M. (1992). *Bright air, brilliant fire: On the matter of the mind*. New York: Basic Books.

*Elkin, I. (1994). The NIMH treatment of depression collaborative research program: Where we began and where we are. In A. E. Bergin and S. L. Garfield (Eds.), *Handbook of psychotherapy and behavior change*. (pp.114–139). New York: Wiley.

*Elkin, I., Shea, M. T., Watkins, J. T., Imber, S. D., Glass, D. R., Pilkonis, P. A., Leber, W. R., Doherty, W. R., Fiester, S. J., & Parloff, M. B. (1989). National Institute of Mental Health Treatment of Depression Collaborative Research Program: General effectiveness of treatments. *Archives of General Psychiatry, 46*, 971–982.

Ellenberger, H. F. (1970). *The discovery of the unconscious*. New York: Basic Books.

*Elliott, J. E. (1993). Using releasing statements to challenge shoulds. *Journal of Cognitive Psychotherapy, 7*, 291–295.

**Ellis, A. (1957a). *How to live with a neurotic: At home and at work*. New York: Crown. Rev. ed., Hollywood, CA: Wilshire Books, 1975.

*Ellis, A. (1957b). Outcome of employing three techniques of psychotherapy. *Journal of Clinical Psychology, 13*, 344–350.

*Ellis, A. (1959). Requisite conditions for basic personality change. *Journal of Consulting Psychology, 23*, 538–540.

*Ellis, A. (1962). *Reason and emotion in psychotherapy*. Secaucus, NJ: Citadel.

*Ellis, A. (1965a). *The treatment of borderline and psychotic individuals*. New York: Institute for Rational-Emotive Therapy. Rev. ed., 1989.

*Ellis, A. (1965b). Workshop in rational-emotive therapy. Institute for Rational-Emotive Therapy, New York City, September 8.

*Ellis, A. (1967). Goals of psychotherapy. In A. H. Mahrer (Ed.), *The goals of psychotherapy* (pp. 206–220). New York: Macmillan.

*Ellis, A. (1968). Is psychoanalysis harmful? *Psychiatric Opinion, 5*, 16–25. Reprinted: New York: Institute for Rational-Emotive Therapy.

*Ellis, A. (1969). A weekend of rational encounter. *Rational Living, 4*(2), 1–8. Reprinted in A. Ellis & W. Dryden (Eds.), *The practice of rational-emotive therapy* (pp. 180–191). New York: Springer, 1987.

*Ellis, A. (1971). *Growth through reason*. North Hollywood, CA: Wilshire Books.

**Ellis, A. (1972a). *Executive leadership: The rational-emotive approach.* New York: Institute for Rational-Emotive Therapy.

*Ellis, A. (1972b). Helping people get better rather than merely feel better. *Rational Living, 7*(2), 2–9.

*Ellis, A. (1972c). Emotional education in the classroom: The living school. *Journal of Clinical and Child Psychology, 1*(3), 19–22.

*Ellis, A. (1972d). *Psychotherapy and the value of a human being.* New York: Institute for Rational-Emotive Therapy. Reprinted in A. Ellis & W. Dryden (Eds.), *The essential Albert Ellis.* New York: Springer, 1990.

**Ellis, A. (1972e). *How to master your fear of flying.* New York: Institute for Rational-Emotive Therapy.

**Ellis, A. (Speaker). (1973a). *How to stubbornly refuse to be ashamed of anything.* Cassette recording. New York: Institute for Rational-Emotive Therapy.

*Ellis, A. (1973b). *Humanistic psychotherapy: The rational-emotive approach.* New York: McGraw-Hill.

**Ellis, A. (Speaker). (1973c). *Twenty-one ways to stop worrying.* Cassette recording. New York: Institute for Rational-Emotive Therapy.

*Ellis, A. (1974a). Cognitive aspects of abreactive therapy. *Voices, 10*(1), 48–56. Reprinted: New York: Institute for Rational-Emotive Therapy. Rev. ed., 1992.

**Ellis, A. (Speaker). (1974b). *Rational living in an irrational world.* Cassette recording. New York: Institute for Rational-Emotive Therapy.

*Ellis, A. (1974c). *Techniques of disputing irrational beliefs (DIBS).* New York: Institute for Rational-Emotive Therapy.

**Ellis, A. (1975a). *How to live with a neurotic,* Rev. ed. North Hollywood, CA: Wilshire Books.

**Ellis, A. (Speaker). (1975b). *RET and assertiveness training.* Cassette recording. New York: Institute for Rational-Emotive Therapy.

*Ellis, A. (1976a). The biological basis of human irrationality. *Journal of Individual Psychology, 32,* 145–168. Reprinted: New York: Institute for Rational-Emotive Therapy.

**Ellis, A. (Speaker). (1976b). *Conquering low frustration tolerance.* Cassette recording. New York: Institute for Rational-Emotive Therapy.

*Ellis, A. (1976c). RET abolishes most of the human ego. *Psychotherapy, 13,* 343–348. Reprinted: New York: Institute for Rational-Emotive Therapy. Rev. ed., 1991.

**Ellis, A. (1977a). *Anger—how to live with and without it.* Secaucus, NJ: Citadel Press.

**Ellis, A. (Speaker). (1977b). *Conquering the dire need for love.* Cassette recording. New York: Institute for Rational-Emotive Therapy.

*Ellis, A. (1977c). Fun as psychotherapy. *Rational Living, 12*(1), 2–6. Also: Cassette recording. New York: Institute for Rational-Emotive Therapy.

**Ellis, A. (Speaker). (1977d). *A garland of rational humorous songs.* Cassette recording and songbook. New York: Institute for Rational-Emotive Therapy.

**Ellis, A. (Speaker) (1978). *I'd like to stop but...Dealing with addictions.* Cassette recording. New York: Institute for Rational-Emotive Therapy.

*Ellis, A. (1979a). Discomfort anxiety: A new cognitive behavioral construct. Part 1. *Rational Living, 14*(2), 3–8.

**Ellis, A. (1979b). *The intelligent woman's guide to dating and mating.* Secaucus, NJ: Lyle Stuart.

*Ellis, A. (1979c). A note on the treatment of agoraphobia with cognitive modification versus prolonged exposure. *Behavior Research and Therapy, 17,* 162–164.

*Ellis, A. (1979d). Rational-emotive therapy: Research data that support the clinical and personality hypotheses of RET and other modes of cognitive-behavior therapy. In A. Ellis & J. M. Whiteley (Eds.), *Theoretical and empirical foundations of rational-emotive therapy* (pp. 101–173). Monterey, CA: Brooks/Cole.

*Ellis, A. (1979e). Rejoinder: Elegant and inelegant RET. In A. Ellis & J. M. Whiteley (Eds.), *Theoretical and empirical foundations of rational-emotive therapy* (pp. 240–267). Monterey, CA: Brooks/Cole.

*Ellis, A. (1980a). Discomfort anxiety: A new cognitive-behavioral construct. Part 2. *Rational Living, 15*(1), 25–30.

*Ellis, A. (1980b). Rational-emotive therapy and cognitive-behavior therapy: Similarities and differences. *Cognitive Therapy and Research, 4,* 325–340.

**Ellis, A. (Speaker). (1980c). *Twenty-two ways to brighten up your love life.* Cassette recording. New York: Institute for Rational-Emotive Therapy.

*Ellis, A. (1980d). The value of efficiency in psychotherapy. *Psychotherapy, 17,* 414–419. Reprinted in A. Ellis & W. Dryden (1990), *The essential Albert Ellis* (pp. 237–247). New York: Springer.

*Ellis, A. (1980e). Psychotherapy and atheistic values. *Journal of Consulting and Clinical Psychology, 48,* 635–639.

*Ellis, A. (1981). The use of rational humorous songs in psychotherapy. *Voices, 16*(4), 29–36.

**Ellis, A. (Speaker). (1982). *Solving emotional problems.* Cassette recording. New York: Institute for Rational-Emotive Therapy.

*Ellis, A. (1983a). *The case against religiosity.* New York: Institute for Rational-Emotive Therapy. Rev. ed., 1991.

*Ellis, A. (1983b). Failures in rational-emotive therapy. In E. B. Foa and P. M. G. Emmelkamp (Eds.), *Failures in behavior therapy* (pp. 159–171). New York: Wiley.

*Ellis, A. (1983c). The philosophic implications and dangers of some popular behavior therapy techniques. In M. Rosenbaum, C. M. Franks, & Y. Jaffe (Eds.), *Perspectives in behavior therapy in the eighties* (pp. 138–151). New York: Springer.

*Ellis, A. (1984a). Introduction to H. S. Young, *The work of Howard S. Young.*

Edited by W. Dryden. *British Journal of Cognitive Psychotherapy, Special Issue,* 2(2), 1–5.

*Ellis, A. (1984b). The place of meditation in cognitive-behavior therapy and rational-emotive therapy. In D. H. Shapiro & R. Walsh (Eds.), *Meditation* (pp. 671–673). New York: Aldine.

*Ellis, A. (1984c). The use of hypnosis with rational-emotive therapy. *International Journal of Eclectic Psychotherapy, 3*(3), 15–22.

*Ellis, A. (1985a). *Intellectual fascism.* New York: Institute for Rational-Emotive Therapy. Rev. ed., 1991.

*Ellis, A. (1985b). *Overcoming resistance: Rational-emotive therapy with difficult clients.* New York: Springer.

*Ellis, A. (1985c). A rational-emotive approach to acceptance and its relationship to EAPs. In S. H. Klarreich, J. L. Francek, & C. E. Moore (Eds.), *The human resources management handbook* (pp. 325–333). New York: Praeger.

*Ellis, A. (1986a). Anxiety about anxiety: The use of hypnosis with rational-emotive therapy. In E. T. Dowd & J. M. Healy (Eds.), *Case studies in hypnotherapy* (pp. 3–11). New York: Guilford. Reprinted in A. Ellis & W. Dryden, *The practice of rational-emotive therapy.* New York: Springer, 1987.

**Ellis, A. (Speaker). (1986b). *Effective self-assertion.* Cassette recording. Washington, DC: Psychology Today Tapes.

*Ellis, A. (1986c). Rational-emotive therapy applied to relationship therapy. *Journal of Rational-Emotive Therapy,* 4–21.

*Ellis, A. (1987a). The evolution of rational-emotive therapy (RET) and cognitive-behavior therapy (CBT). In J. K. Zeig (Ed.), *The evolution of psychotherapy* (pp. 107–132). New York: Brunner/Mazel.

*Ellis, A. (1987b). The impossibility of achieving consistently good mental health. *American Psychologist, 42,* 364–375.

*Ellis, A. (1987c). Integrative developments in rational-emotive therapy (RET). *Journal of Integrative and Eclectic Psychotherapy, 6,* 470–479.

*Ellis, A. (1987d). A sadly neglected cognitive element in depression. *Cognitive Therapy and Research, 11,* 121–146.

*Ellis, A. (1987e). The use of rational humorous songs in psychotherapy. In W. F. Fry, Jr., & W. A. Salamed (Eds.), *Handbook of humor and psychotherapy* (pp. 265–287). Sarasota, FL: Professional Resource Exchange.

*Ellis, A. (1988a). *How to stubbornly refuse to make yourself miserable about anything—yes, anything!* Secaucus, NJ: Lyle Stuart.

**Ellis, A. (1988b). How to live with a neurotic man. *Journal of Rational-Emotive and Cognitive-Behavior Therapy, 6,* 129–136.

**Ellis, A. (Speaker). (1988c). *Unconditionally accepting yourself and others.* Cassette recording. New York: Institute for Rational-Emotive Therapy.

*Ellis, A. (1989a). Comments on my critics. In M. E. Bernard & R. DiGiuseppe (Eds.), *Inside rational-emotive therapy* (pp.199–233). San Diego, CA: Academic Press.

*Ellis, A. (1989b). Comments on Sandra Warnock's "Rational-Emotive

Therapy and the Christian client." *Journal of Rational-Emotive and Cognitive-Behavior Therapy, 7,* 275–277.

*Ellis, A. (1989c). The history of cognition in psychotherapy. In A. Freeman, K. M. Simon, L. E. Beutler, & H. Aronowitz (Eds.), *Comprehensive handbook of cognitive therapy* (pp. 5–19). New York: Plenum.

**Ellis, A. (Speaker). (1989d). *Overcoming the influence of the past.* Cassette recording. New York: Institute for Rational-Emotive Therapy.

*Ellis, A. (1989e). *The treatment of psychotic and borderline individuals with RET.* (Orig. publication, 1965). New York: Institute for Rational-Emotive Therapy.

*Ellis, A. (1989f). Using rational-emotive therapy (RET) as crisis intervention: A single session with a suicidal client. *Individual Psychology, 45* (1 & 2), 75–81.

**Ellis, A. (Speaker). (1990a). *Albert Ellis live at the Learning Annex.* 2 cassettes. New York: Institute for Rational-Emotive Therapy.

*Ellis, A. (1990b). Is rational-emotive therapy (RET) "rationalist" or "constructivist"? In A. Ellis, & W. Dryden. *The essential Albert Ellis* (pp. 114–141). New York: Springer.

*Ellis, A. (1990c). Let's not ignore individuality. *American Psychologist, 45,* 781.

*Ellis, A. (1990d). My life in clinical psychology. In C. E. Walker (Eds.) *History of clinical psychology in autobiography,* Vol. 1 (pp. 1–37). Homewood, IL: Dorsey.

*Ellis, A. (1990e). Rational and irrational beliefs in counseling psychology. *Journal of Rational-Emotive and Cognitive-Behavior Therapy.*

*Ellis, A. (1990f). Special features of rational-emotive therapy. In W. Dryden & R. DiGiuseppe, *A primer of rational-emotive therapy* (pp. 79–93). Champaign, IL: Research Press.

*Ellis, A. (1991a). Achieving self-actualization. *Journal of Social Behavior and Personality, 6*(5), 1–18. Reprinted: New York: Institute for Rational-Emotive Therapy.

*Ellis, A. (1991b). Are all methods of counseling and psychotherapy equally effective? *New York State Association for Counseling and Development Journal, 6*(2), 9–13.

*Ellis, A. (1991c). *Cognitive aspects of abreactive therapy,* rev. ed. New York: Institute for Rational-Emotive Therapy.

*Ellis, A. (1991d). How can psychological treatment aim to be briefer and better. The rational-emotive approach to brief therapy. In K. N. Anchor (Ed.), *The handbook of medical psychotherapy* (pp. 51–88). Toronto: Hografe & Huber. Also in J. K. Zeig & S. G. Gilligan (Eds.), *Brief therapy: Myths, methods and metaphors* (pp. 291–302). New York: Brunner/Mazel.

**Ellis, A. (Speaker). (1991e). *How to get along with difficult people.* Cassette recording. New York: Institute for Rational-Emotive Therapy.

**Ellis, A. (Speaker). (1991f). *How to refuse to be angry, vindictive, and unforgiving.* Cassette recording. New York: Institute for Rational-Emotive Therapy.

*Ellis, A. (1991g). *Humanism and psychotherapy: A revolutionary approach*, rev. ed. New York: Institute for Rational-Emotive Therapy. Original publication, 1972.

*Ellis, A. (1991h). The philosophical basis of rational-emotive therapy (RET). *Psychotherapy In Private Practice, 8*(4), 97–106.

*Ellis, A. (1991i). *Rational-emotive family therapy*. In A. M. Horne & J. L. Passmore (Eds.), *Family counseling and therapy*, 2nd edition (pp. 403–434). Itasca, IL: F. E. Peacock.

*Ellis, A. (1991j). The revised ABCs of rational-emotive therapy. In J. Zeig (Ed.), *The evolution of psychotherapy: The second conference* (pp. 79–99). New York: Brunner/Mazel. Expanded version: *Journal of Rational-Emotive and Cognitive-Behavior Therapy, 9*, 139–172.

**Ellis, A. (1991k). *Self-management workbook: Strategies for personal success*. New York: Institute for Rational-Emotive Therapy.

*Ellis, A. (1991l). Suggestibility, irrational beliefs, and emotional disturbance. In J. F. Schumaner (Ed.). *Human suggestibility* (pp. 309–325). New York: Routledge.

*Ellis, A. (1991m). Using RET effectively: Reflections and interview. In M. E. Bernard (Ed.). *Using rational-emotive therapy effectively* (pp. 1–33). New York: Plenum.

*Ellis, A. (1992a). Brief therapy: The rational-emotive method. In S. H. Budman, M. F. Hoyt, & S. Fiedman (Eds.), *The first session in brief therapy* (pp. 36–58). New York: Guilford.

*Ellis, A. (1992b). Foreword to Paul Hauck, *Overcoming the rating game* (pp. 1–4). Louisville, KY: Westminster/John Knox.

**Ellis, A. (Speaker). (1992c). *How to age with style*. Cassette recording. New York: Institute for Rational-Emotive Therapy.

*Ellis, A. (1992d). Group rational-emotive and cognitive-behavioral therapy. *International Journal of Group Psychotherapy, 42*, 63–80.

*Ellis, A. (1992e). My current views on rational-emotive therapy (RET) and religiousness. *Journal of Rational-Emotive and Cognitive-Behavior Therapy, 10*, 37–40.

*Ellis, A. (1992f). Rational-emotive approaches to peace. *Journal of Cognitive Psychotherapy, 6*, 79–104.

*Ellis, A. (1993a). The advantages and disadvantages of self-help therapy materials. *Professional Psychology: Research and Practice, 24*, 335–339.

*Ellis, A. (1993b). Changing rational-emotive therapy (RET) to rational emotive behavior therapy (REBT). *Behavior Therapist, 16*, 257–258.

*Ellis, A. (Speaker). (1993c). *Coping with the suicide of a loved one*. Video cassette. New York: Institute for Rational-Emotive Therapy.

*Ellis, A. (1993d). Fundamentals of rational-emotive therapy for the 1990s. In W. Dryden & L. K. Hill (Eds.), *Innovations in rational-emotive therapy* (pp. 1–32). Newbury Park, CA: Sage.

*Ellis, A. (1993e). General semantics and rational emotive behavior therapy.

Bulletin of General Semantics, No. 58, 12–28. Also in P. D. Johnston, D. D. Bourland, Jr., & J. Klein (Eds.), *More E-prime* (pp. 213–240). Concord, CA: International Society for General Semantics.

**Ellis, A. (Speaker). (1993f). *How to be a perfect non-perfectionist.* Cassette recording. New York: Institute for Rational-Emotive Therapy.

**Ellis, A. (Speaker). (1993g). *Living fully and in balance: This isn't a dress rehearsal—This is it!* Cassette recording. New York: Institute for Rational-Emotive Therapy.

*Ellis, A. (1993h). Rational-emotive therapy and hypnosis. In J. W. Rhue, S. J. Lynn, & I. Kirsh (Eds.), *Handbook of clinical hypnosis* (pp. 173–186). Washington, DC: American Psychological Association.

*Ellis, A. (1993i). The rational-emotive therapy (RET) approach to marriage and family therapy. *Family Journal: Counseling and Therapy for Couples and Families, 1,* 292–307.

*Ellis, A. (1993j). Rational emotive imagery: RET version. In M. E. Bernard & J. L. Wolfe (Eds.), *The RET resource book for practitioners* (pp. II8–II10). New York: Institute for Rational-Emotive Therapy.

*Ellis, A. (1993k). Reflections on rational-emotive therapy. *Journal of Consulting and Clinical Psychology, 61,* 199–201.

**Ellis, A. (Speaker). (1993l). *Releasing your creative energy.* Cassette recording. New York: Institute for Rational-Emotive Therapy.

*Ellis, A. (1993m). Vigorous RET disputing. In M. E. Bernard & J. L. Wolfe (Eds.), *The RET resource book for practitioners* (p. II7). New York: Institute for Rational-Emotive Therapy.

*Ellis, A. (Speaker). (1993n). *Rational-emotive approach to brief therapy.* 2 cassette recordings. Phoenix, AZ: Milton H. Erickson Foundation.

*Ellis, A. (1994a). Foreword to P. D. Johnston, D. D. Bourland, Jr., & J. Klein (Eds.), *More E-prime* (pp. xiii–xviii). Concord, CA: International Society for General Semantics.

*Ellis, A. (1994b). Post-traumatic stress disorder (PTSD) in rape victims: A rational emotive behavioral theory. *Journal of Rational-Emotive and Cognitive-Behavior Therapy, 12,* 3–25.

*Ellis, A. (1994c). Radical behavioral treatment of private events: A response to Michael Dougher. *Behavior Therapist, 17,* 219–221.

*Ellis, A. (1994d). Rational emotive behavior therapy approaches to obsessive-compulsive disorder (OCD). *Journal of Rational-Emotive and Cognitive-Behavior Therapy, 12,* 121–141.

*Ellis, A. (1994e). *Reason and emotion in psychotherapy.* Revised and updated. New York: Birch Lane Press.

*Ellis, A. (1994f). Secular humanism. In F. Wertz (Ed.), *The humanistic movement* (pp. 233–242). Lakeworth, FL: Gardner Press.

*Ellis, A. (1994g). The treatment of borderline personalities with rational emotive behavior therapy. *Journal of Rational-Emotive and Cognitive-Behavior Therapy, 12,* 101–119.

*Ellis, A. (1994h). Life in a box. Review of D. W. Bjork, *B. F. Skinner: A Life.*
Readings, 9(4), 16–21.

*Ellis, A. (1994i). The sport of avoiding sports and exercise. *Sport Psychologist,*
8, 248–261.

*Ellis, A. (1995a). Rational emotive behavior therapy. In R. Corsini & D.
Wedding, (Eds.), *Current psychotherapies* 5th ed. (pp. 162–196). Itasca, IL:
Peacock.

*Ellis, A. (1995b). A social constructionist position for mental health counsel-
ing: A response to Jeffrey A Guterman. *Journal of Mental Health Counseling.*
7, 97–104.

*Ellis, A. (1995c, March 6). Dogmatic religion doesn't help, it hurts. *Insight in*
the News, pp. 20–22.

*Ellis, A., & Abrahms, E. (1978). *Brief psychotherapy in medical and health practice.*
New York: Springer.

**Ellis, A., & Abrams, M. (1994). *How to cope with a fatal disease.* New York:
Barricade Books.

**Ellis, A., Abrams, M., & Dengelegi, L. (1992). *The art and science of rational*
eating. New York: Barricade Books.

**Ellis, A., & Becker, I. (1982). *A guide to personal happiness.* North Hollywood,
CA: Wilshire Books.

*Ellis, A., & Bernard, M.E. (Eds.). (1983). *Rational-emotive approaches to the*
problems of childhood. New York: Plenum.

*Ellis, A., & Bernard, M. E. (Eds.). (1985). *Clinical applications of rational-*
emotive therapy. New York: Plenum.

*Ellis, A., & DiGiuseppe, R. (Speakers). (1994). *Dealing with addictions.*
Videotape. New York: Institute for Rational-Emotive Therapy.

**Ellis, A., & DiMattia, D. (1991). *Self-management: Strategies for personal success.*
New York: Institute for Rational-Emotive Therapy.

*Ellis, A., & Dryden, W. (1985). Dilemmas in giving warmth or love to clients:
An interview with Windy Dryden. In W. Dryden, *Therapists' Dilemmas*
(pp. 5–16). London: Harper & Row.

*Ellis, A., & Dryden, W. (1987). *The practice of rational-emotive therapy.* New
York: Springer.

*Ellis, A., & Dryden, W. (1990). *The essential Albert Ellis.* New York: Springer.

*Ellis, A., & Dryden, W. (1991). *A dialogue with Albert Ellis: Against dogma.*
Philadelphia: Open University Press.

*Ellis, A., & Dryden, W. (1993). A therapy by any other name? An interview.
The Rational Emotive Therapist, 1(2), 34–37.

*Ellis, A., & Grieger, R. (Eds.). (1977). *Handbook of rational-emotive therapy*
(vol. 1.). New York: Springer.

*Ellis, A., & Grieger, R. (Eds.). (1986). *Handbook of rational-emotive therapy*
(vol. 2.). New York: Springer.

**Ellis, A., & Harper, R. A. (1961). *A guide to successful marriage.* North
Hollywood, CA: Wilshire Books.

**Ellis, A., & Harper, R. A. (1975). *A new guide to rational living.* North Hollywood, CA: Wilshire Books.

**Ellis, A., & Hunter, P. (1991). *Why am I always broke?* New York: Carol Publications.

**Ellis, A., & Knaus, W. (1977). *Overcoming procrastination.* New York: New American Library.

*Ellis, A., Krasner, P., & Wilson, R. A. (1960). An impolite interview with Dr. Albert Ellis. *Realist,* Issue *16,* 1, 9–14; Issue *17,* 7–12. Rev. ed., New York: Institute for Rational-Emotive Therapy, 1985.

**Ellis, A., & Lange, A. (1994). *How to keep people from pushing your buttons.* New York: Carol Publications.

*Ellis, A., McInerney, J. F., DiGiuseppe, R., & Yeager, R. J. (1988). *Rational-emotive therapy with alcoholics and substance abusers.* Needham, MA: Allyn & Bacon.

*Ellis, A., & Robb, H. (1994). Acceptance in rational-emotive therapy. In S. C. Hayes, N. S. Jacobson, V. M. Follette, & M. J. Dougher (Eds.), *Acceptance and change: Content and context in psychotherapy* (pp. 91–102). Reno, NV: Context Press.

*Ellis, A., Sichel, J., Leaf, R. C., & Mass, R. (1989). Countering perfectionism in research on clinical practice. I: Surveying rationality changes after a single intensive RET intervention. *Journal of Rational-Emotive and Cognitive-Behavior Therapy, 7,* 197–218.

*Ellis, A., Sichel, J. L., Yeager, R. J., DiMattia, D. J., & DiGiuseppe, R. A. (1989). *Rational-emotive couples therapy.* Needham, MA: Allyn & Bacon.

**Ellis, A., & Velten, E. (1992). *When AA doesn't work for you: Rational steps for quitting alcohol.* New York: Barricade Books.

*Ellis, A., & Whiteley, J. M. (1979). *Theoretical and empirical foundations of rational-emotive therapy.* Monterey, CA: Brooks/Cole.

**Ellis, A., Wolfe, J. L., & Moseley, S. (1966). *How to raise an emotionally healthy, happy child.* North Hollywood, CA: Wilshire Books.

*Ellis, A., & Yeager, R. (1989). *Why some therapies don't work: The dangers of transpersonal psychology.* Buffalo, NY: Prometheus.

*Ellis, A., Young, J., & Lockwood, G. (1987). Cognitive therapy and rational emotive therapy: A dialogue. *Journal of Cognitive Psychotherapy, 1*(4), 137–187.

*Engels, G. I., Garnefski, N., Diekstra, R. F. W. (1993). Efficacy of rational-emotive therapy: A quantitative analysis. *Journal of Consulting and Clinical Psychology, 61,* 1083–1090.

*Epictetus. (1890). *The collected works of Epictetus.* Boston: Little, Brown.

*Epicurus (1994). *Letter on happiness.* San Francisco: Chronicle Books.

**Epstein, S. (1993). *You're smarter than you think.* New York: Simon & Schuster.

*Epstein, S. (1994). Integration of the cognitive and the psychodynamic unconscious. *American Psychologist, 49,* 709.

Erickson, M. H. (1980). *Collected papers.* New York: Irvington.

Erickson, M. H., & Rossi, E. L. (1979). *Hypnotherapy.* New York: Irvington.

Esterson, A. (1993). *Seductive mirage: An exploration of the work of Sigmund Freud.* Open Court.

Evans, R. (1978). Conversations with Karl Jung. New York: Bantam.

Eysenck, H. J. (1985). *Decline and fall of the Freudian empire.* New York: Penguin.

*Eysenck, M. W. (1992). *Anxiety: The cognitive perspective.* Hillside, NJ: Erlbaum.

Fava, M., Bless, E., Otto, M. W., Pava, A., et al. (1994). Dysfunctional attitudes in major depression: Change with pharmacotherapy. *Journal of Nervous and Mental Disease, 182,* 45–49.

Fenichel, O. (1945). *Psychoanalytic theory of neurosis.* New York: Norton.

Fenichel, O. (1954). *The collected papers of Otto Fenichel.* New York: Norton.

Ferenczi, S. (1952). *Further contributions to the theory and technique of psychoanalysis.* New York: Basic Books.

*FitzMaurice, K. (1989). *Self-concept: The enemy within.* Omaha, NE: FitzMaurice Publishing Co.

*FitzMaurice, K. (1991). *We're all insane.* Omaha, NE: Palmtree Publishers.

*FitzMaurice, K. (1994). *Introducing the 12 steps of emotional disturbances.* Omaha, NE: Author.

**Foa, E. B., & Wilson, R. (1991). *Stop obsessing: How to overcome your obsessions and compulsions.* New York: Bantam.

*Forest, J. (1987). Effects of self-actualization of paperbacks about psychological self-help. *Psychological Reports, 60,* 1243–1246.

Frank, J. (1985). Therapeutic components shared by all psychotherapies. In M. Mahoney & A. Freeman (Eds.), *Cognition and psychotherapy* (pp. 49–79). New York: Plenum.

*Frank, J. D., & Frank, J. B. (1991). *Persuasion and healing.* Baltimore, MD: Johns Hopkins University Press.

*Frankl, V. (1959). *Man's search for meaning.* New York: Pocket Books.

*Franklin, R. (1993). *Overcoming the myth of self-worth.* Appleton, WI: Focus Press.

Freedheim, D. K. (Ed.). (1992). *History of psychotherapy: A century of change.* Washington, DC: American Psychological Association.

*Freeman, A. (1994). *Short-term therapy for the long-term patient: Workshop syllabus.* Chapel Hill, NC: Author.

*Freeman, A., & Dattilo, F. W. (1992). *Comprehensive casebook of cognitive therapy.* New York: Plenum.

**Freeman, A., & DeWolfe, R. (1993). *The ten dumbest mistakes smart people make and how to avoid them.* New York: Harper Perennial.

Freud, S. (1965). *Standard edition of the complete psychological works of Sigmund Freud.* New York: Basic Books.

*Fried, R. (1993). *The psychology and physiology of breathing.* New York: Plenum.

*Friedman, M. I., & Lackey, G. H., Jr. (1991). *The psychology of human control.* New York: Praeger.

Friedman, S., (Ed.). (1993). *The new language of change: Constructive collaboration in psychotherapy.* New York: Guilford.

**Froggatt, W. (1993). *Choose to be happy.* New Zealand: Harper-Collins.

Fromm, E. (1955). *The sane society.* New York: Rinehart.

Gazzaniga, M. S. (1993). *Nature's mind.* New York: Basic Books.

*Gelber, D. M. (1993). Re: Exposure therapy. *Behavior Therapist, 16*(2), 13.

Gendlin, E. (1981). *Focusing* (2nd ed.). New York: Bantam.

*Gerald, M., & Eyman, W. (1981). *Thinking straight and talking sense: An emotional education program.* New York: Institute for Rational-Emotive Therapy.

Gergen, R. J. (1991). *The saturated self.* New York: Basic Books.

Gilovich, T. (1992). *How we know what isn't so: The fallibility of human reason in everyday life.* New York: Free Press.

*Glasser, W. (1965). *Reality therapy.* New York: Harper & Row.

*Glasser, W. (1992a). Reality therapy. In J. K. Zeig (Ed.), *The evolution of psychotherapy: The second conference* (pp. 270–282). New York: Brunner/ Mazel.

*Glasser, W. (1992b). Discussion of Jay Haley, *Zen and the art of therapy.* In J. K. Zeig (Ed.). *The evolution of psychotherapy: The second conference* (pp. 34–35). New York: Brunner/Mazel.

*Golden, W. L., Dowd, E. T., & Friedberg, F. (1987). *Hypnotherapy: A modern approach.* New York: Pergamon.

*Goldfried, M. R., & Castonguay, L. G. (1993). Behavior therapy: Redefining strengths and limitations. *Behavior Therapy, 24,* 505–526.

*Goldfried, M. R., & Davison, G. C. (1991). *Clinical behavior therapy* (3rd ed.). New York: Holt Rinehart & Winston.

Goldsmith, T. H. (1991). *The biological roots of human nature.* New York: Oxford.

*Goleman, D. (1989, July 6). Feeling gloomy? A good self-help book may actually help. *New York Times,* p. B6.

*Goleman, D. (1993a, March 21). A slow methodical calming of the mind. *The New York Times Magazine,* pp. 20–21.

Goleman, D. (1993b, April 4). Studying the secrets of childhood memory. *The New York Times,* pp. C1, C11.

**Gordon, S. (1994). *"Is there anything I can do?" Helping a friend when times are tough.* New York: Delacorte.

*Gould, R. A., Clum, G. A., & Shapiro, D. (1993). The use of bibliotherapy in the treatment of panic: A preliminary investigation. *Behavior Therapy, 24,* 241–252.

*Goulding, M. M. (1992). Short-term redecision therapy in the treatment of clients who suffered childhood abuse. In J. K. Zeig (Ed.), *The evolution of* *psychotherapy: The second conference* (pp. 239–251). New York: Brunner/ Mazel.

*Granvold, D. K. (Ed.). (1994). *Cognitive and behavioral treatment: Methods and applications.* Pacific Grove, CA: Brooks/Cole.

Greenberg, L., Elliott, R., & Litaer, B. (1994). Research on experiential psychotherapies. In A. E. Bergin and S. L. Garfield (Eds.), *Handbook of psychotherapy and behavior change* (pp. 509–539). New York: Wiley.

*Greenberg, L. S., & Safran, J. D. (1987). *Emotion in psychotherapy.* New York: Guilford.

*Greenwald, H. (1987). *Direct decision therapy.* San Diego, CA: Edits.

*Greist, J. H. (1993). *Obsessive compulsive disorder.* Madison, WI: Dean Foundation for Health and Education.

*Grieger, R. M. (1988). From a linear to a contextual model of the ABCs of RET. In W. Dryden and P. Trower (Eds.), *Developments in cognitive psychotherapy* (pp. 71–105). London: Sage.

*Grieger, R., & Boyd, J. (1980). *Rational-emotive therapy: A skills-based approach.* New York: Van Nostrand Reinhold.

**Grieger, R. M., & Woods, P. J. (1993). *The rational-emotive therapy companion.* Roanoke, VA: Scholars Press.

*Grossack, M. (1976). *Love and reason.* Boston: Institute for Rational Living.

Grunbaum, A. (1993). *Validation in the clinical theory of psychoanalysis.* New York: International Universities Press.

*Guidano, V. F. (1991). *The self in progress.* New York: Guilford.

Guisinger, S., & Blatt, S. J. (1994). Individuality and relatedness: Evolution of a fundamental dialectic. *American Psychologist, 49*, 104–111.

Guterman, J. T. (1994). A social constructionist position for mental health counseling. *Journal of Mental Health Counseling, 16*, 226–244.

Gutsch, K. U., & Ritenoor, J. V. (1983). In Gutsch, K. U., Sisemore, D. A., & Williams, R. L. (Eds.), *Systems of psychotherapy* (pp. 276–286). Springfield, IL: Thomas.

Gyorky, Z. K., Royalty, G. M., & Johnson, D. H. (1994). Time-limited therapy in university centers: Do time-limited and time-unlimited centers differ? *Professional Psychology, 25*, 50–54.

*Haaga, D. A., & Davison, G. C. (1989). Outcome studies of rational-emotive therapy. In M. E. Bernard & R. DiGiuseppe (Eds.), *Inside rational-emotive therapy* (pp. 155–197). San Diego, CA: Academic Press.

*Hajzler, D., & Bernard, M. E. (1991). A review of rational-emotive outcome studies. *School Psychology Quarterly, 6*(1), 27–49.

*Haley, J. (1963). *Strategies of psychotherapy.* New York: Grune & Stratton.

Haley, J. (1973). *Uncommon therapy: The psychiatric techniques of Milton H. Erickson.* New York: Norton.

*Haley, J. (1990). *Problem solving therapy.* San Francisco: Jossey-Bass.

Haley, J. (1992). Zen and the art of therapy. In J. K. Zeig (Ed.), *The evolution*

of psychotherapy: The second conference (pp. 24–38). New York: Brunner/
Mazel.

*Hammond, D. C., & Stanfield, K. (1977). *Multi-dimensional psychotherapy*.
Chicago: Institute for Personality and Ability Testing.

Hartman, R. S. (1967). *The measurement of value*. Carbondale, IL: University of
Southern Illinois Press.

**Hauck, P. A. (1973). *Overcoming depression*. Philadelphia: Westminster.

**Hauck, P. A. (1974). *Overcoming frustration and anger*. Philadelphia:
Westminster.

**Hauck, P. A. (1977). *Marriage is a loving business*. Philadelphia: Westminster.

**Hauck, P. A. (1991). *Overcoming the rating game: Beyond self-love—beyond self-
esteem*. Louisville, KY: Westminster/John Knox.

Hayakawa, S. I. (1965). *Language in action*. New York: Harcourt, Brace and
World.

Hayakawa, S. I. (1968). The fully functioning personality. In S. I. Hayakawa
(Ed.), *Symbol, status, personality* (pp. 51–69). New York: Harcourt Brace
Jovanovich.

*Hayes, S. C. (1995). Why cognitions are not causes. *Behavior Therapist, 18*,
59–60.

*Hayes, S. C., & Hayes, L. J. (1992). Some clinical implications of
contextualistic behaviorism: The example of cognition. *Behavior Therapy,
23*, 225–249.

*Hayes, S. C., McCurry, S. M., Afan, N., & Wilson, K. (1991). *Acceptance and
commitment therapy (ACT)*. Reno, NV: University of Nevada.

*Hayes, S. C., & Melancon, S. M. (1989). Comprehensive distancing, paradox,
and the treatment of emotional avoidance. In M. Ascher (Ed.), *Paradoxical
procedures in psychotherapy* (pp. 110–130). New York: Guilford.

Hearn, R. J. (1994). Zen Buddism. In R. J. Corsini (Ed.), *Encyclopedia of
psychology* (2nd ed.). (vol. 3, pp. 593–595).

Heidegger, M. (1962). *Being and time*. New York: Harper & Row.

Hendlin, S. J. (1992). *When good enough is never enough*. New York: Putnam.

*Herzberg, A. (1945). *Active psychotherapy*. New York: Grune & Stratton.

Higgins, G. O'C. (1994). *Resilient adults: Overcoming a cruel past*. San Francisco:
Jossey-Bass.

Hillman, J. (1992). One hundred years of solitude, or can the soul ever get out
of analysis? In J. K. Zeig (Ed.), *The evolution of psychotherapy: The second
conference* (pp. 313–321). New York: Brunner/Mazel.

Hoffer, E. (1951). *The true believer*. New York: Harper & Row.

*Hollon, S. D., & Beck, A. T. (1994). Cognitive and cognitive/behavioral
therapies. In A. E. Bergin & S. L. Garfield (Eds.), *Handbook of psychotherapy
and behavior change* (pp. 428–466). New York: Wiley.

Horney, K. (1937). *Neurotic personality of our time*. New York: Norton.

Horney, K. (1950). *Neurosis and human growth*. New York: Norton.

Hornstein, G. A. (1992). The return of the repressed: Psychology's problem-
atic relations with psychoanalysis. *American Psychologist, 47*, 254–263.

Horvath, A. O., & Luborsky, L. (1993). The role of the therapeutic alliance in psychotherapy. *Journal of Consulting and Clinical Psychology, 61,* 561–573.

Huber, C. H. & Baruth, L. G. (1989). *Rational-emotive and systems family therapy.* New York: Springer.

Hunt, M. (1977). *Sexual behavior in the 1970s.* Chicago: Playboy Press.

*Janet, P. (1898). *Neurosis et idée fixes.* 2 vols. Paris: Alcan.

*Janis, I. L. (1983). *Short-term counseling.* New Haven, CT: Yale University Press.

*Janis, I. L., & Mann, L. (1977). *Decision making.* New York: Free Press.

Jacobson, E. (1938). *You must relax.* New York: McGraw-Hill.

*Jacobson, N. S. (1992). Behavioral couple therapy: A new beginning. *Behavior Therapy, 23,* 491–506.

*Johnson, W. (1946). *People in quandaries.* New York: Harper & Row.

*Johnson, W. R. (1981). *So desperate the fight.* New York: Institute for Rational-Emotive Therapy.

Johnston, P. D., Bourland, D. D., Jr., & Klein, J. (Eds.). (1994). *More E-prime: To be or not to be.* Concord, CA: International Society for General Semantics.

Jung, C. G. (1954). *The practice of psychotherapy.* New York: Pantheon.

Kahneman, S., Slovic, P., & Tversky, A. (Eds.). (1982). *Judgment under uncertainty: Heuristics and biases.* New York: Cambridge University Press.

Kaminer, W. (1993). *I'm dysfunctional you're dysfunctional.* New York: Vintage.

*Kanfer, F. H., & Goldstein, A. P. (Eds.). (1986). *Helping people change* (3rd ed.). New York: Pergamon.

*Kanfer, F. H., & Schefft, B. K. (1988). *Guiding the process of therapeutic change.* New York: Pergamon.

Kant, I. (1929). *Critique of pure reason.* New York: St. Martin's.

Kardiner, A. (1941). *The traumatic neuroses of war.* New York: Hoeber.

Kayser, K., & Himle, D. P. (1994). Dysfunctional beliefs about intimacy. *Journal of Cognitive Therapy, 8,* 127–140.

*Kazdin, A. E. (1994). Psychotherapy for children and adolescents. In A. E. Bergin & S. L. Garfield (Eds.), *Handbook of psychotherapy and behavior change* (pp. 543–594). New York: Wiley.

Kellerman, P. F. (1992). *Focus on psychodrama.* London: Jessica Kingsley.

*Kelly, G. (1955). *The psychology of personal constructs.* 2 vols. New York: Norton.

Kendall, P. C. (1991). *Child and adolescent therapy.* New York: Guilford.

*Kiser, D. J., Piercy, E. P., & Lipchik, E. (1993). The integration of emotion in solution-focused therapy. *Journal of Marital and Family Therapy, 19,* 233–242.

Klein, M. (1984). *Envy and gratitude and other works.* New York: Free Press.

Kleinke, C. L. (1993). *Common principles of psychotherapy.* Pacific Grove, CA: Brooks/Cole.

*Knaus, W. (1974). *Rational-emotive education.* New York: Institute for Rational-Emotive Therapy.

Kopata, S. M., Howard, K. I., Lowry, J. L., & Beutler, L. E. (1994). Patterns of symptomatic recovery in psychotherapy. *Journal of Consulting and Clinical Psychology, 62,* 1009–1016.

*Kopec, A. M., Beal, D., & DiGiuseppe, R. (1994). Training in RET: Disputational strategies. *Journal of Rational-Emotive and Cognitive-Behavior Therapy, 12, 47–60.*

Korzybski, A. (1933). *Science and sanity.* San Francisco: International Society for General Semantics.

Koss, M. P., & Shiang, J. (1994). Research on brief psychotherapy. In A. E. Bergin & S. L. Garfield (Eds.), *Handbook of psychotherapy and behavior* (pp. 664–700). New York: Wiley.

*Kottler, J. A. (1991). *The complete therapist.* San Francisco: Jossey-Bass.

Kramer, P. D. (1993). *Listening to prozac.* New York: Penguin.

*Kuehlwein, K. T., & Rosen, H. (Eds.). (1993). *Cognitive therapies in action.* San Francisco: Jossey-Bass.

Kurtz, P. (1986). *The transcendental temptation.* Buffalo, NY: Prometheus.

*Kwee, M. G. T. (1982). Psychotherapy and the practice of general semantics. *Methodology and Science, 15,* 236–256.

*Kwee, M. (1991). Cognitive and behavioral approaches to meditation. In M. G. Kwee, *Psychotherapy, meditation and health* (pp. 36–53). London: East/West Publications.

*Kwee, M. G. T. (1991). *Psychotherapy, meditation, and health: A cognitive behavioral perspective.* London: East/West Publications.

Lambert, M. J., & Bergin, A. E. (1994). The effectiveness of psychotherapy. In A. E. Bergin and S. L. Garfield (Eds.), *Handbook of psychotherapy and behavior change* (pp. 143–189). New York: Wiley.

**Lange, A., & Jakubowski, P. (1976). *Responsible assertive behavior.* Champaign, IL: Research Press.

Langley, M. H. (1994). *Self-management for borderline personality disorder.* New York: Springer.

Lao-Tse (1975). *Tao: A new way of thinking.* New York: Harper & Row.

Lasch, C. (1978). *The culture of narcissism.* New York: Norton.

*Laydon, M. A., & Newman, C. F. (1993). *Cognitive therapy of borderline disorder.* Des Moines, IA: Longwood Division, Allyn & Bacon.

*Lazarus, A. A. (1977). Toward an egoless state of being. In A. Ellis & R. Grieger (Eds.), *Handbook of rational-emotive therapy.* (vol. 1, pp. 113–116). New York: Springer.

**Lazarus, A. A. (1985). *Marital myths.* San Luis Obispo, CA: Impact.

*Lazarus, A. A. (1989). *The practice of multimodal therapy.* Baltimore, MD: Johns Hopkins.

*Lazarus, A. A. (1992). Clinical/therapeutic effectiveness: Banning the procrustean bed and challenging 10 prevalent myths. In J. K. Zeig (Ed.), *The evolution of psychotherapy: The second conference* (pp. 100–113). New York: Brunner/Mazel.

**Lazarus, A. A., Lazarus, C., & Fay, A. (1993). *Don't believe it for a minute:*

Forty toxic ideas that are driving you crazy. San Luis Obispo, CA: Impact Publishers.

*Lazarus, R. S. (1966). *Psychological stress and the coping process.* New York: McGraw-Hill.

*Lazarus, R. S. (1994). *Emotion and adaptation.* New York: Oxford.

*Lazarus, R. S., & Folkman, S. (1984). *Stress, appraisal, and coping.* New York: Springer.

*Lazarus, R. S., & Lazarus, B. N. (1994). *Passion and reason.* New York: Oxford.

**Lewinsohn, P., Antonuccio, D., Breckenridge, J., & Teri, L. (1984). *The "coping with depression course."* Eugene, OR: Castalia.

*Levey, A. B., Aldaz, J. A., Watts, F. N., & Coyle, K. (1991). Articulatory suppression and the treatment of insomnia. *Behavior Research and Therapy, 29,* 85–89.

*Lichtenberg, J. W., Johnson, D. D., & Arachtingi, B. M. (1992). Physical illness and subscription to Ellis's irrational beliefs. *Journal of Counseling and Development, 71,* 157–163.

*Lightsey, O. R., Jr. (1994). "Thinking positive" as a stress buffer: Role of positive automatic cognitions in depression and happiness. *Journal of Counseling Psychology, 41,* 325–334.

*Linehan, M. M. (1993). *Cognitive-behavioral treatment of borderline personality disorders.* New York: Guilford.

*Lipsey, M. W., & Wilson, D. B. (1993). The efficacy of psychological, educational, and behavior treatment: Confirmation from meta-analysis. *American Psychologist, 48,* 1181–1209.

**Low, A. A. (1952). *Mental health through will training.* Boston: Christopher.

*Lyons, L. C., & Woods, P. J. (1991). The efficacy of rational-emotive therapy: A quantitative review of the outcome research. *Clinical Psychology Review, 11,* 357–369.

Mahoney, M. J. (1976). *Scientist as subject.* Cambridge, MA: Ballinger.

*Mahoney, M. J. (1991). *Human change processes.* New York: Basic Books.

*Mahoney, M. J. (Ed.). (1995). *Cognitive and constructive psychotherapies: Theory, research and practice.* New York: Springer.

Mahrer, A. R. (1989). *How to do experiential psychotherapy: A manual for practitioners.* Ottawa, Canada: University of Ottawa Press.

Malan, D. H. (1963). *A study of brief psychotherapy.* London: Tavistock.

Maltz, M. (1965). *Psychocybernetics.* Englewood Cliffs, NJ: Prentice-Hall.

Mann, J. (1973). *Time-limited psychotherapy.* Cambridge, MA: Harvard University.

**Marcus Aurelius. (1890). *Meditations.* Boston: Little, Brown.

*Marks, I. (1994). Behavior therapy as an aid to self-care. *Current Directions in Psychological Science, 3*(1), 19–22.

*Marlatt, G. A., & Gordon, J. R. (Eds.). (1989). *Relapse prevention: Maintenance strategies in the treatment of addictive behaviors.* New York: Guilford.

Marmor, J. (1962). A re-evaluation of certain aspects of psychoanalytic theory and practice. In L. Salzman & J. H. Masserman (Eds.), *Modern concepts of psychoanalysis* (pp. 189–205). New York: Philosophical Library.

*Marmor, J. (1987). The psychotherapeutic process: Common denominators on diverse approaches. In J. K. Zeig (Ed.), *The evolution of psychotherapy* (pp. 266–282). New York: Brunner/Mazel.

Marmor, J. (1992). The essence of dynamic psychotherapy. In J. K. Zeig (Ed.), *The evolution of psychotherapy: The second conference* (pp. 189–200). New York: Brunner/Mazel.

Maslow, A. H. (1973). *The farther reaches of human nature.* Harmondsworth, UK: Penguin.

Masters, W. H., Johnson, V. E., & Kolodny, R. C. (1982). *Human sexuality.* Boston: Houghton Mifflin.

*Maultsby, M. C., Jr. (1971a). Rational emotive imagery. *Rational Living, 6*(1), 24–27.

*Maultsby, M. C., Jr. (1971b). Systematic written homework in psychotherapy. *Psychotherapy, 8,* 195–198.

*Maultsby, M. C., Jr. (1984). *Rational behavior therapy.* Englewood Cliffs, NJ: Prentice-Hall.

May, R. (1969). *Love and will.* New York: Norton.

May, R. (1986). Transpersonal. *APA Monitor, 17*(5), 2.

McCrae, R. R., & Costa, P. T., Jr. (1994). The stability of personality: Observations and evaluations. *Current Directions in Psychological Science, 3,* 173–175.

*McGovern, T. E., & Silverman, M. S. (1984). A review of outcome studies of rational-emotive therapy from 1977 to 1982. *Journal of Rational-Emotive Therapy, 2*(1), 7–18.

McIntyre, A. (1988). *After virtue.* London: Duckworth.

**McKay, G. D., & Dinkmeyer, D. (1994). *How you feel is up to you.* San Luis Obispo, CA: Impact Publishers.

*McMullin, R. (1986). *Handbook of cognitive therapy techniques.* New York: Norton.

**McWilliams, P. (1994). *Life 101.* Los Angeles: Prelude Press.

Meehl, P. E. (1962). Schizotaxia, schizotypy, schizophrenia. *American Psychologist, 17,* 827–838.

*Meichenbaum, D. (1977). *Cognitive-behavior modification.* New York: Plenum.

*Meichenbaum, D. (1992). Evolution of cognitive behavior therapy: Origins, tenets, and clinical examples. In J. K. Zeig (Ed.), *The evolution of psychotherapy: The second conference* (pp. 114–128). New York: Brunner/Mazel.

*Meichenbaum, D., & Cameron, R. (1983). Stress inoculation training. In D. Meichenbaum & M. E. Jaremko (Eds.), *Stress reduction and prevention* (pp. 115–154). New York: Plenum.

**Miller, T. (1986). *The unfair advantage.* Manlius, NY: Horsesense, Inc.

**Mills, D. (1993). *Overcoming self-esteem*. New York: Institute for Rational-Emotive Therapy.

Mohr, D. C. (1995). Negative outcome in psychotherapy. *Clinical Psychology, 2*, 1–27.

Moore, R. H. (1993). Traumatic incident reduction. In W. Dryden & L. Hill (Eds.), *Innovations in rational-emotive therapy* (pp. 116–159). Newbury Park, CA: Sage.

Moore, S. (1994). Meditation. In R. J. Corsini (Ed.), *Encyclopedia of psychology*. (2nd ed.) (vol. 2, pp. 381–382). New York: Wiley.

Moore, T. (1992). *Care of the soul*. New York: Harper Perennial.

Moreno, J. L. (1990). *The essential J. L. Moreno*. New York: Springer.

*Neimeyer, G. J. (1993). The challenge of change: Reflections on constructive psychotherapy. *Journal of Cognitive Psychotherapy, 7*, 183–194.

*Neimeyer, R. A. (1993). Constructivism and the cognitive psychotherapies: Some conceptual and strategic contrasts. *Journal of Cognitive Psychotherapy, 7*, 159–171.

*Nezu, A. M. (1985). Differences in psychological distress between effective and ineffective problem solvers. *Journal of Counseling Psychology, 54*, 135–138.

*Nezu, A. M. (1986). Efficacy of a social problem-solving therapy approach for unipolar depression. *Journal of Consulting and Clinical Psychology, 54*, 42–48.

*Norcross, J. C., & Goldfried, M. R. (1992). *Handbook of psychotherapy integration*. New York: Basic Books.

**Nottingham, E. (1992). *It's not as bad as it seems: A thinking approach to happiness*. Memphis, TN: Castle Books.

**Nye, B. (1993). *Understanding and managing your anger and aggression*. Federal Way, WA: BCA Publishing.

*O'Hanlon, B., & Beadle, S. (1994). *A field guide to possibility land: Possibility therapy methods*. Omaha, NE: Possibility Press.

*O'Hanlon, B., & Wilk, J. (1987). *Shifting contexts: The generation of effective psychotherapy*. New York: Guilford.

Oldham, J. M. (Ed.). (1991). *Personality disorder*. Washington, DC: American Psychiatric Press.

*Olkin, R. (1994). The use of a paradoxical intervention for the treatment of recalcitrant temper tantrums. *Behavior Therapist, 17*, 37–40.

Orlinsky, D. E., Grawe, K., & Parks, B. K. (1994). Process and outcome in psychotherapy—Noch einmal. In A. E. Bergin & S. L. Garfield (Eds.), *Handbook of psychotherapy and behavior change* (pp. 270–371). New York: Wiley.

*Palmer, S., Dryden, W., Ellis, A., & Yapp, R. (1995). *Rational interviews*. London: Centre for Rational Emotive Behavior Therapy.

*Palmer, S., & Ellis, A. (1994). In the counselor's chair. *The Rational Emotive Therapist, 2*(1), 6–15. From *Counseling Journal*, 1993, *4*, 171–174.

Paul, G. L. (1967). Strategy of outcome research in psychotherapy. *Journal of Consulting Psychology, 31,* 109–118.

**Peale, N. V. (1952). *The power of positive thinking.* New York: Fawcett.

Perls, F. (1969). *Gestalt therapy verbatim.* New York: Delta.

*Peterson, C., Maier, S. F., & Seligman, M. E. P. (1993). *Learned helplessness.* New York: Oxford.

*Phadke, K. M. (1982). Some innovations in RET theory and practice. *Rational Living, 17*(2), 25–30.

*Phillips, E. L., & Wiener, D. N. (1966). *Short-term psychotherapy and structured behavior change.* New York: McGraw-Hill.

Piaget, J. (1954). *The construction of reality in the child.* New York: Basic Books.

*Pietsch, W. V. (1993). *The serenity prayer.* San Francisco: Harper San Francisco.

Plomin, R., & McClearn, G. E. (1994). *Nature, nurture, and psychology.* Washington, DC: American Psychological Association.

*Plutchik, R., & Kellerman, H. (1990). *Emotion, psychopathology, and psychotherapy.* San Diego, CA: Academic Press.

Popper, K. R. (1962). *Objective knowledge.* London: Oxford.

Popper, K. R. (1985). *Popper selections.* David Miller (Ed.). Princeton, NJ: University Press.

**Powell, J. (1976). *Fully human, fully alive.* Niles, IL: Argus.

*Prochaska, J. O., DiClemente, C. C., & Norcross, J. C. (1992). In search of how people change: Applications to addictive behaviors. *American Psychologist, 47,* 1102–1114.

Quintana, S. M., & Holahan, W. (1992). Termination in short-term counseling: Comparison of successful and unsuccessful cases. *Journal of Counseling Psychology, 39,* 299–305.

*Raimy, V. (1975). *Misunderstandings of the self.* San Francisco: Jossey-Bass.

Rand, A. (1961). *For the new intellectual.* New York: New American Library.

Randi, J. (1987). *The faith-healers.* Buffalo, NY: Prometheus.

Rank, O. (1945). *Will therapy and truth and reality.* New York: Knopf.

Reandeau, S. G., & Wampold, B. E. (1991). Relationship of power and involvement to working alliance: A multiple-case sequential analysis of brief therapy. *Journal of Counseling Psychology, 38,* 107–114.

Reason, J. (1990). *Human error.* Cambridge, England: Cambridge University.

Reich, W. (1960). *Selected writings.* New York: Farrar, Straus and Cudahy.

*Resick, P. A., & Schicke, M. K. (1993). *Cognitive processing therapy for rape victims.* Newbury Park, CA: Sage.

Rhue, J. W., Lynn, S. J., & Kirsch, I. (Eds.). (1993). *Handbook of clinical hypnosis.* New York: Guilford.

*Robin, M. W., & DiGiuseppe, R. (1993). Rational-emotive therapy with an avoidant personality. In K. T. Kuehlwein & H. Rosen (Eds.), *Cognitive therapies in action* (pp. 143-159). New York: Guilford.

Rogers, C. R. (1957). The necessary and sufficient conditions of therapeutic personality change. *Journal of Consulting Psychology, 21,* 95–103.

Rogers, C R. (1961). *On becoming a person*. Boston: Houghton-Mifflin.

*Rorer, L. G. (1989). Rational-emotive theory: I. An integrated psychological and philosophic basis. II. Explication and evaluation. *Cognitive Therapy and Research, 13*, 475–492; 531–548.

Rosenbaum, R. (1994). Single session therapies: Intrinsic integration. *Journal of Psychotherapy Integration, 4*, 229–252.

*Rotter, J. B. (1954). *Social learning and clinical psychology*. Englewood Cliffs, NJ: Prentice-Hall.

*Rush, A. J. (1989). The therapeutic alliance in short-term cognitive-behavior therapy. In W. Dryden & P. Trower (Eds.), *Cognitive psychotherapy: Stasis and change* (pp. 59–72). London: Cassell.

**Russell, B. (1950). *The conquest of happiness*. New York: New American Library.

Russell, B. (1965). *The basic writings of Bertrand Russell*. New York: Simon & Schuster.

*Safran, J. D., & Greenberg, L. S. (Eds.). (1991). *Emotion, psychotherapy, and change*. New York: Guilford.

*Salter, A. (1949). *Conditioned reflex therapy*. New York: Creative Age.

Salter, A. (1952). *The case against psychoanalysis*. New York: Creative Age.

Sampson, E. E. (1989) The challenge of social change in psychology. Globalization and psychology's theory of the person. *American Psychologist, 44*, 914–921.

Santrock, J. W., Minnett, A. M., & Campbell, B. D. (1994). *The authoritative guide to self-help books*. New York: Guilford.

*Satir, V. (1978). *People making*. Palo Alto: Science & Behavior Books.

Schneider, K. (1987). The deified self: A "centaur" response to Wilber and the transpersonal movement. *Journal of Humanistic Psychology, 27*, 196–216.

Schofield, W. (1964). *Psychotherapy: The purchase of friendship*. Englewood Cliffs, NJ: Prentice-Hall.

Schutz, W. (1967). *Joy*. New York: Grove.

*Schwartz, R. (1993). The idea of balance and integrative psychotherapy. *Journal of Psychotherapy Integration, 3*, 159–181.

*Scoggin, F., Bynum, J., Stephens, G., & Calhoun, S. (1990). Efficacy of self-administered treatment programs: Meta-analytic review. *Professional Psychology, 21*, 42–47.

*Scoggin, F. & McElreath, L. (1994). Efficacy of psychosocial treatment for geriatric depression: A quantitative review. *Journal of Consulting and Clinical Psychology, 62*, 68–74.

*Seligman, M. E. P. (1991). *Learned optimism*. New York: Knopf.

Seltzer, A. (1986). *Paradoxical strategies in psychotherapy*. New York: Wiley.

*Shapiro, D. H., & Walsh, R. N. (Eds.). (1984). *Meditation: Classic and contemporary perspectives*. New York: Aldine.

Shedler, J., Mayman, M., & Manis, M. (1993). The illusion of mental health. *American Psychologist, 48*, 1117–1131.

*Shibles, W. (1974). *Emotion: The method of philosophical therapy*. Whitewater, WI: Language Press.

*Shoham, V., & Rohrbaugh, M. (1994). Paradoxical intervention. In R. J. Corsini (Ed.), *Encyclopedia of psychology.* vol. 3, pp. 5–8. New York: Wiley.

*Shostrom, E. L. (1976). *Actualizing therapy.* San Diego, CA: Edits.

**Sichel, J., & Ellis, A. (1984). *RET self-help form.* New York: Institute for Rational-Emotive Therapy.

Sifneos, P. E. (1972). *Short-term psychotherapy and emotional crisis.* Cambridge, MA: Harvard University.

Silver, D., & Rosenbluth, M. (Eds.). (1992). *Handbook of borderline disorders.* CT: International Universities Press.

*Silverman, M. S., McCarthy, M., & McGovern, T. (1992). A review of outcome studies of rational-emotive therapy from 1982–1989. *Journal of Rational-Emotive and Cognitive-Behavior Therapy, 10*(3), 111–186.

**Simon, J. L. (1993). *Good mood.* LaSalle, IL: Open Court.

Skinner, B. F. (1954). Critique of psychoanalytic concepts. *Scientific Monthly, 79,* 300–335.

Skinner, B. F. (1971). *Beyond freedom and dignity.* New York: Knopf.

Slater, R. (1964). Karen Horney on psychoanalytic technique. In H. Helman (Ed.), *Advances in psychoanalysis* (pp. 242–250). New York: Norton.

Small, L. (1979). *The briefer psychotherapies.* rev. ed. New York: Brunner/Mazel.

Smith, M. B. (1973). On self-actualization. *Journal of Humanistic Psychology, 13*(2), 17–33.

*Smith, M. L., & Glass, G. V. (1977). Meta-analysis of psychotherapy outcome studies. *American Psychologist, 32,* 752–760.

*Smith, M. L., Glass, G. V., & Miller, T. I. (1980). *The benefits of psychotherapy.* Baltimore: Johns Hopkins University Press.

Snyder, M. (1994). The development of social intelligence in psychotherapy. *Journal of Humanistic Psychology, 34*(1), 84–108.

Socarides, C. W. (1968). The overt homosexual. New York: Grune & Stratton.

*Sookman, D., Pinard, G., & Beauchemin, N. (1994). Multidimensional schematic restructuring treatment for obsessions: Theory and practice. *Journal of Cognitive Psychotherapy, 8,* 175–207.

**Spillane, R. (1985). *Achieving peak performance: A psychology of success in the organization.* Sydney, Australia: Harper & Row.

*Spivack, G., Platt, J., & Shure, M. (1976). *The problem-solving approach to adjustment.* San Francisco: Jossey-Bass.

*Spivack, G., & Shure, M. (1974). *Social adjustment in young children.* San Francisco: Jossey-Bass.

Stace, W. T. (1960). *The teachings of the mystics.* New York: New American Library.

Stampfl, T. G., & Levis, D. J. (1967). Essentials of implosive therapy. *Journal of Abnormal Psychology, 72,* 496–503.

*Stanton, H. (1977). The utilization of suggestions derived from rational-emotive therapy. *International Journal of Clinical and Experimental Hypnosis, 25,* 18–26.

*Stanton, H. E. (1989). Hypnosis and rational-emotive therapy–A de-stressing combination. *International Journal of Clinical and Experimental Hypnosis, 37,* 95–99.

*Starker, S. (1988a). Do-it-yourself therapy. *Psychotherapy, 25,* 142–146.

*Starker, S. (1988b). Psychologists and self-help books. *American Journal of Psychotherapy, 43,* 448–455.

Stekel, W. (1950). *Technique of analytical psychotherapy.* New York: Liveright.

Steenberger, B. N. (1994). Duration and outcome in psychotherapy: An integrative review. *Professional Psychology, 25,* 111–119.

*Steketee, G. S. (1993). *Treatment of obsessive compulsive disorder.* New York: Guilford.

Stricker, G., & Gold, J. R. (1993). *Comprehensive handbook of psychotherapy integration.* New York: Plenum.

*Stroud, W. L., Jr. (1994). A cognitive-behavioral view of agency and freedom. *American Psychologist, 44,* 142–143.

Strupp, H. H., & Binder, J. L. (1984). *Psychotherapy in a new key.* New York: Basic Books.

Sullivan, H. S. (1953). *The interpersonal theory of psychiatry.* New York: Norton.

Suzuki, D. T. (1956). *Zen Buddhism.* New York: Doubleday Anchor Books.

Suzuki, D. T., Fromm, E., & DeMartino, R. (1963). *Zen Buddhism and psychoanalysis.* New York: Grove.

Tart, C. T. (1992). *Transpersonal psychologies.* New York: HarperCollins.

Tate, P. (1993). *Alcohol: How to give it up and be glad you did.* Altamonte Springs, Fl: Rational Self-Help Press.

Tavris, C. (1983). *Anger: The misunderstood emotion.* New York: Simon and Schuster.

Taylor, S. E. (1990). *Positive illusions: Creative self-deception and the healthy mind.* New York: Basic Books.

*Thorne, F. C. (1950). *Principles of personality counseling.* Brandon, VT: Journal of Clinical Psychology Press.

Tillich, P. (1953). *The courage to be.* New York: Oxford.

*Tosi, D. J., & Baisen, B. S. (1984). Cognitive experiential therapy and hypnosis. In W. Wester & J. Smith (Eds.), *Clinical hypnosis* (pp. 155–178). Philadelphia: Lippincott.

*Tosi, D. J., Fuller, J., & Gwynne, P. (1980, June). The treatment of hyperactivity and learning disabilities through RSDH. Paper presented at the Third Annual Conference in Rational Emotive Therapy, New York.

*Tosi, D. J., Judah, S. M., & Murphy, M. M. (1989). The effects of a cognitive experiential therapy utilizing hypnosis, cognitive restructuring, and developmental staging on psychological factors associated with duodenal ulcer. *Journal of Cognitive Psychotherapy, 3,* 273–290.

*Tosi, D., & Marzella, J. N. (1977). The treatment of guilt through rational stage directed therapy. In J. L. Wolfe & E. Brand (Eds.), *Twenty years of* *rational therapy* (pp. 234–240). New York: Institute for Rational-Emotive Therapy.

*Tosi, D., & Reardon, J. P. (1976). The treatment of guilt through rational stage directed therapy. *Rational Living, 11*(1), 8–11.

*Tosi, D. J., Rudy, D. R., Lewis, J., & Murphy, M. A. (1992). The psychobiological effects of cognitive experiential therapy, hypnosis, cognitive restructuring, and attention placebo control in the treatment of essential hypertension. *Psychotherapy, 29,* 274–284.

**Trimpey, J. (1989). *Rational recovery from alcoholism: The small book.* New York: Delacorte.

*Trimpey, J. (1993). Step zero: Addiction voice recognition technique. *Journal of Rational Recovery, 6*(1), 5–7.

*Trimpey, J. (1994). AVRT in a nutshell. *Journal of Rational Recovery, 6*(2), 1–3.

*Trimpey, J., & Trimpey, L. (1990). *Rational recovery from fatness.* Lotus, CA: Lotus Press.

Tyler, F. B., Brome, D. B., & Williams, J. E. (1991). *Ethnic validity, ecology and psychotherapy.* New York: Plenum.

Underhill, E. (1974). *Mysticism.* New York: New American Library.

**Velten, E. (Speaker). (1987). *How to be unhappy at work.* Cassette recording. New York: Institute for Rational-Emotive Therapy.

*Vernon, A. (1989). *Thinking, feeling, behaving: An emotional education curriculum for children.* Champaign, IL: Research Press.

Wachs, T. D. (1992). *The nature of nurture.* Newbury, CA: Sage.

*Wachtel, P. L. (1977). *Psychoanalysis and behavior therapy: Toward an integration.* New York: Basic Books.

*Wachtel, P. L. (1994). Cyclical processes in personality and psychopathology. *Journal of Abnormal Psychology, 103,* 51–54.

*Walen, S., DiGiuseppe, R., & Dryden, W. (1992). *A practitioner's guide to rational-emotive therapy.* New York: Oxford University Press.

*Walen, S. R., Rader, M. W. (1991). Depression and RET. In M. E. Bernard, (Ed.). *Using rational-emotive therapy effectively* (pp. 219–264). New York: Plenum.

Walker, J. & others (Speakers). (1992). *Ayn Rand. Ideas,* May 19, 26, 1992. Toronto: CBC Ideas Transcripts.

Walsh, R., & Vaughan, F. (1994). *Paths beyond ego: The transpersonal vision.* Stanford, CA: J.T.P. Books.

**Walter, M. (1994). *Personal resilience.* Kanata, Ontario, Canada: Resilience Training International.

*Warga, C. (1988, September). Profile of psychologist Albert Ellis. *Psychology Today,* pp. 18–33. Rev. ed., New York: Institute for Rational-Emotive Therapy, 1989.

*Warnock, S. (1989). Rational-emotive therapy and the Christian client. *Journal of Rational-Emotive and Cognitive-Behavior Therapy, 7*, 263–274.

*Warren, R., & Zgourides, G. D. (1991). *Anxiety disorders: A rational-emotive perspective.* Des Moines, IA: Longwood Division, Allyn & Bacon.

*Watson, C. G., Vassar, P., Plemel, D., & Herder, J. (1990). A factor analysis of Ellis' irrational beliefs. *Journal of Clinical Psychology, 46*, 412–415.

**Watson, D., & Tharp, R. (1993). *Self-directed behavior,* 6th ed. Pacific Grove, CA: Brooks/Cole.

Watson, J. B. (1919). *Psychology from the standpoint of a behaviorist.* Philadelphia: Lippincott.

Watson, J. B., & Rayner, R. (1920). Conditioned emotional reactions. *Journal of Experimental Psychology, 3*, 1–14.

Watzlawick, P. (1978). *The language of change.* New York: Basic Books.

Watzlawick, P., Beaven, A., & Jackson, D. (1967). *Pragmatics of human communication.* New York: Norton.

*Watzlawick, P., Weakland, J., & Fisch, R. (1974). *Change.* New York: Norton.

*Weinberger, J. (1995). Some common factors aren't so common. *Clinical Psychology, 3*, 58–69.

*Weinrach, S. G. (1980). Unconventional therapist: Albert Ellis. *Personnel and Guidance Journal, 59*, 152–160.

*Wessler, R. L. (1988). Affect and nonconscious processes in cognitive psychotherapy. In W. Dryden & P.Trower (Eds.), *Developments in cognitive psychotherapy* (pp. 23–40). London: Sage.

*Wessler, R. A., & Wessler, R. L. (1980). *The principles and practice of rational-emotive therapy.* San Francisco: Jossey-Bass.

Whitaker, C. A. (1992). Symbolic experiential family therapy: Model and methodology. In J. K. Zeig (Ed.), *The evolution of psychotherapy: The second conference* (pp. 13–23). New York: Brunner/Mazel.

*Wiener, D. (1988). *Albert Ellis: Passionate skeptic.* New York: Praeger.

Wiggins, J. G. (1994). New study supports psychotherapy but challenges psychologists. *Psychotherapy Bulletin, 29*(3), 45–46.

Wilber, K. (1990). *Eye to eye,* rev. ed. Boston: Shambhala.

Wilson, E. O. (1975). *Sociobiology: The new synthesis.* Cambridge, MA: Harvard University Press.

*Wilson, P. H. (1992). *Principles and practice of relapse prevention.* New York: Guilford.

*Winston, A., Laikin, M., Pollack, J., &Samstag, L.W. (1994). Short-term psychotherapy of personality disorders. *American Journal of Psychiatry, 151*, 190–194.

Wittgenstein, L. (1922). *Tractatus logico-philosophicus.* London: Kegan Paul.

*Wolberg, L. R. (1954). *Technique of psychotherapy.* New York: Grune & Stratton.

*Wolberg, L. R. (1965). *Short-term psychotherapy.* New York: Grune & Stratton.

*Wolfe, J. L. (Speaker). (1977). *Assertiveness training for women.* Cassette recording. New York: BMA Audio Cassettes.

*Wolfe, J. L. (Speaker). (1980). *Woman—assert yourself.* Cassette recording. New York: Institute for Rational-Emotive Therapy.

**Wolfe, J. L. (1992). *What to do when he has a headache.* New York: Hyperion.

**Wolfe, J. L. (1993). *How not to give yourself a headache when your partner isn't acting the way you'd like.* New York: Institute for Rational-Emotive Therapy.

**Wolfe, J. L. (Speaker). (1994). *Overcoming low frustration tolerance.* Video Cassette. New York: Institute for Rational-Emotive Therapy.

*Wolfe, J. L., & Brand, E. (Eds.). (1977). *Twenty years of rational therapy.* New York: Institute for Rational-Emotive Therapy.

*Wolfe, J. L., & Fodor, I. G. (1975). A cognitive-behavioral approach to modifying assertive behavior in women. *Counseling Psychologist, 5*(4), 45–52.

*Wolfe, J. L., & Naimark, H. (1991). Psychological messages and social context. Strategies for increasing RET's effectiveness with women. In M. Bernard (Ed.), *Using rational-emotive therapy effectively.* New York: Plenum.

Wolpe, J. (1990). *The practice of behavior therapy,* 4th ed. Needham Heights, MA: Allyn & Bacon.

Woods, P. J. (1974). A taxonomy of instrumental conditioning. *American Psychologist, 29,* 584–597.

Woods, P. J. (1983). Improving behavioral-change strategies with clients. *Journal of Rational-Emotive Therapy, 1,* 26–28.

Woods, P. J. (1985). Learning paradigms expectancies and behavioral control: An expanded classification for learned behavior. *British Journal of Cognitive Psychotherapy, 3*(1), 43–58.

**Woods, P. J. (1990a). *Controlling your smoking: A comprehensive set of strategies for smoking reduction.* Roanoke, VA: Scholars' Press.

*Woods, P. J. (1992). A study of belief and non-belief items from the Jones' irrational beliefs test with implications for the theory of RET. *Journal of Rational-Emotive and Cognitive-Behavior Therapy, 10,* 41–52.

*Woods, P. J. (1993). Building positive self-regard. In M. E. Bernard & J. L. Wolfe (Eds.), *The RET resource book for practitioners* (158–161). New York: Institute for Rational-Emotive Therapy.

Yalom, I. (1990). *Existential psychotherapy.* New York: Basic Books.

Yankura, J., & Dryden, W. (1990). *Doing RET: Albert Ellis in action.* New York: Springer.

Yankura, J., & Dryden, W. (1994). *Albert Ellis.* London: Sage.

Yates, A. (1970). *Behavior therapy.* New York: Wiley.

**Young, H. S. (1974). *A rational counseling primer.* New York: Institute for Rational-Emotive Therapy.

*Young, H. S. (1984). Special issue: The work of Howard S. Young. *British Journal of Cognitive Psychotherapy, 2*(2), 1–101.

Zeig, J. K. (1992). The virtues of our faults: A key concept of Ericksonian therapy. In J. K. Zeig (Ed.), *The evolution of psychotherapy: The second conference* (pp. 252–269). New York: Brunner/Mazel.

Zeig, J. K., & Gilligan, S. G. (Eds.). (1990). *Brief Therapy: Myths, Methods and Metapohors.* New York: Brunner/Mazel.

*Zilbergeld, B. (1983). *The shrinking of America.* Boston: Little, Brown.

Name Index

Subject Index